The Last Caravan

Also by Thurston Clarke

Dirty Money
(with John J. Tigue, Jr.)

The Last Caravan
by Thurston Clarke

G. P. PUTNAM'S SONS

New York

SBN: 399-11900-0

Library of Congress Cataloging in Publication Data

Clarke, Thurston.
  The last caravan.

  Includes index.
  1. Tuaregs. 2. Sahara—Social conditions.
I. Title.
DT346.T7C55 1977   966'.004'933   77-9533

PRINTED IN THE UNITED STATES OF AMERICA

For my two fathers—Thurston and Esmond. And for the many friends who have supported me—particularly Carolyn, Marilyn, and Steven.

Acknowledgments

I began my research for *The Last Caravan* in the summer of 1975. At the United Nations, Michael Platzer directed me to reports from various U.N. agencies and arranged interviews with officials involved in famine relief and development programs in the sahel. Bonnie Schultz and Joy Zollner of the African-American Institute, and Lorraine Watriss, a veteran of many expeditions to the sahel, were all helpful in recommending people and documents that I should consult, both in New York and in Niger.

In London I used the library of the School of Oriental and African Studies. Books and articles about Niger, the drought, and the Tuareg by Edmond Bernus, Robert Murphy, Johannes Nicolaisen, Francis Nicolas (some of the poems included in the text were translated from Tamashek into French by Nicolas), and Jeremy Swift were all especially perceptive and useful. All of these men are (or were) distinguished anthropologists who have spent many years living with the Tuareg. I am also in debt to Victor DuBois, an American political scientist, for his moving eyewitness account of the Tuareg refugees at Lazaret. While I was in Britain I enjoyed the generous hospitality of Jamie and Damaris Fletcher and Margaret and Ronan Nelson.

In Niger, Boucli Najim and Khamed Moussa spent many days with me as friends and interpreters, both of their language and their culture.

They also introduced me to Tuareg in Niamey and in the bush whose stories are the basis for this book. It was a traumatic experience for many of these Taureg to recount, and in some cases reenact, what had been sad and painful experiences and I am grateful to them, particularly to Sidi and Hassan.

I would also like to thank Dioulde Laya (the Director of the Nigerien Research Institute), his staff, Amadou Ousmane, and numerous other officials and citizens of Niger who gave generously of their time.

The European and American residents of Niger who offered advice, rides, and rooms in which to work and sleep are too numerous to list. I am especially grateful to Al Baron, Sidney Bliss, Craig Buxton, Jim Conway, Douglas and Ernie Heck, Gene Stone, and Peggy Zirker.

I am also thankful for the support and encouragement that I received from my friends and relatives while I was writing *The Last Caravan*. Among those who deserve special mention are John Brim, Alice Geller, Frank Hendrickson, Dexter Hunneman, David McEwan, and Julie Toland. My mother the novelist read the first chapters of the manuscript and told me how to make them better. I followed her suggestions.

Ann Glasser not only convinced me that this was a book that should be written, she also gave excellent advice as to how it should be written. I am grateful to my publisher for understanding that the research for this book would present me with unique obstacles and difficulties.

Finally, I am indebted most of all to Hugh Howard, for his wise and sensitive editing, and for his devotion to this book.

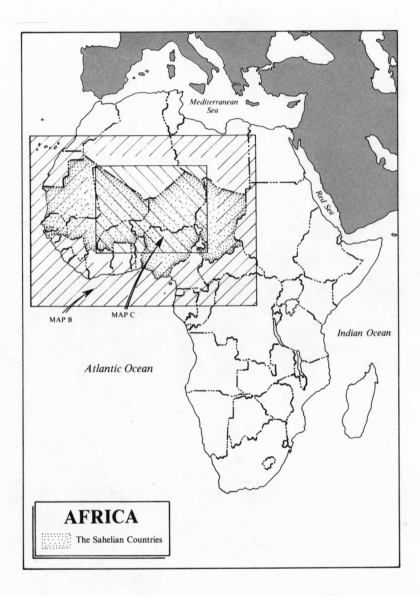

MAP B

MAP C

Mediterranean
Sea

Red Sea

Indian Ocean

Atlantic Ocean

AFRICA

The Sahelian Countries

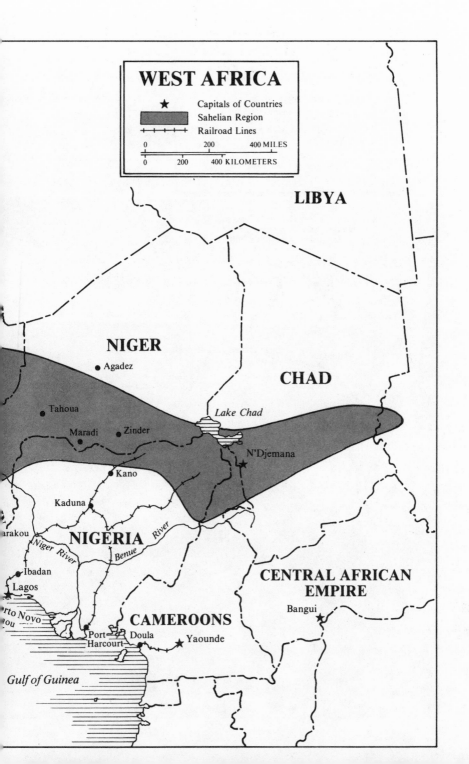

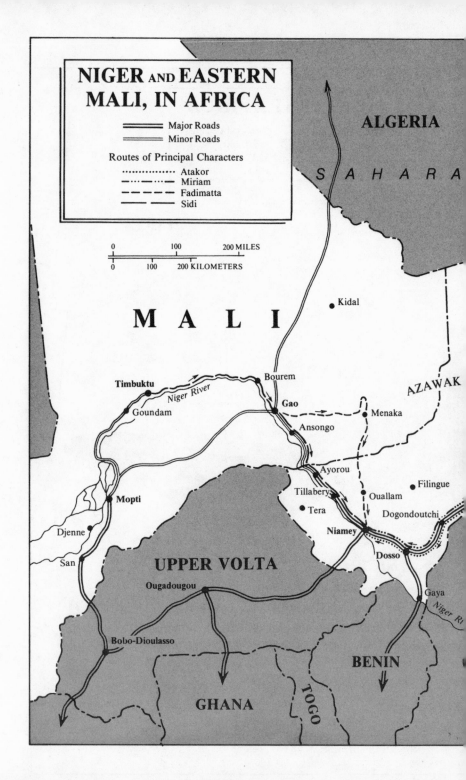

Author's Note

Between 1968 and 1974 a drought ravaged the people, animals, and land of the six countries that make up West Africa's sahelian region.

The most serious years of this drought were the last two, from September 1972 to September 1974, when the cumulative effects of years of substandard rainfall resulted in a famine. During these two years the sahelian country of Niger endured the most devastating losses of crops and livestock.

Niger contains four major ethnic groups: the Hausa and Djerma farming peoples and the Peul and Tuareg nomads. All suffered during the drought, but because the Tuareg suffered and were transformed the most, I decided that they should be the subject of this book. In 1975 I went to Niger and interviewed individual Tuareg about their experiences.

Besides questioning Tuareg who had survived the drought, I visited most of the cities, towns, and nomadic areas in which the events described in this book took place. I went to In Waggeur, and on camel and on foot retraced the route followed by Atakor in the prologue. I went to Gao and visited the Mokhtar, Rissa, the animal market, and the port—the people and places described in chapter four. In Niamey, I arranged for the participants in the incidents described in the final chapter to re-enact their movements.

The people portrayed in this book are typical; the events factual. In some instances I have changed names and expanded individual stories with incidents that happened to other Tuareg from the same tribe or region during the same period of time.

Instead of assuming what people were thinking, I have decided to let them speak for themselves. Throughout the book I have consolidated their responses to my questions into longer statements.

Sympathy and aid for the victims of poverty and disaster in wealthy countries is often solicited by emphasizing individual tragedies. In poor countries, suffering is normally expressed in terms of mortality rates, health, diet, and life expectancy.

People become collages of gaunt faces pushing babies and empty bowls into the lens of a camera. It is easy to forget that these malnourished millions are comprised of unique *peoples,* whose struggle to survive is grounded in their own particular history and culture, and that these peoples are individuals, each drawing on his or her own genius, as well as that of their people, to wage a battle against extinction.

June 1973

Vicinity of In Waggeur, Niger

*A*takor woke up nightblind. Flashes exploded in his eyes as he strained to adjust to the light of dawn. Usually they disappeared in a few seconds. Now they were prolonged by vitamin deficiencies.

He searched for his clothes. His feet swept the sand until they found his sandals. He lifted a blue robe, a *boubou,* over his head, strapped a sword to his waist, and hung red leather pouches around his neck. Sealed in each pouch were verses from the Koran. He patted them with the soft touch of the blind.

He pulled a swatch of indigo cloth through his right hand. The darkblue dye that colored the material smudged his hands, and he then rubbed the blue residue onto his forehead and sunken cheeks. Previous applications had left a sediment in the lines in his face, making them dark and prominent.

The cloth was eighteen inches wide and twelve feet long. He draped it over his head like a shawl, the short left end hanging a foot below his chin, and gathered the remaining material in his right hand. He looped it once under his chin and wound the rest into a turban that covered his head. Then he drew the loop from under his chin over the bridge of his nose and pulled down a swath of the turban to shade his forehead like a visor. Veil and turban covered his face. Nightblind eyes stared through a medieval slit.

"Never uncover your mouth in front of your wife's parents or Tuareg from other tribes. Before your own family or when you are among the blacks it is not necessary to be modest; you may expose your mouth." Twenty years ago a *marabout,* a member of a caste of Tuareg religious teachers, had recited these instructions as he wound the turban around Atakor's head for the first time. Atakor had been fourteen.

During the last week hunger and sadness had drawn him into a fitful delirium. Time stopped, a past in which history had become myth and myth history slid into the present, and his exploits became confused with those of ancestors. The marabout's words came back to Atakor. He wore the veil, he thought, because Tuareg men had always worn it. It protected the face from the sun and the nose and throat from the sandy winds.

The women who sing, remember, and compose history had another explanation. Atakor's wife Miriam recited a poem which claimed that once only Tuareg women wore veils. When a group of Tuareg warriors had been routed after a fierce battle and their camels seized, they straggled back to their camp on foot. Their wives had screamed, "You have disgraced our eyes, vanquished warriors! In the future it is you who shall hide your faces!" The women ripped off their veils and threw them at their husbands' feet. The men had put them on.

Atakor's taut, brown skin was visible only around his eyes. His mouth, his nose, the rest of his face were hidden. Clues to his emotions were found elsewhere. Frowns, smiles, scowls were reflected in his hollow hermit's eyes, or in how he wrapped his veil: how tight, how close to the eyes, how high over the nose.

His movements revealed his feelings, and he had a repertory of shy, fluid, feminine gestures. With his thin arms and fine hands he smoothed his veil like a woman pulling the hem of her dress over her knees. Shaking hands, he followed the ritual of snapping his fingers and then touching his heart; when he served tea, he was like a geisha, pouring from a great height, arranging glasses in a neat pattern, smoothing and brushing the blanket for a guest.

14

These gestures were watched intently by others, and admired and criticized. On Niger's plains, the Taureg recognized each other from great distances by gait or a particular physical disability: A limp was a scar, a slouch a mole, a twitch a birthmark.

As he finished dressing, Atakor's eyes registered the first strong light since he awoke. He walked east, toward it. One of his loose sandals slapped on the dry riverbed. He heard his wife stir, sigh, and gather her robes under the skin tent he had just left. His infant daughter cried. From a neighboring tent a tubercular cough answered.

He bent down, felt for his feet, and pulled off the sandal. He was too late. Miriam was awake.

"Where are you going so early?"

"To save myself."

Not understanding, she swept the baby under her black cloak and comforted it. When mother and child were quiet, he went on his way.

The Tuareg call themselves the Kel Tamashek, the "people who speak Tamashek." Tuareg is an Arabic word meaning "the abandoned of God." Some linguistic authorities believe instead that the word refers to a particularly desolate place in the Sahara desert. In both cases the name has unwanted connotations, and the Tuareg themselves do not use it.

The Tuareg who live in Niger are accustomed to an annual hunger. The French who colonized Niger called this time of famine *la soudure,* "the soldering." The image is of lips and fingers soldered together, of people unable to feed themselves.

The soudure begins during the spring hot season. The temperature rises to 120° Fahrenheit; the udders of cows, goats, and camels are dry, and the stores of millet, sorghum, and wild grains are exhausted. For the farmers the soudure lasts until the autumn harvests. For the Tuareg nomads it breaks in August, when summer rains renew pastures and animals give milk.

By June of 1973, however, five consecutive years of drought had triggered a human and ecological catastrophe. Atakor's animals were not dry, they were dead. Farmlands had become arid pastures, arid pastures deserts, and the soudure lasted twelve months.

Before the soudure of 1969 Atakor had owned fifteen camels, a hundred cows, and more than two hundred goats. He was unsure of the numbers because, he said, "I owned so many that I rarely counted." Half of them died in 1969, a few during the next three years, and the rest in 1973: first the donkeys, sheep, and cows, and then the camels and goats. When his last and favorite camel died, he squatted on the ground, covered his forehead with the palms of his hands, rocked back and forth on his heels, and cried for two days. His wife, his infant daughter, and his two sons by a previous marriage were fed by his cousin, the head of one of the other six families who shared his camp and lived among the thorn trees that bordered the dry river. His cousin was fortunate enough to have saved a few of his goats and cows.

After two days of sleepless misery, Atakor decided to "save himself," to walk alone into the bush without food or water. He knew that after he left the camp the members of his family would have larger portions of the food that remained. This knowledge brought him immediate comfort. He imagined that afterwards Miriam would recite poems celebrating his heroism in saving his family, describing how he had tried to survive in a land in which even goats starved, telling how he tried to save himself because suicide is forbidden.

After walking for five minutes, Atakor stopped and, facing east to where the sun was balanced on the horizon, knelt to wash his hands and arms by rubbing them with sand. Then he stood, bowed his head, bent forward from the waist, fell to his knees, and, prostrate, touched the earth gently with his head.

"In the name of God, the merciful, the compassionate, praise belongs to God, the Lord of all being, the all-merciful, the all-compassionate, the Master of the day of doom."

He rose, paused as if awaiting a reply, and repeated the ritual. Thousands of miles of identical arid landscape separated him from Mecca. Among other Moslems, the Tuareg have a reputation as unorthodox followers of Mohammed. Their knowledge of the Koran is limited, their sexuality is considered indecent, their women are unveiled, and their praying is thought to be sporadic and clumsy. Yet Atakor performed the ritual of prayer with grace and attention to detail.

His prayers finished, Atakor walked southeast, away from the water pump in the small nomadic village of In Waggeur and the dirt track that ran through the village and connected the desert oasis of In Gall, 50 miles to the north, to the market city of Tahoua, 145 miles to the south. He left behind him the carcass of his last and favorite camel, and his family. He walked with long strides, his tall, thin body erect and his eyes straight ahead.

He was in the Tadarast, a sandy, monotonous plain in the center of Niger's northern nomadic zone. Scattered across it were bushes and short, thick-trunked trees. Beneath them clumps of dying grass hugged the ground, their extensive network of roots searching futilely for moisture.

The trees and bushes seemed geometrically spaced, an ordered labyrinth of bare branches which during a sandstorm appeared to be puffs of fossilized smoke. The landscape repeated itself endlessly, as if surrounded by gigantic mirrors that intensified heat, trapped dust, and reflected an infinity of trees and bushes.

Seen closely, the trees were unique in their deformities. Branches had been hacked off or bark stripped for firewood. Lower branches had been ripped off by goats and the higher ones cut by nomads and fed to animals. Trunks were scarred by termites and surrounded by ant castles. Sand had smothered saplings. Erosion had exposed roots which were then buried by sandstorms until summer floods exposed them again or washed away the entire tree.

In another time, Atakor, mounted on a camel above the tree line, could identify individual trees. They directed him to neighboring camps, wells, and seasonal pools of water. During the months just past many had been cut down, altering the landscape. Now, on foot, he missed these familiar signposts.

By midmorning a red wall of dust, the kind of intense sandstorm that often precedes a summer thunderstorm, rolled across the Tadarast. The winds stripped away the thin covering of soil. As the edge of the storm advanced toward Atakor, it rippled the sand into wavelets. More sand seemed to pour from the sky, plugging his nostrils, scouring his eyes, clogging his throat. He tightened his veil and breathed with difficulty. Finally he stopped and sat, leaning against a withered tree, sand drifting at his back.

As the drought destroyed their material wealth, many Tuareg withdrew into the familiar and comforting myths and oral histories of their people. They resembled impoverished aristocrats wandering through crumbling mansions, doting on heirlooms, recreating the past, escaping the present. Now even this comfort eluded Atakor. Since leaving his camp that morning to "save himself," he had thought of Tanut.

Although the French had claimed Niger as a colony in 1900, not until seventeen years later did they succeed in crushing the last major Tuareg uprising that challenged their rule. Atakor's Tuareg tribe, the Illabakan, then numbered around a thousand. The Illabakan and about twenty other tribes of varying sizes were all members of the Kel Dennik confederation. In 1917 Ikhesi, a member of the Kel Nan tribé, had just become the chief of the Kel Dennik. Ikhesi was reluctant to join the general Tuareg rebellion against the French. He wanted to consolidate his own power, and his people were more accessible to French reprisals than dissident confederations to the north.

Ikhesi was therefore receptive when, in March 1917, he received a communication from a Captain Sadoux urging him not to join the revolt. Sadoux promised that if Ikhesi complied, the French would formally recognize his leadership. Sadoux himself was coming north from the French fort at Tahoua with a column of troops to conduct the ceremony.

Having waited for twelve years to become chief, Ikhesi was determined to let nothing stand in his way. He waited for the French column at Tanut, a collection of small wells in a tree-lined valley southeast of In Waggeur, near where Atakor now leaned against the withered tree. With Ikhesi were over a thousand warriors, most of the Kel Dennik nobles, and many of their vassals, wives, children, marabouts, and slaves.

On March 12, 1917, Sadoux and a column of ninety men left Tahoua. The column consisted of three French officers, African soldiers from the French colony of Senegal, and warriors and interpreters from the Kel Gress, a Tuareg confederation that had frequently fought against the Kel Dennik during the nineteenth century. On April 8 they arrived at the Tanut wells. Sadoux sent two Tuareg interpreters, Al-Qasem and Afangarom, to Ikhesi's tent. They told Ikhesi that the French had come on a peaceful mission, had marched for a day without food or water, and were hungry and thirsty. Ikhesi and the Kel Dennik moved away from the wells and gave them food. The soldiers ate and drank and camped among the trees.

The next morning the French column built an enclosure of wood and thorn branches. The walls were six feet high, and there was one exit. "You will gather here tomorrow to name your chief," Captain Sadoux explained.

The following day, the Tuareg were led in and the entrance closed. Turbaned and veiled, their ancient swords at their sides, daggers tied to their forearms, some carrying spears, they talked and stared at the stockade walls, waiting to vote. The women sat inside as well, their black cloaks pulled over their heads but not their mouths. They wore silver earrings and bracelets. Silver pendants anchored their black braids.

Although there were only a few of his tribe, the Illabakan, at Tanut, one had been a relative of Atakor's. Atakor remembered the scar on the man's forehead. He touched his own forehead and recalled a poem that was still recited at Kel Dennik gatherings:

O God my saviour
I will soon join my dead parents.
Al-Qasem is on my trail.
He accompanies the lieutenant who will kill me.
They are going to return with my head
And earn a great reward.
The lieutenant has called Afangarom and given him a double reward
So that he can seek his fortune among the black women.
O God my saviour,
During the night which will hear my last sigh,
The women will stay by my side,
Weeping as they stitch my shroud.
O God, divide my inheritance among my women:
Saoudata, Echchehidet, Errilata,
Aminata and Elfelilet,
Because the lieutenant will pierce my side,
His sword will cut my throat.

Thirst interrupted Atakor's reverie. He was suddenly alert, rescued from his vision of Tanut. The wind had slackened and he stood up, his back to the tree. A hundred yards away he saw black shapes merge and then separate. They sky had cleared and dust devils, small tornadoes of sand fifty to a hundred feet in diameter, formed as hot currents of air met above the ground. They danced between the trees, disappeared and reappeared on the horizon, swallowing the black forms.

Atakor remembered a nearby well used by the Peul, the other nomadic people of the Tadarast. Hoping to find water, he reversed his direction and walked west, back toward In Waggeur.

When even the stunted bushes disappeared, Atakor knew he was close to the Peul well. Trees, stripped of their branches, looked like poles. Sand slithered around clumps of inedible grasses, encircling them.

During five years of drought, circular deserts had formed around the wells, pools, and pumping stations of the Tadarast and the fossilized Azawak valley on whose eastern fringes the Tadarast is located. The radius of these deserts was usually less than ten miles, or half the distance a cow could walk before it needed water. Once the cows had consumed the edible grasses within this circle, they had to be led to another water point. On such journeys, many died of thirst. But the alternative was to die of hunger. Peul and Tuareg nomads had to choose: Would they watch their animals die of thirst outside this ten-mile radius, or of starvation inside?

The land around the well was barren. Beyond the crest of a small, newly formed sand dune, Atakor saw a Peul, dressed in skins and wearing a conical straw hat. He was bent over the well, pulling up a leather bucket.

The ground sloped away from the mouth of the well on three sides. At the foot of the little hill, thirty severed cows' heads were arranged in semicircular rows. Bloated tongues hung from their mouths and enormous horns, a matador's nightmare, stuck out like wings. There were whitened skulls and decomposing heads. Under a recent casualty a pool of blood reddened the sand.

The Peul ignored Atakor. He carried his bucket from the well and dashed water on the remains of his dead herd. Behind the well three young boys, his sons, stood in a line holding each others' arms like a string of paper dolls.

20

His wife was crouched behind them. Naked breasts that looked like badgers' tails hung to her waist. As Atakor approached her husband, she lifted one breast, then the other. They slapped against her stomach. "Dry," she whispered. "Dry."

The Peul began the elaborate ceremony of greeting.

"Welcome on your arrival."

"How is your health?" asked Atakor.

"Fine, thanks be to God. How is your health?"

"Fine. How is your work?"

"My work goes well," answered the Peul.

"How is your family?"

"All well, thanks be to God." (The Peul's wife smiled.)

"And your animals?"

"All are in good health," the Peul replied.

The greetings continued, each man repeating the same questions and giving the same answers, always replying that everything—animals, family, health, and work—was fine. Any other response would have been rude.

When the ritual was completed the Peul asked if Atakor wanted some water. He threw the bucket into the well, hauled on the rope, and poured water into a gourd. As Atakor drank, the Peul filled another bucket and wandered among his garden of heads, pouring water into pools in front of the bloated tongues. He tapped a stick against the horns, urging his cows to drink.

Like the Sahara, the Tadarast is characterized by a sterile silence that magnifies the slightest sound—the groan of a camel, the slap of a sandal, the buzzing of a fly. As the Peul finished watering the heads, Atakor sensed that someone else had invaded this silence. Hoping to avoid whoever it was, he left the well. He walked west, back over his earlier tracks.

Two hours later he crossed the In Gall-Tahoua track within sight of In Waggeur, whose dozen mud houses, cement school, and water pump made it similar to other small villages scattered across Niger's nomadic zone. He continued west, following one of the dry rivers that filled with brown water during the rainy season and ran into the In Waggeur pond. Many of these riverbeds had been formed thousands of years earlier,

21

when the climate was more humid. Their fossilized promise of water taunted the rest of the landscape.

On one bank of the riverbed, a few miles from In Waggeur, was a camp that had been built by the Tuareg slave caste, the *bouzous*. It was empty. The bouzous had joined the exodus. Atakor poked at piles of ashes, picked up tattered mats, and kicked broken gourds as he looked for food. A donkey brayed, and he turned to see some shadows merge with those of the thorn trees. Again he was not alone. Instead of investigating, he climbed into a four-foot-high enclosure made of woven thorn branches meant to prevent young goats from wandering. He sat down inside and stared at the wall of thorns opposite. In a few minutes he was asleep.

In 1917 the French had called the Tuareg out of the Tanut enclosure one by one, presumably to cast a secret ballot for their next chief, for Ikhesi. The most famous warriors were called by name.

As each man emerged, he was seized from behind and thrown to the ground. His turban was ripped away. If he wore his hair long and braided in the style of the Tuareg nobles, his throat was cut. His body was stripped of weapons and jewelry and tossed into a growing heap. Only the marabouts, who were not warriors and were identified by their shaved heads, were spared.

After some dozens of their comrades had "voted," the men remaining within the enclosure became suspicious that they failed to return. They rushed toward the narrow entrance. The French blocked it. The Tuareg shrieked when they climbed over the walls and saw the bodies of their comrades. Those who could, jumped out and ran. The troops pursued them into the bush with knives and rifles. The African mercenaries and the Kel Gress burst inside the enclosure and fired point-blank into the survivors.

Ikhesi was wounded in the abdomen, then shot again by a Senegalese mercenary. His head was cut off and stuck onto a pole. His long braids waved over the massacre.

Some people survived. One wounded Illabakan lay under a pile of bodies, feigning death. Others simply outran their pursuers. But the

22

bloodshed was devastating. Nearly all of the 207 Tuareg warriors at Tanut perished. As late as 1965, nomads who visited the Tanut wells were
still digging up the jewelry of the victims.

According to Atakor, Tanut proved that the Kel Dennik were truly
courageous. "They were afraid of us, so they had to resort to treachery
to defeat us."

Awakened by a sharp cry, Atakor stood up and looked out of the enclosure. Nothing was visible. The sun was setting and the surrounding
trees threw their shadows on him. He paced uneasily around the circumference of the enclosure until he reached the entrance. Outside he could
hear someone calling his name.

Atakor whirled and leaped over the wall of the enclosure. The voices
continued to call his name. He crouched close to the ground and they
sprang from the other side of the enclosure. He jumped into the dry riverbed. They followed.

At sunset, the temperature in the Tadarast can drop as much as 30 degrees. The sun disappears and the moon is suddenly visible. Action is
suspended between night and day, moon and sun, cold and heat. Caught
between Tanut and the drought, vision and blindness, Atakor unsheathed his sword and turned to face his pursuers.

As they separated, he whirled and slashed. Limbs crashed down from
a thorn tree, and as he lifted the sword again it became entangled. Sha-
dowy black forms were holding the ends of a rope that fell across his
chest. The forms ran in opposite directions, drawing closer as the rope
bound his body, tying his legs and binding his hands to his sides. The
shapes met in front of him and knotted the rope. His vision cleared, and
they became Miriam and his sister Fani.

Other Tuareg men had already tried to kill themselves by walking off
into the bush without food or water. When Atakor hadn't returned by
midmorning, Miriam remembered what he had said and understood his
intention. She told Fani, borrowed a rope and a donkey, and set off after
him.

Miriam was thirty-two. When she married Atakor in 1967 she had

23

been, by her own account, "large and beautiful." Seven years later she was thin, and the robes that once stretched tightly around her waist hung in folds.

Miriam's skin had been soft and pale. It had become hard and dark, because she "worked, walked in the sun, and had no milk to drink." Once she had spent hours arranging her jewelry, braiding her hair, and coloring her fingernails with a dye squeezed from red berries.

She was certain that large and white she was more beautiful. The drought had melted away the attractive fat and left her arms scrawny and her cheekbones prominent. During the soudure of 1973 she aged years in a few weeks. Her thick black hair dropped out and her braids became thin. Coughs cut every breath. Wrinkles creased her forehead and her eyes became dry and red.

Miriam was a conventional Tuareg woman. She had been divorced, and she had enjoyed numerous lovers. Also, like many Tuareg wives, she often intimidated her husband. That she should rescue him was not unusual.

Miriam and Fani tied Atakor onto the donkey and walked back to In Waggeur. The next day they took him to Emouzakoum, a marabout.

Insanity was rare in the Tadarast before the drought, but in 1973 it was epidemic. The Tadarast resembled an open-air madhouse, and Atakor was one of many inmates. Others slept all day rather than tend their dying herds. They refused to eat and their eyes watered with tears. They attempted suicide, and if they succeeded their deaths were attributed to "sadness."

A Peul tried to jump into a well when his last cow died. His wife grabbed him by the heels and held him suspended for hours.

The wife of a marabout sat naked under the midday sun. She crooned a mad song that blamed God for her dead animals and begged Him to take her life. The Tuareg believed that to blame God for a calamity was madness.

An elderly man, Abrika, began searching for his dead sheep in January. During February he rode a camel. When it became too weak to carry him he traded it for a donkey. When the donkey died he walked. He became enraged when his kinsmen suggested his sheep were not lost, but dead. He continued his search, and sometime during the soudure he vanished.

Miriam left Atakor alone with the marabout. The men were friends but their meeting under the circumstances was dignified and formal. They clasped hands and then slid them apart until only their fingertips touched. As they lost contact they each snapped fingers against palms. This traditional handshake was followed by an involved ritual of verbal greetings.

The marabout had lost most of his own animals, but he could still afford to buy tea, sugar, millet, and tobacco from the trader at In Waggeur. The drought had forced him to lower the price of his magic but had increased the demand for it.

Before, a potent amulet that protected the wearer against death and disease, that made him invulnerable to sword wounds, promoted good fortune, and prevented camels from straying, cost a cow or a combination of less valuable animals. With few surviving animals, charms were sold for whatever a client could pay. People asked for an amulet that would protect their animals from the drought, but the marabout had been unable to find a fitting Koranic verse and had to admit that there was no amulet to prevent the drought.

After he and Atakor had drunk three glasses of green tea, the marabout offered advice instead of an amulet. "Since you can no longer support your wife, you must send her to her parents. Since you have no animals, you must beg. Since you loved your animals, you must find a way to buy new ones." Before Atakor left, the marabout gave him a fistful of green tea and a branch of dates.

In Waggeur is located on one of the major trans-Saharan routes, and four-wheel-drive vehicles, mostly Land Rovers and Toyotas, and large diesel trucks, some private and some belonging to SNTN (the Nigerien government transportation agency), pass through the village several times a day. Many stop for a few minutes. The drivers and passengers relieve themselves, fill canteens from the pump, and buy hard candies and stale cigarettes from an open pack kept by a merchant.

Trucks are the sole form of public transportation in northern Niger. Passengers bargain with the drivers over the fare and ride sitting on the cargo. Most of the trucks are old and slow. Along the In Gall-Tahoua

25

road they average less than twenty miles an hour. It takes them at least twelve hours to cover the two hundred miles between the two towns. Breakdowns and flat tires are frequent. Often a driver and his passengers will camp next to a stalled truck for days waiting for a spare part to arrive from Niger's capital, Niamey. Pumps at the infrequent petrol stations are apt to run out of fuel.

At In Waggeur a single tree stands at the side of the In Gall-Tahoua road. Since it provides shade, it is the truck depot. Two days after Atakor visited the marabout, he and Miriam sat under this tree waiting for a truck. They had been there since late afternoon, and now it was getting dark.

During the hot season most trucks travel at night. Twenty minutes before they arrive at In Waggeur their headlights flicker on the horizon like artillery flashes. They disappear and reappear, again and again, finally becoming a dull glow accompanied by a grinding of worn gears and a bubbling of broken mufflers.

About midnight one of these trucks stopped in front of the In Waggeur tree. Atakor paid the driver with money he had begged the day before from a Land Rover full of English tourists (following the marabout's advice) and climbed over the side to join the other passengers, most of whom were Tuaregs and bouzous, a cargo of silent, veiled heads. When he was settled Miriam handed up his sword and a bundle wrapped in a blue cloth that had once been a boubou. Inside were the dates, a rusty lock and key, and green twigs for cleaning his teeth.

The route Atakor was about to travel was familiar. Three or four times a year he and other Illabakan had formed small caravans of between ten and a hundred animals and gone south to the markets of Abalack, Kao, Barmou, and Chadawanka. All were located on the fringes of the nomadic zone, between 60 and 150 miles south of In Waggeur. They were meeting places for farmers and nomads.

The Illabakan caravans were gone for a couple of weeks. They left with herds of sheep and goats and returned with their donkeys and camels laden with millet, cloth, tea, sugar, and tobacco. But on this trip Atakor had nothing to trade. He was following this familiar caravan route for the last time.

26

1

The Tuareg

They [the Tuareg] have their old ideals perhaps
as a veiled and unconscious goal; something definite
and real they still do keep. If their outlook is sad
and their eyes seem to be forever wandering away to a
further horizon, their melancholy is not that of
pessimism. It is merely that they are aware of
something which is now beyond their reach.

—Francis Rodd (British explorer
who lived among the Tuareg of
Niger during the 1920s)

i

S*ahel* is an Arabic word meaning "border" or "shore." The West African sahel is a 300- to 600-mile-wide border separating desert and tropics, a 2,600-mile-long shore of arid and semiarid land on the southern edge of the Sahara. It runs from west to east, from the Atlantic beaches of Senegal to the center of the African continent.

Its people are tested by a harsh climate. A short and unpredictable rainy season gives farmers one yearly harvest and herders three months of good pasture. In the space of a few hours, both farmers and herders can be scorched by walls of wind-blown sand, drenched by pounding rains, and suffocated by temperatures of over 100 degrees Fahrenheit.

The sahel's land is poor. In the north it is mostly sandy plains with scattered bushes, nearly a desert; in the south, more plains of hard red clay and more bushes, almost fertile.

The sahel's people are poor. Twenty-five million live in six nations which were French colonies until 1960. Except for a tiny upper class of merchants and government functionaries, the people are either herders or farmers. Some are both, farmers who own animals and herders who scatter seeds.

The farming people have black skins and negroid features, and live in the south. They have not always been farmers. Many were also, and some still are, clever traders, brave warriors, and efficient administrators.

The herders have skin that shades from white to black, facial features which can be caucasian, negroid, or a mixture, and live in the north. They too were once traders and warriors.

The sahelian farmers and herders are separated by history, vocation, and race, but unified by malnutrition, illiteracy, and disease. They are among the poorest people in the world. Whenever the United Nations or the World Bank publishes world economic summaries, the people of four sahel countries—Niger, Mali, Upper Volta, and Chad—compete with a half-dozen others for the distinction of having the lowest per capita income in the world. The people of the other sahel countries—Senegal, Gambia,[1] and Mauritania—are close behind them.

Of the six West African countries—Chad, Mali, Mauritania, Niger, Senegal, and Upper Volta—which contain sahelian land, Niger has by far the most. Niger is also the largest country in West Africa, covering 489,000 square miles,[2] more than Texas and California combined.

Most of the 4.5 million people who inhabit this huge country belong to one of four ethnic groups. They are either Hausa or Djerma farmers, or Peul or Tuareg herders. Niger's farmers are concentrated in a narrow strip of fertile land running parallel to the border with Benin and Nigeria. Two million Hausa farmers and traders live in the eastern portion of this strip, and one million Djerma, who dominate Niger's government, live in the west.

In the semiarid grasslands to the north of this farming belt, Niger's two nomadic peoples, the Tuareg and the Peul, raise cattle, camels, sheep, and goats. The Peul, who number 600,000 in Niger, are an extremely mobile nomadic people found throughout West Africa. Their

[1]Gambia is a small, ex-British colony surrounded by an ex-French colony, Senegal. Although its land is not sahelian, it has become classified with these countries for political purposes because it is totally within the borders of Senegal, a country that does contain sahelian land.

[2]Statistics for the drought, the sahel, and Niger vary greatly and are extremely unreliable. According to some sources, Niger has 459,000 square miles, while others give it 465,000. If these figures are accepted, Mali, rather than Niger, becomes the largest West African country. Some of the confusion about Niger's precise area stems from uncertainty as to the exact location of the Saharan border with Libya.

skin is dark red, their faces oval, and their features Hamitic. The Peul who inhabit Niger's Tadarast plateau are generally darker, their features more negroid than those found in many other regions of West Africa.

The Tuareg consider themselves a caucasian people and, although many do have light-colored skin and European facial features, they are, in fact, racially a very heterogeneous people. Their skin color ranges from light brown to almost black.

ii

*T*he Tuareg are indigenous to three African countries. There are 10,000 of them living in the vicinity of the Hoggar Mountains of southern Algeria, 250,000 in northeastern Mali, and another 250,000 scattered throughout central and northern Niger. (These figures exclude the Tuareg slave caste, the bouzou, of whom there are almost an equal number.)

Some Saharan historians and explorers believe that the Tuareg are the descendants of a valiant band of twelfth-century European crusaders who, cut off from and later abandoned by the Christian armies in Palestine, wandered across Egypt and North Africa and finally settled in the southern Sahara. Another theory is that they are the survivors of the Garamantes, Christian knights descended from Roman legionnaires who built fortresses in the Libyan oases.

Such theories suggest that the racial and cultural similarities between the Tuareg and these early Christians are more than coincidental, that the Tuareg's intricate codes of chivalry and courage, their feudal social structure, and their weapons—two-edged swords, javelins, skin shields, and sheathed daggers—are inherited from European warriors.

Some evidence supports these theories. Heraldic lions have been found engraved on the hilts of ancient Tuareg swords, as has the Wolf of Passau, the mark of medieval German swordsmiths that was later copied by Spanish craftsmen. Tuareg swords, which are shaped like

, resemble those of the crusaders. The stylized crosses that deco-
hields and women's jewelry, especially the famous cross of
ez, are thought to have been inspired by the Christian cross. Some
reg, in greeting each other, kiss the crossed thumb and forefinger of
the right hand, a gesture that was one of the secret signs of the early
Christian church, a sign still used among some Spanish Christians.

However, the most likely reason for these similarities between the
Tuareg and European Christians is that the Agadez cross is derived from
an ancient Egyptian fertility symbol, that the European swords were
brought not by crusaders but by traders, and that the other resemblances
are coincidental.

A more logical explanation for the presence of the Tuareg in West
Africa is that they were once Berbers, a caucasian people who were the
original inhabitants of North Africa and whose occasional blue eyes and
blond hair are the legacy of the Roman and Vandal invasions.

The largest Arab invasion of North Africa took place in 1045. Fleeing
a famine in Egypt, the Arabs arrived in North Africa with wives, children, and slaves. They were colonizers who wanted to convert and as-
similate the native Berbers. Many Berber tribes evacuated the coastal
plains and isolated themselves in the mountains. Others, presumably the
original Tuareg, fled into the Sahara Desert to preserve their unique culture and language.

Between the twelfth and the nineteenth centuries, as the climate of
the Sahara became drier and men and animals increased and required
more abundant pastures, many Tuareg migrated further south into the
Air Mountains and the plateaus of northern Niger and Mali. They pros-
pered in this region. Not because of what was buried under its land—
there was no gold or minerals—or what could be grown on it—a small
harvest in the oasis and pasture grasses that supported modest herds.
But because of what traveled through it—caravans that brought slaves
and gold from tropical Africa to the Mediterranean and cloth from the
Mediterranean to tropical Africa. The Tuareg were able to "tax" these
caravans, either by guarding them or, if their services were spurned or
they were being guarded by a rival confederation, by plundering them.
Both occupations encouraged them to become skillful warriors.

As the Tuareg moved south into the northern regions of the sahel, they also found another source of profit and comfort, slavery. They enslaved the indigenous black sedentary people in their path and recruited others by raiding more southerly villages and carrying away their inhabitants. These black slaves, known as bouzous, were soon absorbed into the culture of their masters. They wore veils, learned Tamashek, and became a distinct people in their own right.

The bouzous enabled the Tuareg to become overseers. When they weren't raiding or warring, they needed only to make decisions as to where and when their animals would graze and drink, which animals would be traded, and how much millet should be bought to enable them to survive the soudure.

The bouzous did the work. They usually milked the animals, led them to the wells, and then pulled up buckets of water. Sometimes they fought in Tuareg armies as spear-carrying foot soldiers.

The Tuareg women became ladies of leisure. They nursed children, gossiped, recited poetry, played violins, and managed the bouzou women who pounded and cooked millet, gathered wood, made fires, swept the camp, and looked for emergency foods such as wild grasses and melons. Rarely did a Tuareg woman perform these tasks herself.

In Niger's nomadic zones wealth was measured by the size of herds, and many Tuareg were wealthy. Animals were a capital resource that multiplied and produced income when pasture was plentiful. They enabled the Tuareg to "pay" their bouzous with milk, skins, and an occasional yearling, and to enjoy a life of leisure surprising for a nomadic people living in so harsh an environment.

Blacks seized in Tuareg raids had both more liberty and security than those sent to America. Tuareg and bouzou lived in the same camp, in similar shelters, and ate the same meals, often from the same pot. In many respects the bouzous were members of the Tuareg families. Atakor said, "I loved them all. Of course you love someone who works for you. Sometimes, though, they were naughty children and had to be beaten." These beatings, however, usually consisted of only a few swats with a light stick.

An elaborate ritual discouraged harsh treatment of the bouzous and enabled them to change masters. When a bouzou was dissatisfied with his master, he chose a new one and cut an insignificant slit in the ear of one of his anmials. Responsible for his slave's actions, the embarrassed and unwanted master then had to give the slave to the owner of the injured animal as compensation. A Tuareg master did not have an equal right. Involuntary manumission was prohibited, and it was a master's duty to feed, clothe, and shelter a bouzou until he either died or ran away.

iii

*D*uring the nineteenth century, the Europeans who explored West Africa wove a schizophrenic myth around the Tuareg which was to influence the actions of European colonizers in the early years of the twentieth century and, later, those of European philanthropists. One part of this myth portrayed the Tuareg as cruel and treacherous primitives who signed treaties one minute and massacred the signers the next, a people never to be trusted. The second part of the European myth portrayed them more sympathetically, even romantically.

The first European explorer to reach Timbuctoo, Gordon Laing, was slain in 1826 by a Tuareg. His murderer, Sheikh Labeida, was rabid in his hatred of Christians, and acted with a religious fanaticism that was unusual among the Tuareg. As a sign of his contempt for infidels, Labeida held his nose while Laing's possessions burned. Laing's death was the first in a series of nineteenth-century atrocities that gave the Tuareg a reputation for treachery and barbarity.

(In 1910, eighty-four years later, a French army officer, Bonnel de Mézières, visited Timbuctoo and sought out the eighty-two-year-old nephew of Sheikh Labeida. This nephew said that he had been told by Labeida that "we burned his [Laing's] cases and buried them because he had come to poison the land, and we held our noses as we burned them." The nephew was able to direct de Mézières to a tree outside

Timbuctoo under which, he said, Laing had been murdered and buried. De Mézières dug beneath the tree and uncovered charred bones which a French army doctor later identified as having belonged to a European adult. No evidence of Laing's diaries was ever found; presumably, they were burned with the cases. The written records of the first European to reach Timbuctoo were lost, but the Tuareg histories had preserved an amazingly accurate account of his murder for almost a century.)

In 1828 a young French adventurer named René Caillié became the first European to visit Timbuctoo (now located in Mali) and return alive. In his widely read journals, he said, "The trade of Timbuctoo is considerably cramped by the Tooariks [Tuareg], a warlike nation who render the inhabitants of the town their tributaries. . . . They are cruel as they are warlike. Their nose is aquiline, their eyes large, their mouth finely formed, the face long and the forehead rather elevated. The expression of the countenance is however savage and barbarous."

Caillié was particularly sympathetic to the blacks of Timbuctoo: "The Tooariks have terrified the negroes of their neighborhood into subjection, and they inflict upon them the most cruel depredations and exactions. Like the Arabs, they have fine horses which facilitate their marauding expeditions. The people exposed to their attacks stand in such awe of them that the appearance of three or four Tooariks is sufficient to strike terror into five or six villages."

Although Caillié was probably correct about the exploitation of the inhabitants of Timbuctoo by the Tuareg, many of his other judgments were erroneous. However, since he was the first European to have visited and returned from Timbuctoo, his journals were the most important single source of European prejudices against the Tuareg.

The Tuareg reputation for treachery was renewed some fifty years later. In 1881 a column of ninety-seven men, including French engineers and soldiers, left Ouargla in southern Algeria under the command of Colonel Flatters. The purpose of the expedition was to explore possible routes for a trans-Saharan railway. A year later twelve men returned. The rest had been attacked and murdered or fed poisoned dates by hostile Tuareg. Some had died of thirst and been cannibalized by their comrades.

For decades this disaster convinced the French that, if their colonization of the Sahara and the sahel was to be successful, the Tuareg would have to be eliminated. They ignored the fact that Flatters had unwisely allied himself with a weak Tuareg confederation and was considered fair game when he entered their rivals' territory.

The first and most important proponent of the second part of the schizophrenic European myth depicting the Tuareg as noble and brave warriors, a beautiful and hospitable people, was Henri Duveyrier. A Frenchman, Duveyrier, at the age of twenty-one, lived with the Tuareg for nine months. His experience made him a sympathetic expert.

In his book *The Tuareg of the North*, Duveyrier spoke of the Tuareg's grace, chivalry, and respect for their women. He even found beauty in their war charge:

> To see a Tuareg war charge is to feel complete and utter fear creep through one's body. Great serried squadrons of tall, blue-veiled men, mounted on fast white camels, crashing forward like a vast roller. The shrill cries of the warriors, the thrilling sound of the javelins flashing through the air, and the long lugubrious beat of the tobol [drum] combine to make it one of the most stunning spectacles to be seen on any battlefield.

Duveyrier had stayed with the Tuareg in 1860. Two decades later, when Flatters was preparing for his ill-fated expedition, Duveyrier warned him that the Hoggar Tuareg, in whose territory Flatters was to travel, were in a state of anarchy and that he should not try to pass from the territory of one Tuareg tribe into that of another without a guarantee of safe conduct. Flatters disregarded the advice and entered Hoggar lands despite a further warning from a Tuareg chief that he could not expect to be protected. Ironically, Duveyrier was accused of complicity in the ensuing tragedy because of his sympathetic portrayal of the Algerian Tuareg. These accusations were to drive him to suicide.

Although some Tuareg were handsome and had a graceful physique, there were countless others who were withered and emaciated from years of sun, wind, and desert hardship. Although most had black hair, curly or straight, and brown, almost black eyes, there were blond Kel Ajjar Tuareg in northern oases, as well as short, almost negroid Tuareg among the southern confederations.

Most early explorers and visitors saw only the handsome Tuareg. Their descriptions were, for the most part, similar to that of Lord Rodd, an English explorer who visited the Air Mountains in the early twentieth century:

> The beauty and grace of their bodies are the principal characteristics of the Tuareg. They are tall, more commonly in the neighbourhood of six feet than shorter. They look much taller owing to their flowing robes. When at rest they have little superficial muscular development; their bodies are not corrugated and knobbly like the powerfully built Latin: they are more like Nordic folk in that their limbs and backs are smooth until exerted, when the muscles stand up hard and tough. Their arms and legs are long and shapely and exceedingly graceful; they never have flaccid or cylindrical limbs like Abyssinians or certain Indian races. Their bones are small. They have wrists and ankles as slender as a woman's; it is noteworthy that whatever the degree of negro admixture this sign of high breeding is the last to disappear. It is a most infallible mark of pure Tuareg parentage. With it, of course, go slenderness and refinement of hands and fingers. The men never grow fat: they are hard and fit and dry like the nerve of a bow, or a spring in tension. Of all their characteristics the one I have most vividly in mind is their grace of carriage. The men are born to walk and move as kings, they stride along swiftly and easily, like Princes of the Earth, fearing no man, cringing before none, and consciously superior to other people.

The nineteenth-century romanticization and vilification of the Tuareg endured well into the twentieth. In 1944 a British Intelligence handbook on West Africa expressed the confusion succinctly: "On the whole they are proud, brave, courteous, and hospitable, but they are also greedy, deceitful, and treacherous." The acceptance of the latter part of this caricature guided French treatment of the Tuareg, and particularly the Kel Dennik confederation, during the first two decades of French rule in Niger.

* * *

*N*iger was one of the last African countries to be invaded by Europeans. It boasted no known precious metals, no tropical products, and no strategic trading outposts. There was no vast pool of native labor to exploit, no wealthy people to pillage. There was only desert, arid plateau, and a small fertile stretch along the Niger River, underpopulated because of disease.

The largest sahelian countries—Niger, Mali, and Chad—were blanks on colonial maps. During the scramble for African territory at the turn of the century, geographic continuity, land quantity rather than quality, and rivalry with other colonial powers were more important to the French than plunder and profit. It was this hunger for land area, coupled with a fear that if they failed to colonize unoccupied African regions the British would, that brought the French to Niger.

Unlike the richer West African countries on the coast, Niger was colonized first by soldiers, to be followed later by missionaries and traders. The French treasury did not profit from Niger, but the businessmen who built and supplied the modest western infrastructure, the roads, telegraph lines, new cities, and military outposts, did.

The country's harsh climate and vast, hostile deserts offered the French military a grand adventure. Britain's prime minister, Lord Salisbury, commented that by colonizing Niger and the rest of the western Sudan, "the French gained a lot of sand where its cockerel could use its spurs." A French politician saw the new empire as a desert where "nothing can be grown except the decorations that flourish on the uniforms of officers impatient for promotion."

With the French army in control, the colonization of the sahel was planned like a gigantic military maneuver. One French column was to move south from Algeria, and a number of others westward from Senegal. They were to make treaties, annex land, and converge at Lake Chad, thereby uniting the north, west, and equatorial French African empires.

One of the earliest engagements between the French army and the

Tuareg in Niger occurred in June 1895. A column of French and Senegalese troops under the command of a Colonel Toutée were proceeding alongside the Niger River, exploring southern Niger. According to Toutée's diary, "For the last three days my trip has taken on a new interest. We are constantly encircled by many fine-featured white faces. They give us unsettling looks, many give outward demonstrations of their friendship, but others, fleeting signs of hatred and treachery."

When Toutée saw a fleet of empty, flat-bottomed boats being poled across the Niger by a handful of armed Tuareg, he gave the order to load weapons and form a single rank. The Tuareg were so certain of victory that they had already arranged transportation for the booty.

The twenty-nine men in the column (twenty-four Senegalese and Dahomian troops, two servants, Toutée, and two other French officers) were armed with pistols and short rifles. A hundred feet away, facing their single rank, was a line of fifty Tuareg warriors. The skin shields they held in front of themselves touched and formed a wall capable of protecting them against javelins and swords but not bullets. According to Toutée, they were "jumping, dancing, and leaping in the air like trampolinists." Behind these leaping foot soldiers were a hundred horsemen. (The more southerly Tuareg confederations were likely to ride horses, while the desert Tuareg preferred camels.)

Before the foot soldiers began to advance, the Tuareg chief rode to within fifty feet of the French column and shouted, "There is only one God and Mohammed is his prophet; Christians, my father has decided that today you will stop living like dogs and blacks and you will meet the only God."

After this threat, Toutée reported, the Tuareg "screamed, performed savage dances, and exploded with cries of delight when they saw how few we were." The foot soldiers advanced to within sixty feet of the column and threw their lances; these fell short without injuring anyone.

The French opened fire. Immediately the Tuareg fell to the ground and tried to crawl forward under their shields. They offered a vulnerable target. Many were killed. None of the French troops was wounded. After a few minutes, the Tuareg retreated under the steady French fire, and soon "the rest of these fanatics disappeared."

After his troops had been beaten back, the chief rode alone against the French and was cut down. Toutée said, "This son of Bouboukar was a beautiful boy, white as milk, with fine arms and legs. The bracelet that I took after the battle was too small for a normal man to slip over his wrist. Only women were able to wear it."

The French learned from this encounter that a small, well-armed detachment of troops had to fear the Tuareg only if they charged en masse. "It is certain," said Toutée, "that if the Tuareg, instead of advancing slowly, had rushed us, like their magnificently courageous chief, we would have all been killed or taken and they would have lost only a dozen men." Toutée also learned that his Senegalese troops "don't fight to kill but to capture." He recommended that they be instructed to kill.

In 1898 the Battle of Izewan between the Kel Dennik and the Kel Ahaggar, an Algerian Tuareg confederation, reinforced the Nigerien Tuareg's fear of rifles. Before the battle, Mohammad ag El Kumati, the chief of the Kel Dennik, wrote to the Kel Ahaggar chief demanding that his tribe put down their guns and fight, as before, with the traditional Tuareg weapons—a six-foot iron spear, a straight sword, and a short dagger whose sheath was attached to the left wrist by a leather armlet.

The Algerians refused. Their rifles mowed down the Kel Dennik before they could use their knives and swords. The Nigerien Tuareg learned again that courage, traditional tactics, and physical force could be overcome by a man with a gun. They became reluctant to fight the French or to engage Tuareg raiders who were armed.

By 1900 French rifles had secured much of Niger. The military commander in Zinder created by decree the French Military Region of Niger, a region without a single natural or ethnic boundary, a senseless collection of antagonistic peoples who suddenly found themselves gathered into a colony ignored by the British. (The borders of the modern nation of Niger are roughly similar to those of the military region.)

On December 4, 1900, a French column of 150 Senegalese troops commanded by a Lieutenant Figeac arrived in the market town of Tahoua, 145 miles south of In Waggeur. Most of the town's inhabitants fled, as did those of the surrounding villages. Birni-n'Konni, south of

Tahoua, had already been visited by a similar column, and many of its citizens had been massacred, a common method of "pacification."

(A French officer who had witnessed similar operations in neighboring Mali described the procedure. "The order is given to pillage. Everyone taken is killed. All the prisoners, about 4,000 of them, are herded together. Each European is given a woman of his choice . . . children and those who get tired, en route afterwards, are killed by blows dealt with a rifle butt or run through with a bayonet.")

"It is necessary to show that we are the strongest," said Lieutenant Figeac. And so, throughout 1901 small, well-armed detachments of French troops marched north from Tahoua to pacify the Azawak Tuareg. As these detachments pushed toward the edge of the Sahara, they were resisted by more warlike "natives" than those they had encountered in Birni-n'Konni. Protected by their isolation, their harsh environment, and their reputation as cruel, courageous, and skillful warriors, the Kel Dennik Tuareg had preserved a feudal society centered around warfare.

As if transported in a time machine to medieval Europe, the French were confronted by tall, veiled warriors fighting small-scale battles with medieval weapons and adhering to elaborate codes of chivalry. In the vast, empty Nigerien landscape, the warriors appeared romantic, mythical, larger than life. The French were frightened and intrigued.

The Kel Dennik resisted the French as they would any alien people or rival confederation. They signed treaties to create a lull in what was foreseen as a continual skirmish. Each ensuing peace allowed the Tuareg to regroup their forces, to assemble more warriors. The French considered this Tuareg strategy of signing then violating treaties treachery.

Before some of their conflicts, the Kel Dennik tried to persuade the French—as they had the Algerians a few years earlier—to be courageous and fight on equal terms. The French columns refused, and their rifles enabled them to win the numerous minor battles fought between 1901 and 1905.

At the time that the French were pacifying the Azawak, the Kel Dennik, like other Tuareg confederations, were organized into five distinct

41

classes. Class was inherited, mobility rare, and each caste distinguished by vocation and, to a degree, by racial characteristics. These castes were in addition segregated into their own tribes. There is a Kel Dennik saying: "As long as people are unequal there will be cream, as long as they are on the same foot there will be hatred." It means that order and peace can only exist in a society organized on strict hierarchical lines.

At the top of the Kel Dennik social order were noble tribes such as the Kel Nan and the Tiggermat, composed of warriors who planned and led wars and raids. Beneath them were vassal tribes such as Atakor's Illaba-kan, each under the protection of a particular noble tribe. The vassals fought beside their nobles and shared their booty. They owned animals and slaves, and paid the nobles a yearly tithe of animals and milk.

Some vassal tribes, the Illabakan among them, considered them-selves, according to Atakor, "almost nobles." They dressed like nobles and wore their hair in long tresses under their turbans. Some had once been nobles, but had been demoted after losing crucial battles.

The maraboutique tribes were also in the middle of the Tuareg hier-archy. They comprised religious leaders who taught the Koran, admin-istered religious justice, and wrote the verses from the Koran on slates and pieces of paper that were believed to have magical powers.

At the bottom of the society were the blacksmiths and then the bou-zous. The legal (but not, initially, economic) status of this slave class was altered by the French conquest of Niger. In 1907 a French army officer, Lieutenant Peignol, pointed out that liberating the bouzous was an "excellent way of reducing the Tuareg race to nothing." He predict-ed that many of the Tuareg nobles would literally not be able to feed themselves without the help of their slaves.

After the bouzous were liberated, however, the French failed to offer them any alternatives other than starvation and the ironically named "liberty villages."

The few adventuresome bouzous who left their masters were interned in these villages and forced to build the French administrative centers. But so many of them escaped from their new French masters that it was decreed that anyone leaving a "liberty village" would be pursued and imprisoned for a month when captured. Nonetheless, many bouzous continued to run away and rejoin their former Tuareg masters, who didn't starve until some sixty-five years after Peignol's prediction, twelve years after the French had left.

In many respects slavery became more commonplace and vicious in West African countries during the French occupation. While French decrees were freeing bouzous, purportedly for humanitarian reasons, French soldiers were pillaging villages and giving the survivors to their mercenaries as wages. Later the French instituted their own pharaonic slavery to guarantee that all the sahelians, and not just the bouzous, worked for them. They rounded up their new subjects and forced them to build roads, public edifices, and plantations. Those who refused, or committed other crimes, were punished under the *Indigenat*, a legal code which gave French administrators the right to arrest and imprison an African subject for fifteen days without bringing him to trial. There was no right of appeal, and consecutive fifteen-day sentences could be limitless.

The experience of Atakor's people, the Kel Dennik Tuareg, is illustrative of that of other Tuareg confederations under French rule. At the time of the French conquest, Mohammed ag El Kumati, a noble, was the chief of the Kel Dennik and ruled over all of the noble, vassal, and maraboutique tribes of the confederation. When he died in 1905 there were two candidates for the chieftaincy, Ikhesi and Ismaril. The majority of the Kel Dennik wanted Ikhesi to succeed Mohammed as chief. Only one noble tribe and their vassal tribes, including the Illabakan, preferred Ismaril.

Previously, a Kel Dennik chief had been chosen by a consensus of the nobles with the concurrence of their allied vassals. When there was no consensus, a successor was usually determined by warfare. But in 1905, instead of fighting or bowing to the majority, Tiggermat leaders asked the newest and most powerful "tribe" in the Azawak—the French—to arbitrate the dispute.

The French commanding officer, Captain Noël, sent his own trusted Tuareg emissaries to poll the Kel Dennik. As a result, they concluded

43

that under tribal law, Mohammed's inheritance—his possessions and his animals—should be given to Ismaril, but since the majority supported Ikhesi, he should be named chief.

Captain Noël summoned the Kel Dennik to Tahoua to implement this rational and democratic compromise.

"All those who love Ismaril raise your hands," he said. A handful of nobles responded.

"All those who love Ikhesi raise your hands." The majority of the tribesmen present raised their hands.

Captain Noël told them to sit. A small Tuareg army, whose arrival in Tahoua ten years earlier would have been cause for major panic, sat. Next to the captain were two red blankets. He handed one to Ismaril and said, "I give you the inheritance." He handed the other to Ikhesi. "He who the people like most will be chief."

Ikhesi's supporters counseled him to accept the chieftaincy and leave the inheritance to Ismaril. He refused. Why should he compromise, he argued, when his more numerous supporters could defeat Ismaril and his followers in battle? "I don't want the drum[3] that is not followed by the animals," he said.

Captain Noël asked Ikhesi again to accept the chieftaincy. Again he refused. Enraged that his compromise had been rejected, Noël snatched the blanket from Ikhesi and gave it to Ismaril, along with a new boubou and a veil.

"You are all witnesses," he said. "The chieftaincy and the animals are all for Ismaril."

Ikhesi fled to In Gall and waged frequent and unsuccessful minor wars against Ismaril, whose chieftaincy had sometimes to be defended by French soldiers from Tahoua. Ismaril died in 1908, and the drum

[3]The Tuareg chief's drum is the skin of a white cow which has been stretched across a hollow tree stump to make a drum so large that it takes two blacksmiths to carry it and beat it with skin-covered batons. It hangs from stakes outside the leader's tent and accompanies him on migrations. It is both a symbol and an instrument of power, much like the briefcase of nuclear codes that follows an American president. In the flat Tadarast, the Tuareg claim, it can be heard a hundred miles away as it summons Kel Dennik for meetings or combat.

was inherited by El Khorer ag Arakabbi. Ikhesi's rebellion continued.

In 1916 the traditional Islamic leader of Libya, the Sanussi of Cyrenaica, had rebelled against Italian rule. The allies were claiming that German agents had instigated the uprising. The Sanussi army, commanded by a black called Kaosan, from the slave caste, defeated the Italians in Libya and the French at Djanet in southern Algeria. The revolt spread to Niger.

By December of 1916 many of Niger's Tuareg tribes had joined Kaosan in besieging the French garrison at Agadez (an action that was later the subject of the book and the movie *Beau Geste*). Agadez was the Tuareg capital, the home of their sultan and an important stop on the trans-Sahara and Bilma salt caravan routes. It is a red city whose maze of one- and two-story mud-and-brick-walled houses is dominated by a tall minaret, also built of mud and bricks. Except for the addition of the infrequent street lights, a few government-owned buildings, two hotels, and the destruction of the French fortress, Agadez has changed little architecturally since the siege.

Kaosan sent messages to the Kel Dennik nobles urging them to join the insurrection. He promised that "soon Agadez will fall and the infidels be chased from all Moslem countries."

The Kel Dennik were divided. Should they join Kaosan at Agadez or once again submit to the French. For one thing, Kaosan was a member of a slave caste. For another, the Kel Dennik were closer to French garrisons and therefore more vulnerable to reprisals than the Tuareg who lived further north, in the Air Mountains. Finally only the chief, El Khorer, and a handful of warriors went to Agadez to support Kaosan. El Khorer was captured, imprisoned, freed from jail, and finally killed in a skirmish east of Agadez.

In March 1917 Kaosan was defeated and Agadez relieved by a French-English column that had marched three hundred miles from Zinder, the capital of the Niger colony. The Tuareg were scattered and pursued by French patrols into the Ténéré Desert and the Air Mountains. Massacres similar to Tanut occurred, the noble tribes were decimated, and the most hostile of the Nigerien Tuareg tribes were pacified.

45

There is evidence that these massacres were not aberrations but part of a deliberate policy of genocide. In 1916, a year before Tanut, the French command at Agadez sent a report which advised:

> If we wish to stay in this desert country at all costs, we must try to pacify it without pity for the Tuareg who, in my opinion, must agree to accept the laws of a master who preaches work and peace.
>
> The Tuareg does not have any more reason to exist than the American Indian, but unhappily the climate of the desert and their fantastic camels have put obstacles in our way that were unknown to the Americans.
>
> It is nevertheless possible to overcome these difficulties. When the European wars are over we can have several squadrons of airplanes at our disposal. These planes will have a radical effect! The camel vanquished? So much the better! Then we will have only to await the arrival of the railroads. . . .
>
> The question of the airplane must be settled as soon as possible, otherwise we should decide to quit these territories that leave so many blank spaces on our tax registers and maps.

The Kel Dennik in particular never forgot the French massacres. They continued to recite the events of Tanut in their poems and histories. For the next fifty years they minimized contact with Europeans, avoided their towns, and often "punished" their slaves by sending their children, instead of the Kel Dennik's own, to the nomadic schools run by the French. Sixteen years after the massacre, a French officer in Niger wrote, "The coolness of their [the Kel Dennik's] welcome contrasts with the familiarity of the other Tuaregs of the colony."

v

*A*fter 1917, the resistance to the French occupation ceased. Wars between Tuareg tribes and raids against black farmers became less frequent. The wireless radio enabled small but highly mobile detachments of French troops to identify Tuareg raiding parties quickly and frustrate their purposes. By 1920 the French had rearranged the tribal composition of the Tuareg confederations and appointed chiefs whose principal responsibility was not to organize combat but to collect taxes. It was the end of warfare as a way of life for the Tuareg.

The French pacification and the introduction of the truck also weakened the Tuareg's control of trade across the Sahara and within Niger. The largest and most famous Tuareg caravan in Niger had carried salt from the desert oasis of Bilma, located in the northeast corner of the country, west to Agadez and south to Kano in Nigeria. Bilma salt, thought best for animals because of its impurities, was traded for millet and dried meat. In 1908, when this trade was already in decline due to the French invasion, the average salt caravan was made up of twenty thousand camels. By 1926 it contained only seven thousand. By the early 1960s the caravans were composed of less than a thousand camels.

After 1920 the legal and economic ties between the classes were seriously weakened. Nobles retained their moral authority, but without wars and raids lost the source of much of their wealth. Their vassals ceased paying tithes (now they had to pay taxes to the colony). The vassals had traditionally been entrusted with herding the animals the nobles captured on raids. They were more practiced herders, and they soon became richer than many of their masters. However, class status continued, in spite of this upheaval, to be a more important indication of a Tuareg's worth than material goods.

After 1920 the French also were in a better position to prevent Tuareg slave trading and to encourage the bouzous to become independent and pay French taxes. Some bouzous, no longer needing the patronage of one Tuareg warrior to protect them from the attacks of another, drifted south and began to cultivate the lands that had been a buffer between nomadic pastures and the farmlands of the Hausas and Djermas. Most stayed with their Tuareg masters. They considered themselves a Tuareg people. Although no longer slaves, according to French law, they still performed the same tasks and received the same wages—food, shelter, and clothing.

Before the French occupation, Tuareg social and commercial life had revolved around four activities—raiding, trading, slaving, and herding.

47

After the French pacification, the Tuareg were left with no choice but to concentrate their energies on herding.

This simplification of their culture made it more difficult for the Tuareg to survive a drought. Before, they could raid better-supplied Tuareg nomadic camps or villages and steal enough animals to survive and reconstitute their herds. The farmers were their preferred victims, since they were less likely to resist or retaliate. Slaves also provided insurance against drought, since they could be sold to wealthier Tuareg or North Africans. Money and animals could be earned by guarding or guiding caravans, protecting them from raids which the "guards" might otherwise have staged themselves.

Before 1900 animals had been important to the Tuareg for food (milk rather than meat), transportation, a medium of exchange, a store of wealth, and a source of prestige. After 1920 they became the only source of prestige, the only medium of exchange, and leading them to pasture the only activity for Tuareg men.

But despite the ending of organized warfare, the Tuareg men persisted in considering themselves to be heroic. They struggled to find courageous acts that they could perform which could be praised by their women, and envied and discussed by other men. It was a challenge to be a heroic herder, but some managed. They courted beautiful women, saved cattle from thieves, and tried to ride their camels in a graceful, personal style. But the Tuareg recognized that most of these acts of "heroism" were contrived and artificial. They occurred in pastures rather than on battlefields, and it was admitted that they could not compare with the heroic acts of their ancestors.

The only object in wealthier countries which even comes close to being as important as animals were for the Tuareg after 1920 is the automobile. But only if everyone worked on an automobile assembly line, if automobiles could be milked, if houses were constructed of old chassis, and if wealth equaled Cadillacs parked in the backyard—only then would the automobile approach the immense significance of the Tuareg's animals.

Most Tuareg herds contained goats, cows, sheep, and camels. The exact proportions of these animals within each herd depended on the

48

geography and climate of the region and the preferences of the herder. However, practically every Tuareg herder kept at least a few camels. They were considered to be the "most heroic" animals since the warriors had ridden them into raids and battles.

The Tuareg lavished the most attention on these camels. They gave them names and discussed them as if they were human. Special terms denoted a camel's color, size, gait, and behavior. An *arennenas* is a camel with the habit of "neighing for joy when it sees something very agreeable." An *enerregreg* is one which "roars mournfully when it becomes separated from its master or from another camel with whom it has been grazing." There is a special term for a camel which becomes scared walking in a caravan after sunset so that it throws off its load and panics the other camels.

At an early age boys played with miniature camels cut from rock, and with camel puppets made from sheep jaws. Bride wealths were paid in camels, as were indemnities to injured parties. Since different camels have different aesthetic and monetary values, there were elaborate schedules stipulating the age and appearance of camels offered as compensation.

In order to provide pasture and water for their precious herds, the Tuareg depended on a brief annual rainy season and on the preservation of an ecological equilibrium between human and animal populations, water, and the quantity and quality of pasture.

In 1968 this equilibrium was upset by a drought that would continue for six years and precipitate an ecological disaster of devastating magnitude. During this drought, Tuareg herders lost between 50 and a 100 percent of their animals. Suddenly, the last ties binding together their culture and their families were gone.

In the summer of 1969, after surviving the first year of substandard rains, many of Niger's Tuareg gathered at the oasis of In Gall for the Cure Salée, in English, the salt cure, an annual gathering of Tuareg and Peul nomads. One of the purposes of the gathering was to allow the animals to lick salt and drink salty water from the nearby pools of Tegguidda-Tessoum.

At this 1969 Cure Salée there seemed to be nothing exceptional or

49

ominous about the preceding year of drought. True, some men had already seen half of their animals die, but their herds had been excessively large, and enough animals had survived to support them. Both as individuals and as a people they had survived. They could still consider themselves to be wealthy. They were confident that the rains would return to replenish their wells and nurture their pastures. They had no reason to fear that within five years these pastures would be barren and their animals dead.

2

The Illabakan
August-September 1969
Cure Salée, In Gall, Niger

I humbly adore the acts of the most High
Who has given to the violin what is better than a soul,
So that, when it plays, the men are silent,
And their hands cover their lithiams[1] to hide their emotion.
The troubles of love were pushing me into the tomb,
But thanks to the violin,
God has given me back my life.

—Tuareg poem

[1] The dark-blue Tuareg veil.

i

*M*iriam: "I thought I was rich and that we were the richest people in the world. Atakor and I owned hundreds of sheep, cows, goats, and many beautiful camels. I wore beautiful clothes and jewelry. At the Cure Salée we danced, visited friends, and drank fresh milk.''

When they attended the Cure Salée, Miriam and a dozen other Tuareg women from the Illabakan tribe gathered in a circle every day at dusk. Their cloaks were drawn around them and they appeared to be living in black tents decorated with silver earrings, pendants, and bracelets. Their hands emerged from the tents to slap drums and clap.

Miriam sang one of her compositions. "Abouboukoum, the white camel, and Essawagh, the tricolor, galloped, danced, taking Atakor to In Gall . . . . Atakor is only pleased with a beautiful white camel and because he loves Abouboukoum he has given him beautiful ornaments.''

Abouboukoum himself danced around them, Atakor on his back. The camel lifted his feet in time to the drums. His head bobbed, his copper necklace jangled, and Miriam sang.

She praised the camel's beauty and his dancing, named his parents, and described his heroic exploits and how he had survived the preceding year of drought. She wove these themes into a long poem which she

53

sang in a high monotone, creating a counterpoint to the drums and the clapping.

Atakor pushed on Abouboukoum's neck with his bare feet. The camel's forelegs buckled and his knees rested on the ground. Then the drums slowed and Abouboukoum walked forward on his knees, his hindquarters jutting into the air, his head nodding with the rhythm of the drums. Atakor sat erect in his blue robe, staring through the slit in his veil. The men watching shouted their approval.

Atakor: "When I went to the Cure Salée in the first year of the drought, I still owned more than ten camels. Some were lazy, some were bad, but most were, like Abouboukoum, beautiful and courageous.

"Here is how I showed Abouboukoum that I loved him. I hung beautiful ornaments around his neck and put a beautiful saddle on his back. I never galloped him during the hot season. After I watered him I gave him a day of rest. If he became tired and thin I gave him a month of rest. I lifted his testicles so that they wouldn't bang against his legs.

"During the Cure Salée I led him and the rest of my camels to the salt at Tegguidda-Tessoum. I did not trust him to the bouzous. He ate the salt and drank from the pools of salt water. After every meal I gave him a day of rest. Then when I returned to In Gall I treated him gently.

"I could not sell or eat Abouboukoum. It would make me sick with grief to eat my camels. I would not try to sell them, certainly not the ones I loved the most."

Others joined Abouboukoum's dance. Their riders competed for the praise of the women who judged their grace, the elegance of their saddles and ornaments, and the beauty of their camels. When he felt Abouboukoum tiring, Atakor dismounted, withdrew from the light of the women's fire, and walked to the camp of Najim, the chief of the Illabakan.

A musician from the Tuareg blacksmith caste played the amzad, a Tuareg violin that produces shrill, crystalline notes. Its music obeys different laws of harmony from, and contains dissonances not found in, European music. Najim's eldest sons, both old enough to wear veils, sat at their father's side. Behind them was the youngest, eight-year-old

54

Boucli, a student at the In Waggeur nomadic school. Atakor sat down next to Khamed Moussa, an exceptional twenty-five-year-old Illabakan who spoke fluent French and had been a deputy to the National Assembly in Niger's capital, Niamey.

They reclined on blankets and mats around the musician. Some lay on their sides, propped on elbows. Others sat cross-legged or on their haunches. Most of the women sat in a semicircle behind the men, but a few had penetrated the circle and leaned tentatively against their husbands or lovers. The blue-and-white robes of the men and the women's black cloaks overlapped, seeming to be parts of one enormous garment. Callused hands and feet touched, a hand rested on a knee, another on a neighbor's sandal. Absentmindedly they picked nettles off each other's clothing. For two months of every year music flowed through and bound this human circuit, recharging the men and women and preparing them for the more solitary ten months to come.

The dusk had become evening, and a fire provided light for the musician to see his instrument. His songs were poems set to music. The first described the misfortunes of a noble who cheated his musicians. His cows suffered agonizing deaths, his favorite slave was lost in an enemy raid, and his riding camel was stolen by Hausas. The second song praised the wisdom and generosity of a noble who rewarded his troubadour with a camel. As the musician sang in a gravelly voice, the audience joked, commented on the songs, and addressed the singer as "the greatest musician in In Gall."

Beauty, originality, and vigor were appreciated, but rhythm and style were more important when the Tuareg judged the merits of a particular poem. Many of the songs had a special vocabulary, with allusions and puns incomprehensible to an outsider. There were satires on rival Tuareg confederations, descriptions of journeys taken by the men in the audience during the preceding year, journeys to Algeria, Libya, and the markets in southern Niger, and praise for the exceptional beauty of Tuareg women:

> O people from our entire land,
> You who travel everywhere—
> Kano, Zanfara, Agadez—

55

And admire the beautiful women.
You must agree there is none to compare with Rakhmatou.
In goodness, breeding, intelligence, in everything
She is worth more than gold cloth.
When you are ready to depart,
She holds the camel's bridle with all its beautiful ornaments for you.
She is clothed in lithiam from Kano,
And in gold and silver jewelry.
She wears beautiful tresses and long braids.
She is finer than all your young ladies and when she approaches,
They run and hide.

Aside from these poems, artistic expression is rare among the Tuareg. There are no monuments, buildings, paintings, or statues. The Saharan cave drawings of animals were the product of an earlier people who enjoyed a more humid Saharan climate. Tiffinagh, the unique Tuareg written language (mastery of Tiffinagh does not satisfy the Niger government's criteria for "literacy") is similar to ancient Libyan script. Both are very geometric languages. Most of Tiffinagh's twenty-one characters are arrangements of dots, circles with lines and dots inside, and crossed, straight, and double-crossed lines. Tiffinagh can be scribed left, right, up, or down, and appears in passionate epigrams scratched on whatever is available.

Tuareg men have written their names in Tiffinagh, the names of their sweethearts, and sometimes a poem expressing their emotions on rocks and trees throughout the northern sahel. Messages in Tiffinagh are also traced in the sand by friends and erased before they can be deciphered by outsiders. But besides these poems and messages, there is no significant body of literature.

Art is restricted to functional objects—ornate camel saddles, leather purses, silver jewelry, swords and other weapons. These are decorated in the Tuareg's favorite colors, light green and dark red, and are produced by the clever but disdained class of Tuareg blacksmiths.

The carefully crafted and elaborate poems and oral histories are the real embodiment of Tuareg culture. Most of these oral histories are epics, replete with wars that never end, vengeance, treachery, bravery, and chivalry. They are an inseparable fusion of fact and myth, a counterpoint of minute detail and vague mystery that shatters conventional time frames. Hundred-year-old battles are remembered with precision. The dead and the wounded are named and the nature of their wounds is told, as are the numbers of camels and slaves seized as booty. Warriors are courageous, lovers prodigious, camels beautiful and skillful.

Years are titled subjectively, according to memorable events. In different regions they are given different names. In the Tadarast, for example, 1900 was the Year of the Coming of the Infidel, 1917 the Year of Submission, 1924 the Year of the Rain of Stars (a meteor shower), 1930 the Year of the Grasshoppers, 1932 the Year of the Cement Wells (the first built in the Tadarast), 1939 the Year of the Italians (when people spoke much of the Italians in Libya), and 1965 the Year of the Canvas Sacks (when, after a bad harvest in the south, the Nigerien government distributed free millet in canvas bags).

Tuareg women compose, tell, retell, and teach the histories. They can transform cowards into heroes, add and delete incidents, illuminate hidden morals. They remodel the contours of their stories to comfort the present, to alleviate the pain of a fading past and an uncertain future. The histories are one of the many sources of female power.

The histories are also vivid and personal, created by the tribe but interpreted by the individual. Instead of reading books, Atakor learned from his mother, his sisters, his friends, and Miriam. Something that happened more than fifty years ago could be told in as much detail as last week's gossip. He was surrounded by a history in which present heroics reflected ancient ones, and patterns of chivalry recurred.

One of the most famous histories of Atakor's tribe, the Illabakan, told how in the early 1920s Najim had repulsed a raiding party of Arabs who had ridden down from the Spanish Sahara. This was one of the last acts of traditional heroism, and Najim, the hero, had since become chief of the Illabakan. The raid was a crucial turning point in Illabakan history. Atakor, Miriam, and of course Najim himself, knew the story well. As the musician recited it, they and the other Illabakan gathered around him mouthed the words silently.

Fifty years before, during the short, autumnal hot season, two Illabakan men had ridden out of Najim's camp toward the pool of rainwater that formed at In Waggeur after the summer rains. Armed with spears, they intended to hunt the small deer that, like ostriches, gazelles, and giraffes, were plentiful in the Tadarast before the drought and even more so before the French conquest. (Giraffes often ran into the first telegraph lines that the French were building along the Niger River. In 1908 the colonial authorities hired a band of Tuareg, and within a month they had killed ninety giraffes.)

Before they reached the pool, the two men spied smoke coming from a cluster of trees. Hiding behind thorn bushes, they saw that it came from the cooking fires of a dozen well-armed white strangers. Afraid to approach the intruders and assuming that they were either French or Algerian, they returned to the camp. Later they discovered that the men were from the Spanish Sahara.

The news that the raiders were armed terrified the Illabakan. Only Najim owned a rifle, and during the last twenty years they had suffered in battles against the armed French and Algerians. They knew that their swords were useless against rifles.

The next morning two Illabakan slaves led a herd of goats from Najim's camp to the In Waggeur pool. At midday, when the Arab raiders came to the same pool to water their camels, the slaves were asleep in a clump of trees.

While his camel drank, Hamid, the chief of the Arabs, took off his blue boubou, hung it on a nearby tree, and waded into the pool to wash.

The Illabakan indulged their slaves. Since they were considered to be frivolous and irresponsible children, they were permitted to insult their masters and play practical jokes. And so, while Hamid bathed, one of the Illabakan bouzous stole Hamid's boubou and ran back to the camp to present it to Najim, a trophy proving his courage. Hamid and two of his lieutenants mounted their camels and gave chase.

When they saw the Arabs appear on the horizon, the Illabakan panicked. The women wailed that they had come to "steal our animals and hunt our slaves." Women, children, and men fled. Only Najim and his wife remained in the camp. Najim hid. He took the only Illabakan rifle and climbed into the crook of a tree (in some versions of the story he hid behind the tree). His wife walked out from the deserted camp and told Hamid that the French had taken away the men and animals for taxes and census.

58

Hamid ignored her and rode into the camp. Najim steadied the rifle on a limb, aimed, and when Hamid drew close, fired. The bullet hit Hamid in the chest and he fell from his camel, dead. His terrified lieutenants fled. Their leader had been slain by an unseen, unexpectedly armed assassin. When the other Arabs heard of Hamid's death they too fled from In Waggeur.

Najim jumped out of the tree and sliced off Hamid's right arm. A few days later he presented it to a French officer and was rewarded with a sack of cartridges. In the meantime, the other Illabakan returned from the bush with their herds and slaves.

The blacksmith minstrels took the story to other camps. It was recited to the melodies of Tuareg guitars at yearly nomadic gatherings. It became an infant's lullaby, an epic poem, a symbolic legend.

The musician's next ballad praised Najim's bravery and generosity since his famous defense of In Waggeur against the Arab raiders. He sang about blacks timid as sheep, Algerians too cowardly to throw away their rifles and fight with courage, the treacheries of the French. His veil hung below his chin like a bib and his head was bent over his violin as he concentrated on his fingers.

The musician played four identical notes rapidly, paused, and played a drawn-out high note. He repeated the sequence and Atakor, still sitting in the circle, his back erect, danced with his head and his arms. His fine fingers wove fluid and intricate patterns to the first four notes, his bracelets leaving silver trails in the darkness and his hands pantomiming expressions concealed behind his veil. On the fifth note his head sank forward in a motion reminiscent of the dancing camel. When he was finished he nudged his neighbor. The man imitated Atakor's movements and added his own variations. As the dance flowed from man to man, it became more elaborate and difficult to imitate. The women murmured praise, urging the men into more complicated and graceful motions.

As the men wove their patterns, the women moved closer to them, whispering promises and touching their thighs. When the dance was over some of the men kissed their admirers and led them beyond the firelight into the desert.

The women felt that the beauty of a camel, his saddle and ornaments, and the way he was ridden were the things that made his owner desirable. If a camel was beautiful, so was his rider, and because the men were always veiled and their bodies covered with cloaks and trousers, they were most likely to be recognized and appreciated for the way they rode their camels. The poetic songs expressed this joining of men and camels and love:

O woman with white teeth,
My white camel shall not go raiding, shall not leave you.
It shall not go away from you to another country.
I will lead it to the pastures only to visit with love again.
Neither in dreams nor in thought shall it go away from you to another country.

Two years before, when Atakor was thirty and Miriam two years younger, he and Miriam had met in the same way at the Cure Salée. A year ago, also at the Cure Salée, they had married. Now he watched the familiar rituals of courtship as they were performed with a style and grace identical to that of the dancing camel, the subtle poems, the contagious dance of the men.

Even during the other ten months of the year, when they were scattered across the arid plateaus and fossilized valleys of northern Niger, the Illabakan and other Tuareg tribes constrained the natural anarchy of free love with a ritual. (According to a Tamashek dictionary compiled by Father Foucauld, a French missionary who lived among the Algerian Tuareg, Tamashek has no word to express virginity.)

A Tuareg man wishful of feminine company rode his camel or horse to other camps until he found a woman alone in her tent. "*Isalan?*" ("What's your news?") he asked. If she wanted company she answered, "*Nan-i*" ("I have a lot of news"). He would then enter the tent, caress her, compliment her—"talking of honey"—and spend the evening. But many times the woman refused. Unlike most traditional Moslem women, the Tuareg women openly made their wishes known.

Miriam was not a delicate flower who left trading and herding to the men. Tuareg chivalry was not an entirely pure strain: It was motivated in large part by a fear of the consequences if the women became angry. A French lieutenant who saw what happened when a successful Tuareg raiding party failed to pursue the vanquished enemy and exploit the possibility of plunder said of the incident: "Their women, however, cried shame on them, reproaching them for losing such a chance of presents; and to cut short all further discussion, they threatened that any man who was coward enough to flee from an imaginary danger would have to go without his wife. After this threat the men pursued the enemy."

In traditional Moslem societies women are silent slaves. They are seldom allowed to choose their husbands. They can be divorced arbitrarily, and their advice is rarely, if ever, solicited. They cook, carry firewood and water, and nurse children. They labor in kitchens but never sit at table.

Tuareg women are consulted by their husbands, and their preferences and opinions are felt to be important. They inherit wealth, and are often richer than their spouses. Many tribes trace their ancestry to one illustrious, mythical woman.

Moslem laws allow only the husband to initiate a divorce. Even among the Tuareg it is the man who recites the Koranic verses pertaining to divorce. But when Miriam tired of her first husband, she demanded a divorce and he agreed. For a man to cling to a woman who rejects him is considered ignoble.

This same chivalrous rationale gives a divorced woman custody of any children. "What kind of man," reason the men, "would take the children of a mother away from her?" To be so petty and undignified would be disgraceful.

Most Tuareg marriages are monogamous, but the incidence of divorce and promiscuity scandalizes other Moslems. Tuareg women will not allow their men to take a second wife. Men that do know they risk divorce. Many Tuareg in their thirties have been divorced and remarried, and while the first marriage may have been arranged, the second, like Miriam and Atakor's, is often by choice. In this second marriage, physical attraction and love are important.

Whenever Najim's musician paused between songs, Atakor and the Illabakan could hear the drums from a nearby gathering of Peul nomads. At the Cure Salée, as in the Tadarast during the remainder of the year, the two peoples lived in close and not always harmonious proximity.

61

The drums provided the beat for a conga line of Peul men who performed a restless, frantic dance. They wore skin loincloths and glittering ornaments around their waists. Ribbons were tied in their hair. Their bare feet stamped the ground, kicking up sand and brushing back a perimeter of spectators. They dipped their left shoulders, and holding each other's waists with their right hands they leaned over and slapped the gound in unison. They hopped forward, backward, forward again. Their heads revolved and they smiled, showing perfect, milky teeth.

Surrounding the Peul, Najim's musician, and the dancing camels were hundreds of similar gatherings, filling the spaces between them with hybrid symphonies. Their lights became brighter and more frequent until they merged with those of In Gall, an oasis straddling the sahelian "shore" and the Sahara desert.

Camped in the plain around In Gall was a nomadic army—Tuareg from Niger and Mali, Arabs from northern Niger and Algeria, and Peul from as far away as the Cameroons and as close as Niger itself.

Most of the Tuareg at the Cure Salée were from only one of the eight Tuareg groups, the eastern Ouillemeden. (The Kel Dennik were a confederation within this group.) The other groups were all represented, as well. There were caravaneers who led camels loaded with salt from the Bilma mines across the Ténéré desert to Agadez. Kel Ayar from Agadez and the green valleys of the Air Mountains. Ahaggar who lived in the Hoggar Mountains of southern Algeria, remote volcanic islands of red pinnacles surrounded by the Sahara. Western Ouillemeden whose animals grazed on clumps of desert grass growing among the dead dunes near Timbuctoo and the bend of the Niger. Kel Gress from southern Niger whose herds competed for land with crops of millet, cotton, and peanuts. From the surrounding valleys and plateaus of Niger came the tribes of the Kel Dennik, among them the Illabakan. The gathering contained the representatives of a unique and homogeneous people, more than five hundred thousand in all, scattered across a desert and semidesert land shared by three independent countries—Mali, Algeria, and Niger.

French soldiers and diplomats had drawn lines across blank maps of Africa that bisected Tuareg alliances, confederations, families, and the pasturelands where the Tuareg animals grazed. The Tuareg ignored the lines. The real borders, for them, were between tribes, black farmers and white nomads, Tuareg and Peul grazing lands. These were fluid borders, changing as the monsoon rains watered one area and neglected another, as migrations and wars pushed the Tuareg into new territories.

In 1960 the colonial boundaries became frontiers between sovereign states. They remained invisible to the people they separated, historically, geographically, and ethnically absurd. The nomads continued to ignore them, but the French-educated elite who owned the flags, the United Nations memberships, and the other trappings of statehood, did not. The colonial frontiers defined their powers, and they were willing to fight to preserve them. The people to the west of one line were Malians, to the east Nigeriens; to the north of another they were Algerians, and to the south Nigeriens.

Like the French, the new governments issued identity cards, levied taxes, and tried to control the international movements of their new citizens. In the decade following independence, the nomadic migrations occurred as if on a multidimensional game board. As long as the rains were good and the herds large and healthy, the Tuareg could continue to live within the first dimensions of traditional boundaries. Finally, when the drought made the Tuareg dependent on the charity of the new governments, the modern frontiers became the most important ones. A Tuareg who lived in Niger might receive more relief food and better treatment than one who was a citizen of Mali.

Despite a year of drought, the 1969 Cure Salée still affirmed the vitality of the old borders and traditions. It was the annual celebration of nomadic peoples who had survived another year in one of the world's most brutal environments.

ii

*A*takor: "I loved the music, the dancing, and the pretty women at the Cure Salée. If there was good pasture, the animals were fat and beautiful and produced fresh milk. I visited with friends and exchanged news. We admired the animals and discussed how we would spend the year, which pasture and pools of water we would use.

"I could arrange my affairs. I married during the Cure Salée. I bought sugar, tea, and clothing from the Arabs. Miriam bought jewelry.

"I liked the Cure Salée because you could see large herds of sheep, cattle, and camels. All the men wore their most beautiful clothes. When I saw these beautiful men and animals gathered together it reminded me that we were a powerful people."

During the afternoons and evenings Atakor visited different camps, talking, dancing, and singing. He spent the mornings in the market at In Gall.

In Gall is a white oasis town with wide, clean, sandy streets, one- and two-story houses constructed from mud bricks and known as "banco" houses, a deserted fortress, palm trees, and a busy market. Before the French invasion the town was a rest stop for camel caravans carrying salt, slaves, and dates. Desert tracks have now replaced the caravan routes, and diesel trucks, passenger cars, Land Rovers, and even motorcycles crossing the desert frequently stop for food and water.

In Gall offers little for these transients. Opposite the market is a "hotel-restaurant" built of straw mats. Inside are wood tables and benches. The menu is instant coffee and rice with pimento sauce. After the last evening meal the restaurant floor becomes the hotel. Arab traders a block away sell stale Lebanese biscuits, Spanish sardines, pink plastic water canteens, and dented cans of pineapple. In the afternoon they climb onto the counters and sleep on the wares. A Libyan sells huge green bottles of beer that are cooled underneath a wet burlap sack.

It is possible to call In Gall "romantic," to imagine its crumbling fortress besieged by Tuareg warriors, or to consider its palm trees, mud houses, and sand "timeless and biblical."

Hausa and Arab traders know the Cure Salée is a good place to make money. These permanent merchants own stores located in rows of whitewashed banco houses. Nearby is an open area for the itinerant traders who visit In Gall during the Cure Salée. The market is organized by profession and by the type of goods being offered for sale. On one

64

street, rows of tailors push the treadles of antique Singer sewing machines. On another, butchers hang meat from the animal market close by. Around a corner, a line of small girls picks through mounds of dried red peppers.

Atakor made the majority of his yearly purchases at the In Gall market. He could buy sugar, several grades of tea, tobacco, a teapot, small shot glasses for drinking tea, cloth, locks, and camel saddles. Even when he was without funds he visited the market to browse.

He and most of the other Illabakan patronized a favorite Arab merchant. Every morning a group gathered on mats in his store to feel his cloth, argue its price, and accept a calculated hospitality dispensed with rice and tea.

During the 1969 Cure Salée, Atakor, like many other Illabakan, asked the merchant for credit. He told him and the others about his dead animals and about the poor rains of 1968, rains which had been poor more in "usefulness" than in volume.

Atakor: "During the Year of the Long Drought, the pool of water that formed at In Waggeur after the rainy season was dry by November. The rains were too early and there was no food for the animals. I lost fifty of my hundred cows, almost all my sheep, but my goats survived and only three camels died. It was the worst drought I had ever known, although I have heard people talk of worse ones before I was born."

Sitting in the Arab's store drinking tea, chewing tobacco, and spitting in the sand, lying under tents or striding through In Gall—in step, hands clasped behind their backs in the posture of royalty inspecting exhibitions and new nations—Atakor and the Illabakan, like the other Tuareg, discussed with each other how they had survived the first year of drought.

They talked about where the best pastures remained, which pools had dried early, how they had fed their families. They talked about the one factor that more than any other determined their lives—the rains. They would tell similar stories every year at the Cure Salée until 1973, when there was no Cure Salée.

* * *

iii

*T*he Azawak is the name given a region in northwest Niger dominated by an ancient fossilized river valley. It includes the Tadarast plateau and the nomadic town of In Waggeur. Atakor's tribe, the Illabakan, numbered a thousand, and for the ten months of the year when they were not at the Cure Salée, nine hundred of them camped in the vicinity of an automatic water pump which the Nigerien government built at In Waggeur. The other hundred lived fifty miles east of In Waggeur near the Tchin-Tabaraden pump.

In the Azawak, for a rain to be "useful" it must measure over three millimeters in quantity and, since only rains which come at the right intervals allow the grasses to mature, it must be followed by a similar rainfall within a week. Premature storms followed by weeks of drought mean that grasses flower briefly and then perish. Generally, only rains that fall between June 15 and September 15 are considered useful.

During 1968, the first year of the six-year drought, the rains were useless. Two hundred miles south of In Gall, at Niger's fourth largest city of Tahoua, the average yearly rainfall was 15.0 inches. In 1967, a good year, 19.4 inches fell. In 1968, a bad year when many of the Illabakan's animals died, 15.9 inches fell.

The year 1967 was considered excellent because a total of 13.3 inches was measured between June and September, but in 1968 only 6.9 inches fell during the same period. During 1968 most of the rain fell in violent thunderstorms at the end of April. May was dry. What pools of water there were evaporated early in the autumn. Grasses and shrubs blossomed and died before they could be eaten.

The Illabakan called the 1968–1969 dry season that followed these poor rains the Year of Death, Year of Famine, or Year of the Long Drought.

Maps depicting West African rainfall, temperature, soil, vegetation, population density, and agricultural productivity all have similar contours. So do those which indicate literacy, medical care, miles of paved

66

roads, and per capita income. These maps look as if a child dipped his fingers in paint and dragged them horizontally and unevenly across West Africa, leaving wavy lines which are separated by as little as a hundred miles and as much as four hundred.

The lines are markers—inches of rainfall, grams of food per year per person, degrees of average daily temperature, percentages of literacy, numbers of doctors per thousand citizens, dollars of per capita income. These indices of wealth usually diminish as one moves from south to north, from the Gulf of Guinea toward Niger, In Gall, in Waggeur, and the Sahara. The most important determinant of the position of these lines is the annual monsoon.

The West African monsoon begins to move north in January. A thick mass of dark clouds, humid and heavy with moisture from the tropical seas, pushes northwest across the Gulf of Guinea.

The monsoon is shaped like a five-hundred-mile-long wedge. At its advancing edge is the intertropical front (ITF), the border between the monsoon's wet tropical air and the dry, scorching winds from the Sahara called the Harmattan.

One hundred twenty-five miles south from the edge, the wedge thickens in depth. The moist air is six thousand feet thick, but the high ground temperature makes the mass unstable. Periodic, violent storms dump torrents of rain suddenly and unevenly.

Imagine fifty-two climatic maps of West Africa. Drawn across them are a series of horizontal lines measuring average weekly rainfall. The lines at the top indicate the position of the ITF. The cards are flipped rapidly, and like an early flickering movie the lines move northward after January at a speed of five miles a day.

In March the monsoon crosses the fifth parallel and the southern coast of West Africa. Downpours hammer the tin roofs of huts, turn coastal roads into red rivers, wash rich soil into mango swamps, and leave steaming pools on the concrete of Accra, Lagos, Lomé, and Abidjan. Rain drips from the leaves of the tropical rain forests, alive with snakes, butterflies, and monkeys, and choking with underbrush so thick that on the ground there is no light, no grass.

By the end of April the thick edge of the monsoon has blanketed the

67

tropics. The thin edge, the ITF, is 300 miles north, and a six-month rainy season has begun in the Sudanese zone, a 200- to 400-mile-wide band in which trees and bushes become smaller and the ground cover sparser as the monsoon moves north.

Palm trees, dense jungles, and cocoa plantations merge into dry, leafy forests, tall elephant grass, and thick savannah. The railway lines built to haul gold, cocoa, coffee, palm oil, and tropical and agricultural products to coastal ports stop. Certain of the monsoon's arrival, farmers plant their crops on bald patches of land where they have burned off and slashed away the undergrowth. Yams, maize, cassava, millet, and peanuts grow in the south, and millet and peanuts in the north. On the southern borders of the Sudan, at the eighth parallel, sixty inches of rain fall during the rainy season. On the northern border, at the twelfth parallel, twenty-four inches fall during a four-month season.

In Niger, the rains last for three months, and less than twenty-four inches fall in most places. Farmers plant millet, rice, and sorghum to eat, and peanuts and cotton to sell.

For every 3.4 miles that the monsoon moves north, the rainy season is a day shorter and precipitation less by a fifth of an inch. The soil becomes sandier and light red instead of dark, the vegetation sparser, the trees and grasses shorter, and the distance between them greater. Deer, jackals, ostriches, and giraffes roam in these spaces. The thick, umbrella-shaped Gao trees disappear.

There are more bald patches, small ones around villages and wells and widening, circular deserts around the sahelian capitals of Bamako, Ougadougou, and Niamey. Sandstorms turn into rainstorms, and Niamey is pounded by heavy showers which splatter red mud on cars and the white foundations of concrete houses. Gutters overflow, and camels and donkeys wade through instant lakes.

As the edge of the monsoon slides north of Niamey, it passes over regions where farms become increasingly infrequent and poor, where mud-walled towns become smaller and then disappear. There is less laterite in the soil and it turns from reddish to light brown. There are fewer people. Half of Niger's population of 4.5 million is concentrated on one twelfth of the land along the border with Nigeria.

The rains mean everything to northern Niger. A mere few inches can make the difference between grassland and desert, between healthy animals and skeletons. To the north are hot winds, live, moving sand dunes, and fields of black rock. To the south are grasses, shrubs, and thorn and adras trees.

Most of the rain falls during a six-week period. The fragile desert grasses flower quickly and dust the sandy soil with a light-green haze. Trees along the rivers flourish, and the valleys become green veins flowing into seasonal pools. After violent thunderstorms, the sand along usually dry river banks becomes quicksand, and walls of water roll down the valleys. Children dart in front of them as if charging waves breaking on a beach.

Within Niger, the sixteenth parallel is an important dividing line, a sudden border within the sahelian border. It separates the pastures used by the nomads for ten months of the year from those which are normally useful for only two or three. South of this line, yearly rainfall averages twenty inches. To the north the average is eight inches.

Only the thin edge of the monsoon penetrates beyond the sixteenth parallel and reaches the southern edge of the Sahara. In late August it retreats southward across West Africa at twice the speed of its northern movement.

Along the sixteenth parallel the rains are at their most fickle. They water one pasture and leave another dry. The following year the reverse may occur. Only the flexibility of the nomads and the mobility of their herds enables them to exploit land which may be pasture one year and worthless desert the next.

The sixteenth parallel crosses the Azawak three miles south of Tchin-Salatin, seven miles north of Tchin-Tabaraden, seven miles south of In Waggeur, and two miles south of Atakor's winter camp.

Like most Tuareg, Atakor was a cautious nomad. Every year he made one migration to In Gall for the Cure Salée. For the remainder of the year he lived in a winter camp 75 miles south of In Gall at the pumping station of In Waggeur, making small forays to neighboring pastures and water points. Sometimes he might lead a caravan of animals to southern markets, but his winter camp was his home and, like the other Illabakan, he was attached to it.

Living at this winter camp with Atakor were six other families, about thirty-five people in all. When the intertropical front passed over In Waggeur with intense scattered showers, thunderstorms, and high humidity; when pools of water formed along the valleys; and when wild grasses sprouted in the north and the mosquitoes made sleep impossible, only then did Atakor and the other Illabakan join the migration to the Cure Salée.

In August 1969, as in other years, they had gathered their animals, packed their tents and belongings on camels and donkeys, and left for In Gall. They moved slowly, and the seventy-five-mile trip usually took between one and two weeks, depending on the pasturage along the way.

Atakor and the men rode at the head of the procession on camels, the women riding on donkeys behind them. Then came the pack animals, camels and donkeys with the tents, pots, nomadic beds, and locked trunks of jewelry and clothing.

Herds of cattle, goats, and sheep orbited the caravan. Small children chased stragglers, brandishing long sticks which they carried across their shoulders when not in use. They kept their heads straight but their eyes moved rapidly from side to side, counting and watching for strays.

When Atakor arrived at In Gall, he camped on the surrounding plains for six to eight weeks. His animals ate the grasses, and he took them to Tegguidda-Tessoum to drink salty water. In Tamashek, the Tuareg language, this rainy season and the time of the only large migration is called Akasa.

The remainder of Atakor's year was divided into three seasons. His movements during these seasons, the quantity and quality of his food, and his health and the health of his animals were all determined by the timing and the usefulness of the monsoon rains.

When the rains tapered off in September, he returned from In Gall to his winter camp at In Waggeur. This season was called Gharat. It was the time between the summer rains and the winter sandstorms, when grain was harvested in the south. As soon as the rains ended, the temperature in the Tadarast rose quickly, falling again at the end of November after a short, hot season. Unlike the spring, there was usually ample milk and grain during this time.

During Gharat, the Azawak pools still held rainwater, and Atakor took his herds to pastures surrounding the pools that were likely to dry up first. The animals produced milk, which was drunk plain, curdled into hard, pungent tablets of cheese—a favorite snack with tea—or mixed with millet bought from the southern farmers. The Tuareg favored stews—Eshink (plain millet and milk tasting like porridge) or Aghafera (made with the addition of dates and/or pimentos).

When the drought began, a typical Illabakan was consuming 275 pounds of millet, 1,000 pounds of milk, and only 33 pounds of meat a year. It was a diet poor in vitamin A (68 percent of daily requirements) and C (19 percent), but rich in protein (200 percent) because of milk.

Although to most outsiders this diet is bland, monotonous, and unappetizing, Atakor could not imagine varying it. Like most Tuareg, he was conservative, reluctant to eat anything unfamiliar. He felt that the reason he became sick during the drought was that "I didn't have enough milk to drink."

Tagrest, the cold season, lasts from December to mid-March. It is a time of frigid nights that frost the grasses and hot days; of Harmattan winds that cloud the horizon and suck up moisture, dry up the remaining pools of water, evaporate perspiration, shrink wood, shrivel vegetation, crack leather saddles, and split fingernails. Over the years the Harmattan has carved out canyons, flattened hills, and buried rivers. In a few hours it can move enough sand to change the complexion of the landscape.

At the beginning of Tagrest, the Tuareg's bouzou servants gather nettles, pick wild melons, and shake hard red berries from trees with forked sticks. By the end of Tagrest, these foods are an important part of the Tuareg diet. Also, at the end of Tagrest the pools of water have evaporated or been drunk, pastureland has become scarce, and the herds must be divided into smaller units and shifted to wells.

Atakor: "During Tagrest we lived in the same camp and I did the same thing every day.

71

"When I woke I took the small goats out of the pen and then drank tea. Then I went into the bush to look after the older goats, my cows, and the camels. I called them together and counted them. By eight or nine I gathered all the goats together and shook the trees. Leaves and branches fell and the goats ate them.

"Then I gathered the camels. The bouzous watered them and I led them to pasture. It was then midday and I ate a porridge of millet and milk.

"I slept for three hours and then went to make sure that all the camels were still there and to gather the young goats.

"At six o'clock I returned to the camp, put the goats in the enclosure to protect them against jackals, and made tea. Until midnight I watched over my herd and scared away wild animals."

Welen is the hot season, the soudure, when temperatures rise to 120 degrees. It lasts from April until the end of June. To survive, Atakor ate wild grasses that the bouzous harvested in the winter, and millet bought from farmers.

If the rains in the previous year have been inadequate, it is during Welen that pasture around the wells becomes scarce. Losses in a herd are expected during this season. These losses bring the size of the herds into a balance with available pasture. Atakor had a number of strategies he could employ to minimize these losses.

He could split his herds into smaller groups and lead them to where pasture was more plentiful. He could send them to southern pastures, where rainfall was usually greater. Or he could split up his family and relatives, the size of their camps depending on the severity of the season. When Atakor applied these traditional survival techniques during the hot season of 1969, he had no reason to suspect that they would not work as before, or that the drought would last longer than a year or two.

Throughout the entire year Atakor had to make decisions: which water points to use, when to leave one point for another, what kind and how many animals to herd together, when to split the herds, when to reassemble them, how many animals to trade, how much millet to store.

Leading animals to pasture involves more than finding grass and turning them loose. Grasses cannot be eaten before they reseed, or whole stretches of pasture are destroyed for the following year. Each type of grass had to be consumed at a different stage in its growth—when it first buds, when it flowers, or just before it dies. Atakor had to exploit this cycle to the maximum without destroying the grasses.

There were other variables in the nomadic equation. Atakor owned goats, cows, and camels. Each had a different hierarchy of preferences. Camels liked the boughs and leaves of adras and thorn trees. Goats ate almost anything—grass, shrubs, trees, vegetation despised by other animals, even the tough aristada plant that thrived on overgrazed land. Cattle were more discriminating. They preferred the clumps of grass and small shrubs that grew in riverbeds.

Each animal also had different water requirements that fluctuated with the seasons. To allow for good body temperature and digestion, a Tuareg cow needs ten gallons a day, a camel eight, sheep and goats one. The survival minimum for cows is six gallons every two days, and for goats and sheep a little less than a gallon during the same period. At this level only the strongest animals survive.

To reach water and pasture, animals have different levels of stamina at different times of the year. Camels can go for a week without water, leaving their base camp and wandering for a maximum of fifty miles. Since cows can travel twenty miles without water, ten miles is the maximum that can separate their water and pasture, and the distance is less if they are weak and unhealthy. Goats and sheep are less mobile. In the case of the goat, this vulnerability is offset by a willingness to eat almost anything. Sheep are more discerning and therefore extremely vulnerable to drought. In 1969 they and the donkeys were the first to perish.

Every year Atakor considered these variables and matched animals of differing stamina, appetite, and thirst to the water and pasture at In Waggeur, resources which were both dependent on the monsoon and varied considerably from year to year.

His decisions were as impressive for their magnitude as for their complexity. For example, during the dry season one 550-pound cow needed 10 gallons of water and 14 pounds of dry pasture daily. In 1968 Atakor owned abut 100 cows. Every day he had to arrange to find and haul up 1,000 gallons of water, often from a depth of 180 feet, and locate 1,400

73

pounds of suitable grasses. He had to make like arrangements to feed and water his donkeys, goats, sheep, and camels.

Atakor was not a rancher and he did not try to increase his herds for profit. He increased them for prestige, because he liked them, and most of all as insurance against a possible drought. He maximized his herds to lessen his risks, so that no matter how many animals he lost to drought he would still have enough to feed his family and to restock his losses. It was a rational strategy, one that had been tested and proven to be effective.

Droughts in the Azawak were not aberrations. They were cyclical and expected. Although herd maximization was at the center of Atakor's strategy for surviving drought, it was not his only weapon. He could sell animals for millet, eat wild seeds, borrow milk-producing animals from relatives, split herds, hunt wild animals, or migrate to new pastures.

The romantic image of nomads as aimless wanderers, free spirits, is a fantasy. To survive on the ecological margins of the sahel, Atakor followed rational patterns calculated to maximize the probability of his survival, not gratify his whims. He was a prisoner of a seasonal rhythm determined by the monsoon.

He was not part of a quaint, dying race or the remnant of an inevitable doomed culture. (The Tuareg were not American Indians, Bedouin grazing over oil wells, Amazonian aborigines in the path of bulldozers. The land they occupied was some of the most worthless in the world, coveted by no one, productive only for them.) He was instead from a people who had adapted to a demanding land and climate and who had a unique talent for surviving and sometimes prospering where no one else could. The essence of his nomadism—movement to escape threats and seize opportunities—was still functional at the beginning of the drought. In 1962 Johannes Nicolaisen, a Danish anthropologist who spent years living with Tuareg in Southern Algeria and Niger, said of them, "Their most outstanding quality is that of endurance and contempt for hunger and hardship."

Yet between the Cures Salées of 1969 and 1974, many "professional" survivors like Atakor were destroyed. The animals that held together their homogeneous culture died in such numbers that it became impossible for them to survive in the bush. Families were shattered, and the survivors were, in the words of one refugee, "like little twigs that go wherever the wind carries them."

The mystery of why the Tuareg were destroyed is deepened by the fact that it appeared that they were not overcome by an unforeseen calamity but by a familiar—and formerly frequently and easily conquered—enemy, a drought.

But appearances are misleading. There were other villains besides the unpredictable monsoon. Long before the songs and dances of the 1969 Cure Salée, these villains had quite literally prepared the ground for ensuing disaster. As a consequence, between 1969 and 1974 Atakor and hundreds of thousands of Tuareg across Niger and Mali found that their traditional strategies for surviving drought had become ineffective. They became the victims of a total ecological collapse, the sort of collapse that could have been postponed or perhaps averted by money and technology in a rich country, but which in a poor one is called an "act of God."

3

The Pastures Surrounding

In Waqqeur

September 1969-June 1973

The hum of our motors must always mingle with the splendors of the scenery and the memories evoked by it. That hum has a beauty of its own. It is the song of progress, the rhythm of human effort chanting its victory over the elements.

—Georges-Marie Haardt and Louis
Audouin-Dubreuil (the first men
to cross the Sahara by automobile)

i

*A*takor and the Illabakan believed that the drought was not only an *act* of God, but that it was also His will. One man who lost his entire herd said, "God decided that I would have my animals, and then He decided that I would not. I do not blame Him. My animals belonged to Him and if I find more it will be because He decides to give them to me."

The farmers of Niger, animists and Moslems alike, agreed. The chief magician of Bagaji, a village 175 miles southwest of In Waggeur, said, "It's true that I can make the rain fall. That's one of my many powers. Those who preceded me often made the rain fall and I can still do it.

"It is not as easy now because it's necessary to sacrifice an animal and animals now are very expensive. We slit the throat of an animal—a cow or goat depending on the rite. Once the animal is killed its meat is distributed to the villagers and its blood flows into sacred spots. Then we state our needs and wait.

"There was a time when we could persuade the gods to do whatever we wanted. As soon as we asked for something they wouldn't waste a moment in giving it to us, including rain. But so many people are abandoning our traditions that getting results has become more difficult.

"Especially now, during the drought, we have to offer sacrifices be-

79

cause the gods are becoming displeased with our behavior. It is necessary to appease their anger. If we do, they will not be able to refuse our
demands and we will quickly leave the present difficult situation behind
us.''

Many journalists, scientists, and bureaucrats from more economically advanced societies seem also to believe that a metaphorical
"act of God," a natural phenomenon, was solely responsible for the extent of destruction caused by the drought. One variation of their act-of-
God theory proposed that the sahelian drought is part of an ominous and
irreversible worldwide climatic trend. Reid Bryson, a climatologist at
the University of Wisconsin, predicts that the world is entering a period
of unfavorable and colder weather. The new cold weather is said to be
caused by natural and man-made dust, smoke, and other atmospheric
pollutants which have blocked solar radiation and cooled polar regions,
thereby altering the pattern of global winds that determine the world's
weather.

Since these winds push the monsoon rains north to the Tadarast plateau, the sahelian drought is, according to Bryson's theory, just the beginning of decades, if not centuries, of substandard monsoon rains, expanding deserts, and mass starvation. The consequences of this trend
for the rest of the world will also be grim. Enormous migrations and political and economic chaos are anticipated: Canada will lose 50 percent
of its crops, and northern Europe 30 percent.

Bryson's theories are extremely controversial. Other climatologists
believe that droughts such as that experienced by the sahel are routine
deviations from normal weather patterns, not evidence of long-term
shifts in the world's weather. Still other climatologists believe that neither position is conclusively supported by the scientific data. An expert
committee of the National Academy of Sciences has investigated the
possibility of long-term change and concluded that "not only are the basic scientific questions unanswered, but in many cases we do not know
enough to pose the questions.''

Despite this uncertainty some opponents of financial assistance to
poor countries such as Niger have used the "long-term change in the
weather" theories as arguments for terminating this assistance. They

reason that since these weather changes are inevitable, it is senseless to spend money for economic development in nations which are doomed to become deserts. Instead, this money should be invested in programs to increase crop acreage and in building more storage facilities in the agricultural regions of nations, such as the United States, which will be less affected by the global weather changes.

On May 1, 1976, the same day that United States Secretary of State Henry Kissinger spoke in Dakar of "rolling back the desert" in the sahel, the Central Intelligence Agency (CIA) released a twenty-two-month-old internal report titled "A Study of Climatological Research As It Pertains to Intelligence Problems." This report relied heavily on climatological theories which suggest that "rolling back the desert" in the sahel is impossible. Eleven days later, Patrick Buchanan, a conservative columnist and former advisor to President Nixon, wrote in his nationally syndicated column that "recapturing the Sahara from Mother Nature makes as much sense, economically, as planting central Alaska in cotton."

Records of Niger's climate during the twentieth century refute both Bryson and Buchanan. These records show that the drought is not part of a long-term, or even short-term, change in the climate of the sahel. Instead, they reveal that droughts have been frequent and that there have been others almost as severe during the last seventy years, though without the same disastrous consequences.

Niger's weather has been characterized by cyclical and short-term fluctuations in the quantity of rainfall. The recent drought conforms to this pattern. There was a serious drought in 1913, and then alternating periods of drought and average precipitation between 1920 and 1940. During the 1940s the amount of rainfall was average throughout the decade, but with substantial yearly fluctuations. Between 1950 and 1967 Niger's rains were unusually useful, both plentiful (20 percent more than average) and well-spaced. The size of the nomadic herds increased and the area cultivated by farmers expanded.

In 1968 the good rains ended. Rainfall in the Azawak was one fifth below normal (but one third below the high average sustained during the previous twenty years). Between 1970 and 1973 the rains were one third below normal, and in 1973 only one half their average magnitude. Besides being deficient in quantity, they were also poor in timing and spacing. The greatest declines occurred in regions that depended most on the rains, the fragile pastures of the Azawak.

In 1974 the monsoon returned to Niger, and the drought ended with rains so heavy that floods washed away some crops and pastures. These excess rains also spawned plagues of locusts and rats which ate most of what remained. The rainfall in 1975 and 1976 was normal for most of the sahel, and two countries, Upper Volta and Mali, enjoyed agricultural surpluses. As a climatic phenomenon, the drought was over.

According to a study of Niger's climate conducted by the University of Arizona, lengthy droughts were not unknown even before the twentieth century. Since A.D. 1500 the country has undergone six one-year droughts, eight two-year droughts, two lasting three years, one lasting four, four lasting five, and even one that was sixteen years long. Although the calculations are rough, based on travelers' journals and tree rings, they do indicate that the only real abnormality of the most recent drought was the extent of the social and environmental damage it occasioned.

A second variation of the act-of-God theory for the drought appeared in newspaper stories and in the reports of experts and publicists hired by the international relief groups. According to them, the Sahara desert became a mysterious and malevolent force "rolling forward," covering thousands of square miles of pastures and farms. It "marched south" on its "inexorable advance"; it was an "invading desert" whose "creeping sands swallowed" the sahel at a rate of thirty to a hundred miles a year.

The use of such language made the desert the embodiment of evil and concealed the identity of the more human and less impersonal villains behind such a "natural" disaster.

This language also led to the conclusion that, since the responsibility for such disasters rested with God or "fate," any disaster assistance offered by more fortunate nations was always purely charitable. No human agents had an ethical responsibility to the victims.

A natural disaster is actually composed of two principal elements: the act of God itself—the natural phenomenon of a hurricane, an earthquake, or a drought; and a pattern of human settlement which makes people vulnerable to the phenomenon. The disaster is really the economic and social upheaval caused by the natural event. The magnitude of this upheaval is determined not solely by the ferocity of the natural phenomenon but also by the condition of the human settlement at the time it occurs.

For example, in a North American city heavy rainstorms are an inconvenience. They flood roads and basements and delay commuters. But in South America, where political and economic factors have made human settlements more disaster-prone, these heavy rains trigger a disaster. They precipitate landslides, wash away shantytowns, and bury people alive. A disaster occurs because population pressures, the lure of modern cities, and the plantation system have all induced farmers to abandon the countryside and search for wage-paying labor in the cities. The cheapest land available to them in these South American cities is often located on the slopes of steep hills. The farmers cut down trees, clear underbrush, and build flimsy shacks, thereby turning these hills into areas that are disaster-prone. As a result, what would have been merely a heavy rain a decade earlier becomes a disaster.

A similar scenario occurred in the sahel. There, instead of heavy rains, an extended drought was the natural phenomenon that triggered the subsequent disasters: expansion of the desert, famine, and the death of many humans and animals due to starvation. During the ten years prior to the drought, the human settlement pattern in the sahel's nomadic regions had been profoundly transformed by certain foreign economic and technological innovations. These innovations were largely responsible for turning five years of substandard rainfall into a total ecological collapse. If the sahelian drought does fall into any pattern, it is not one of climatic change but of induced disaster due to unwise technological tampering with the environment.

There are indications that the sahel is not the only poor region in the world in which an increase in environmental tampering has also been responsible for an increase in the number and seriousness of what are sometimes mistakenly called natural disasters. During the decade

83

preceding the sahelian drought there was a dramatic increase not only in the number of worldwide disasters but also in the number of what are termed "large-scale" disasters (such as drought and famine) and in the loss of life per disaster, particularly in the poorer countries.

The United Nations has a Disaster Research Organization (UNDRO) to monitor and record natural disasters. In Washington the Agency for International Development (AID) has a computer printout that ranks disasters according to death, injury, and dollar loss. In addition, a number of universities have disaster research programs. Natural events which result in little human suffering but substantial environmental damage are recorded by some of these organizations and ignored by others. The AID computer has been accused of a bias toward including disasters in countries where AID has extensive programs of its own.

Despite the differences between organizations in defining exactly what a disaster is, their statistics do indicate that people in poor countries are becoming steadily more disaster-prone than those in rich ones, and that when similar disasters occur in each, the inhabitants of the poor countries will suffer more. Changing definitions of disasters, population growth, or improved accuracy in reporting disasters in poor countries do not explain such trends.

In 1969, when the sahelian drought began, a private American organization, the Natural Hazard Research Group, published figures showing that in the United States there was an average of 37 deaths per disaster, while in Africa there were 1,065. UNDRO statistics show an average 4.8 disasters a year in the world between 1919 and 1971. But if the twenty years from 1951 to 1971 are isolated, the rate jumps to 10 a year. Between 1968 and 1971 the average is 13. The sahel's drought was part of this trend of more disasters due to technological tampering.

ii

*B*etween December 1936 and February 1937, a joint English-French expedition of geologists and foresters traveled in desert vehicles across Niger. They took the track that connected Agadez, In Gall, and Tahoua. They inspected In Waggeur and the pastures of the Illabakan, lands that would become virtual deserts thirty-five years later. The purpose of their trip was to find evidence that would either substantiate or disprove the widely publicized hypothesis of E. P. Stebbing, an Edinburgh geographer, that the Sahara was moving south rapidly into fertile West African lands.

The expedition observed regions where the desert appeared to be encroaching on southern lands, but this did not seem to pose the immense and generalized threat that had been postulated. Although in some areas the Sahara was "advancing" south, in others it was "retreating" north. The experts were unanimous in their conclusions that "nothing points to increased unproductiveness due to an extension of desert zones in these areas," and that "the Sahara does not seem to have a general tendency to move toward the south."

In the region between In Gall and Tahoua occupied by the Illabakan, the expedition determined that forestation, rather than desertification, was occurring, and that the inhabitants were "menaced" by an "invasion" of acacia trees. The Tuareg they questioned reported sighting more wild animals each year, and they worried about protecting their herds. The Europeans were impressed that the tribesmen understood the importance of the trees and cut them down only when absolutely necessary for firewood or fodder. They reported that "the inhabitants of the Azawak confirmed our impression [that the desert was stationary] and affirmed that their countryside is more verdant today than before."

Thirty-five years later elderly Illabakan would point to barren plains and describe the trees and grass that once flourished, the wild animals they hunted, and the domesticated animals that grazed on the lands. The Illabakan knew that the reasons for their pastures becoming desert were many.

As Niger's population grew, so too did the need for wood. Branches were cut from trees to feed goats and camels. The Illabakan needed wood for cooking fires, for animal enclosures, nomadic beds, tent frames, and tools, and to shore up wells. In the south, wood was cut and sold to the inhabitants of growing cities. Trees that once anchored soil came into Tahoua and Niamey loaded on donkeys, camels, and the heads of small girls. Every year the journey became longer, the circle wider, the price higher. During the drought the average Niamey family spent one tenth of its monthly earnings to buy firewood hauled from as far as thirty miles away.

Wherever trees, bushes, and grasslands disappeared, the desert seemed to expand. Farmers burned off the underbrush to prepare lands for cultivation. Nomads burned the reburned pastures, hoping it would enrich the soil. The raw, burned land was left unprotected, open to erosion by wind and rain. Without any protective covering it became colder at night, warmer in the day. These extreme and rapid shifts in temperature killed living organisms and rendered the land a lifeless desert.

The desert rolled north from eroded farms. In the thirty years between the English-French expedition to the Azawak and the drought, the line of cultivation moved north from the Adar, the agricultural zone south of the Azawak, into the Azawak pastures themselves.

In 1936 most of the lands on the northern fringes of the Adar served as a refuge for Tuareg herds when the monsoon failed to provide adequate pasturage in their homeland further north. These lands, north of Tahoua and south of In Waggeur, are sometimes called marginal because they are located on the borders of the agricultural region and are suitable only for cultivation during periods of exceptionally heavy rains.

During the decade preceding the drought, however, Niger's rains were exceptional. The country's population grew rapidly, and in response to physical, economic, and social pressures these marginal lands were cultivated for the first time.

A frequently overlooked reason for this cultivation is that the soil in the Adar is sandy, loose, and easy to till. Therefore, when the rains in the Adar are good, it is possible to grow as much as in Niger's south, and with less effort. In the southern farmlands the soil is more fertile but is composed of hard clays. To cultivate this land requires strenuous work.

Niger's independence from France in 1960 was marked by the second emancipation of the bouzous (the first came at the time of the French pacification). Since the Adar lands were then largely unoccupied and seemed to be productive because of the good rainfall, the bouzous who left their Tuareg masters settled on them in great numbers.

The government failed to discourage the settlement and cultivation of these fragile lands. Most of the men who ruled Niger were from one of the two farming peoples, the Djerma or the Hausa, and favored farmers over nomads instinctively. Since this ruling elite had been educated in French schools, it had assimilated the prejudices of the French against Niger's nomads.

Like the leaders of many modern states, they considered the nomads a problem. Nomads wander across frontiers without proper papers, and pay no customs duties. They are chronic tax evaders, and they resist schools, hospitals, and other government services which they perceive, sometimes correctly, as part of a plot to control them. They insist on wearing quaint clothes and following quaint customs, which please tourists but embarrass their country's rulers.

The elite in Niger also inherited from the French an economic system stacked against the nomads. Niger was colonized for glory, not for profit. Only after the French had established a military presence did they start to look for a way to make their new subjects pay for the administrative expenses of occupation.

The French administered the Adar and the Azawak from Tahoua. One of the first officers posted to Tahoua, Lieutenant Peignol, wrote a report in 1907 on the economic hazards and potentials of the colony. On the one hand, he recognized the region's fragile ecology. "It will be necessary," he wrote, "little by little to protect the land against the inhabitants that devastate it." And on the other, he saw that "peace, imposed by the French on the warring Tuareg tribes, will favor the growth of the herds," and thereby harm nomadic pastures. In the same dispatch he warned that Niger could conceivably become a liability to France, since "the country doesn't produce anything itself that can be exchanged for products arriving from the outside."

Peignol's assessment was correct. Niger's nomads raised animals which provided them with food and transportation. The farmers grew food which they ate themselves or exchanged with the nomads for animals and cloth. The Nigerien people were self-sufficient; the colonial administration was not.

The French solution to this problem of their own making—to force farmers to cultivate crops that could be exported for cash—reversed the situation. To ensure that the Nigerien farmers grew cash crops such as peanuts and cotton, the French levied taxes that had to be paid in cash and fined farmers who failed to meet production quotas.

As the Nigerien farmers were forced into the cash and market economy, their harvest of food crops shrank and the cohesion of their villages disintegrated. Men migrated to the coast in the winters to work as laborers and earn more cash. The sahelian countries became *bantustans* providing cheap seasonal labor to other French colonies. The French bought Niger's cash crops at artificially low prices, and sold the Nigeriens goods manufactured in France at artificially high ones. Meanwhile, the farmers were forced to produce cash crops.

One of these cash crops, peanuts, was not a French innovation. In Senegal peanuts were already being grown in exportable quantities and used to supplement food crops before the French arrived. But the French forced the Senegalese to expand the cultivation of peanuts at the expense of their food crops. At first, there was enough land so that the farmers could produce food for their own needs and peanuts for the French. Between the world wars the farmers ran out of land. Land that had been planted in peanuts for years deteriorated, and the price for peanuts on the world market fell. Since they were unable to buy enough food with the earnings from their peanut harvests, some farmers tried to return to growing crops they could eat. But in many regions peanuts had weakened the soil so that even when the rains were good the harvests of food crops were poor.

Thirty years later a similar pattern was occurring in Niger. Cash crops do not have to exhaust farmlands, but the manner in which the French encouraged their cultivation guaranteed that they would. Year after year peanuts and then cotton were planted on the same land. Year after year these crops withdrew the same minerals from the soil.

Some crops are complementary. Legumes, for example, remove potash from the soil and manufacture magnesium. Millet requires magnesium. Legumes and millet are therefore complementary, and when they are rotated in the same field, one replenishes the minerals the other has consumed. In Niger, peanuts and cotton were seldom rotated with other crops, and so they consumed the same minerals until they had exhausted the soil.

88

The destructive cycle was endless. As the cash crops destroyed Niger's more fertile soil, farmers were forced to cultivate more acreage and to reduce the harvests of millet and sorghum, their food crops, to maintain export production at a level satisfactory to the French (and, after 1960, to the independent government of Niger). Since the farmers grew only enough food for their own families, their skimpy surpluses declined. The market for food crops shrank, and what food was available became more expensive.

The export crops had other drawbacks. Before the French encouraged the cultivation of cash crops, Nigerien farmers planted a number of different strains of sorghum. Since each strain required a different amount of rainfall for maturation, at least one strain was sure to prosper even when the rains were poor. But when the farmers planted more acreage in peanuts and cotton and less in sorghum, they were able to cultivate only one strain. Naturally they chose the one that yielded the greatest quantity. Unfortunately, this strain also needed the most moisture, and the farmers ran a larger risk than before that their sorghum crops would fail to mature during a drought.

In the twenty-five years before the drought, some of Niger's farmers moved north. Their migration was encouraged by the favorable weather conditions and by government officials who relied on the foreign exchange earned by their export crops to support a life-style centered on imported luxuries. Farmers were also driven from their southern fields by population pressures and by the fact that their lands had been exhausted by decades of peanut cultivation. Starting in the years after World War II the farmers occupied and cultivated pastures on the southern fringes of the Azawak and other nomadic regions. Pastures became farms, and further south, cotton and peanuts were planted instead of food.

Although more lands than ever before were brought into cultivation between 1960 and 1968, the yield per acre of both cash and food crops declined. In the twenty years before the drought the dry agricultural zones in Niger doubled in area without a similar increase in production. And since the marginal lands were more fragile and less fertile than those further south, they became exhausted even sooner, ready to be eroded and turned into desert.

89

When the good rains that had camouflaged the folly of this practice ended in 1968, these marginal farms deteriorated rapidly. Harvests failed. Wind and water carried away the thin layer of fertile soil. Sand dunes formed, and the pastures that had been a safety valve for the Azawak nomads became deserts.

This increase in cultivation in the south was also responsible in part for the great numbers of animals that grazed on the Azawak's shrinking pastures just prior to the drought.

As agriculture became monetized and directed to the export market, the demand for animals fell and their number rose, making them worth less and less. In the Adar, cotton replaced animals as a medium of exchange. Before World War II one cow was worth thirty sacks of millet. Just before the drought it was worth one. The money and the terms of trade the Tuareg received for their animals ceased to have any relation to the time and energy required to raise them.

Every year the Tuareg needed to trade more and more animals in order to obtain enough food to survive the soudure. Therefore, the large Tuareg herds which were soon to magnify the consequences of the drought were not the result of irrational greed. They were instead the specific, rational, and inevitable response to the fact that in the twenty-five years preceding the drought grain had become more precious and animals less valuable.

iii

When the drought began and desert formed in the eroded marginal farms of the Adar, there were more men and animals in the Azawak trying to survive on less pasture. (Niger's human population has been increasing at the rapid rate of 2.7 percent a year, one of the highest rates anywhere in the world.) Small deserts formed throughout the Azawak wherever the animals trampled the ground cover, ate the grasses that anchored the soil, pulled up plants by the roots, and stripped bark from the branches of trees.

90

The survival of men, animals, and pastures depends on the maintenance of a balance between all three. If there is less than an optimal number of animals they tend to graze selectively, and the most desirable species of grass quickly vanish. The plants they ignore become dangerous. Their stiff woody stems pierce animals' nostrils, and the accumulation of old plant material becomes so dense that other species are choked. The consequences of overgrazing are even more serious. In the thirty years between the English-French mission and the drought, the human and the animal populations of the Azawak (and the rest of the sahel) doubled. Most of this growth occurred in the decade preceding the drought. Between 1960 and 1965 alone there was a 50 percent increase in herds of goats and sheep and a 20 percent increase in cattle.

In the Tahoua nomadic zone, which included the Azawak, the government sponsored three vaccination programs during the winters of 1965, 1966, and 1967. Animal deaths declined, and a subsequent census revealed that the size of the Tuareg herds was much greater than government experts had estimated.

As the number of animals increased, so did the people. In 1900 there were 1,200 Peul in the Tahoua district; in 1965 there were 30,000. After the French pacified the Azawak, the Peul drifted north into pastures that had been the sole preserve of the Illabakan and other Kel Dennik tribes. The Peul were more mobile than the Tuareg and not overly attached to a particular region. Formerly, they had wandered into the Azawak, grazed their animals, clashed with the Tuareg, and returned south again. But in the years preceding the drought their migrations were of a different nature: they came more frequently, in greater numbers, and they stayed.

The Peul had been forced out of their own pastures by the expansion of export crop cultivation. They were attracted to Tuareg areas by concrete wells and automatic pumps, built first by the French and then by the Nigerien government. Since these wells were constructed by the government, they were the property of no one tribe or people. Anyone could use them. Since the Illabakan and other Tuareg in the Azawak were powerless to deny the Peul access to these new water points and to the pastures which surrounded them, they lost control of the most important of their resources.

91

Before 1945 watering animals was the most physically exhausting, time-consuming, and unpleasant of all nomadic tasks. It was exhausting because the water requirements of the herds are immense. To provide a cow with a daily ration of ten gallons of water involved hauling a heavy gallon bucket from a deep well ten times. It was time-consuming because the animals had to be supervised; their owners wanted to be sure they drank as much water as they needed to survive until the next water point. It was unpleasant because animals were watered at the hottest part of the day to encourage them to drink to their capacity.

Before 1945 the only wells in the Azawak were those which the Tuareg themselves had dug, or paid Hausa well-diggers to dig. They were constructed and maintained by the families and tribes that lived in their vicinity. They had to be repaired periodically, their mouths reinforced with wood and the ground around them packed down to prevent cave-ins.

The Illabakan also dug shallow holes to tap underground water where it was close to the surface. These holes were ten meters deep at the most, located near the bank of a river, and usually quickly exhausted during the dry season. For the Illabakan they were only practical to tap the shallow water table near Tchin-Tabaraden.

Tuareg from other tribes, Arabs from the north, Peul from the south—all of these could use the wells and the pastures surrounding them only if they received permission from the Illabakan. Since before 1945 visits from these people were infrequent, and the Illabakan had a reputation for hospitality, this permission was usually granted.

The work involved in watering animals, as well as control by different Tuareg tribes over water points and hence surrounding pastures, limited the size of the Azawak herds and maintained the equilibrium between men, animals, pasture, and water. These constraints offset the tendency of individual Tuareg to increase the size of their herds for prestige and as insurance against losses during a drought. They also lessened the natural human impulse to maximize personal profit from a resource, such as a pasture, which is owned by the community.

After World War II French administrators in Niger and other sahelian countries began a program of pastoral well-digging that weakened these constraints, thus destroying the ecological balance, encouraging erosion, and promoting the concentration of large herds of animals on shrinking pastures.

One of the first of these wells in Niger was dug in 1948 at In Waggeur. It was ninety meters deep, and since its mouth was reinforced with concrete there was no danger of cave-ins and no need for maintenance. It was so deep that it reached underground beyond the range of traditional wells and allowed the Illabakan to remain at In Waggeur in semipermanent camps long after the seasonal pools had disappeared. But since it had been built by the government instead of the Illabakan, it was open to anyone who carried a forked stick, a rope, a bucket, and a pulley. Throughout the 1950s and 1960s scores of these wells were sunk in Niger's pastoral zones.

Drawing water from the new cement wells still involved time and effort. A camel or a donkey had to be hitched to a rope and bucket and made to walk ninety meters toward the well to let the bucket reach water level, and then ninety meters away to haul it up. The alternative was for the men themselves to haul up the bucket.

In 1964 the government eliminated even this work by installing at In Waggeur a pump powered by gasoline which would draw water automatically. Not only was this pump open to anyone, but it could also water huge numbers of animals in a short period of time.

This policy of building cement wells and pumps was outlined in a 1960 report from Niger's Ministry of Rural Economy (although the policy had been conceived before independence, and was implemented and administered by French advisors who had remained for that purpose). The report, "Pastoral Hydrology: The Basis for a Politics of Water in the Sahelian Zone," was a turning point for Nigerien Tuareg. It identified a lack of water as their principal problem and recommended that, inasmuch as so many animals seemed to die during the dry season, the government should encourage an increase in the size of herds by tapping the water table with wells fitted with gasoline-powered pumps. The report made no seasonal provisions for increasing the quantity or quality of the pastures surrounding these pumps.

The French hydrologic and livestock experts understood the potential ecological dangers posed by these wells, and the possibility of erosion which would result from the gathering of huge herds around them for a longer period of time than usual, nine months instead of six. But the precautions they took were inadequate, and imposed on the Tuareg without consultation.

The legal codes which authorized the construction of the pumps regulated most aspects of their operation carefully but unrealistically. To protect surrounding pastures, each pump was to be shut down for a predetermined length of time yearly. To guard against an overconcentration of animals, the pumps were to be carefully spaced and the pastures "protected" for a radius of twenty-five miles by government forestry officers. To prevent any pump from being out of service for a long period of time and forcing animals to group around those that did work, spare parts for the pumps were to be stored in accessible locations. To protect the pastures from cultivation, a "northern limit" was fixed on government maps beyond which farmers were forbidden to plant.

If these regulations could have been enforced, they might have had some effect. But the government lacked the necessary administrative ability and political will. The situation had to become imminently disastrous or a disaster itself before ecological safeguards were enforced.

In Niger the government lacked the experts, spare parts, and funds to keep the new pumps in good working order. When the pumps failed, they were closed down for months and herds congregated around those still working. Most farmers had little idea of, and less interest in, the boundary decreed by the functionaries in Niamey to limit cultivation. Any attempts to shut down the wells and pumps for the sake of the nearby pastures, or to restrict them to certain herders "taking into account their traditional rights and patterns," met with no success at all. Guards who tried to enforce such regulations were assaulted, and a few had their throats cut. Most of the new water points were open all the time, to whoever needed water, whenever he needed it.

Each species of nomadic animal needs a minimum amount of both water and pasture to survive. Water and pasture must be close, preferably within one day's walk of each other. As the distance that separates them becomes greater, so does the danger that animals will become thin and unhealthy and eventually die in transit. Pasture without water means they will die of thirst; water without pasture, of starvation.

This would seem to be an elementary concept. Yet, in building too many wells and pumps, Niger's hydrologic program increased the availability of water and stimulated the growth of herds without producing more pasture. In fact, wells and pumps were proliferating at a time when agricultural policies were causing pasturage to shrink. Even when the new water points made other regions available, they were available to too many animals. Simply put, the pumps and wells watered too many animals too easily, thus attracting more animals than could find pasturage within a day's journey under normal climatic conditions.

All these technological improvements—wells and pumps, vaccination programs, and cash crops—upset the nomadic equilibrium in the Azawak. They also had the appearance, but not the substance, of philanthropy. Their real purpose was to increase the size of the herds so that nomads would sell their surplus animals and increase Niger's tax base and its export of cattle to coastal West African countries; to improve conditions in the nomadic regions at a negligible cost (in 1960 the government spent 3 percent of its national budget on development programs in the nomadic area; by 1970 it was spending only 2 percent, but in the intervening ten years the country's national herd had doubled in size); and to make the Tuareg dependent on the pumps, thus drawing them to the nomadic "towns" that sprang up around them and bringing them under the administrative and fiscal control of the new government.

One impetus behind these improvements was the belief that increased production is beneficial and that more is always better. The growth-oriented technology was introduced in the sahel without restraints and without either consultation with or consideration for the people whom it would affect the most. One of the foremost reasons why the nomads were never consulted by their benefactors was the continued belief in the myth that the nomads were unproductive, inefficient, aimless, and irrational wanderers. It was felt that a foreign technology could maximize and rationalize what was mistakenly perceived to be a minimal and irrational use of resources.

* * *

iv

*T*he Illabakan were among the principal "beneficiaries" of this technology. Pumps were built at Abalack in 1961, at In Waggeur in 1964, and at Tchin-Tabaraden in 1966. In the ten years between 1961 and 1971 twenty pumps in all were constructed in the area, and when the drought began sixteen were operational.

When it opened, the pump at In Waggeur was popular. Its inauguration coincided with the liberation of bouzous who had previously hauled the water from traditional wells. Had the pump not opened when it did, the Illabakan themselves would have had to draw water. Instead, the pump provided them with seemingly limitless gallons of cool, fresh water, spilling into black metal troughs or running into a large tank for storage. Instead of saving labor, the pump eliminated it. It also postponed an adaptation to physical labor that the Illabakan would find themselves having to make later during the drought. Leading their animals to the pump and watching them drink, they considered the pump a "remedy for the departure of the bouzous."

The Illabakan men gathered at In Waggeur to enjoy an extended Cure Salée. They visited, drank tea, told stories, and discussed where the best pastures could be found. Some took seasonal jobs or became small traders, usually using their earnings to buy more animals and increase their herds. Men lost touch with their animals and became lazy, observers of their own fate rather than actors in its working.

In the eight years between 1960 and 1968, according to Boucli, the son of Najim, the Illabakan chief, the two hundred people who normally gathered around In Waggeur became two thousand when the well was open. The growing herds of the Illabakan were joined by those of the Peul and Tuareg foreign to the Tadarast. Until 1968 plentiful and well-spaced rains enabled these monster herds to be accommodated. The seasonal pools lasted until January and February, and animals congregated around the In Waggeur pump for only about five months out of the year.

But when the drought began, these pools dried up two or three months sooner. The herds congregated around In Waggeur for eight months instead of five, and the first consequences of this technological tampering became apparent. At In Waggeur, the year-long Cure Salée spirit vanished. Foreign Peul and Tuareg strained hospitality. Animals became so numerous around the pump that proper surveillance was impossible and thievery rife. When the Illabakan tried to keep strangers away from their deteriorating pastures, there were shoving matches, drawn swords, and fights.

The pump at Abalack, forty miles south of In Waggeur, was designed to handle 2,000 cows and an equal number of other animals daily. By the spring of 1973 it was being used by 16,000 animals a day. The trees, bushes, and grass within a ten-mile radius of Abalack, like those at In Waggeur and the other cement wells and pumps throughout the Azawak, had been destroyed by the oversized herds. Bald spots, circular deserts, little blast zones of technology—they all expanded until they met and formed larger deserts.

The pumps and wells now became labor-creating rather than labor-saving. Many Illabakan moved their camps away from In Waggeur. They found pasture but very little water. They had become so dependent on the pump that they had allowed traditional wells to deteriorate and had dug no new ones. They had few reserves to fall back on. In 1970 two Illabakan families tried to dig a well eight miles from In Waggeur, closer to surviving pastures. They failed and their herd perished. Water was so far from the surface that digging wells was work for skilled laborers.

The Illabakan who stayed at In Waggeur had water but no pasture. Whatever they saved in time and labor by using the pump was spent on the long journeys to outlying pastures. Their animals became thin, weak, susceptible to disease. If they could be sold they were worth less. As the distances between water and pasture became greater, they died.

The Illabakan were aware of these dangers before the drought began. In 1968 many of them were interviewed by government livestock experts. The Peul were in favor of the pumps and the wells, but the Illabakan were divided. Those around In Waggeur were least in favor. They said:

"The pumps are useful for the villagers and to wash clothes and they are useless for the animals."

"Because of the pumps the herders of In Waggeur are frustrated, penalized for the benefit of transients attracted by the pump. When the grass has been eaten by their animals they go elsewhere, leaving only a small corner of pasture for the people who live in that region."

"Before the pump was built the only people at In Waggeur were the Illabakan. Since the pump was built numerous other people come to In Waggeur equally: Kel Oui and the Kel Fadet, and Peul from Madaoua, Dakoro, In Gall, and Agadez."

"The people have become lazy because of the pumps. they no longer know how to draw water from a well with a rope or dig puisards."

"Our problem is now a lack of pasture and a lack of trees. Now the wells encourage the desert and our pastures only last three months."

"The bush is the proper pasture for the herds, not the water pumps. Our animals are not fish; most of all they want pastures."

By 1970 the metamorphosis of pasture into desert around In Waggeur was so extensive and the causes so obvious that Khamed Moussa, an Illabakan who had been a government deputy, wrote to Niamey demanding that the pump be closed to allow the pastures to recover. The government refused. More and more animals died, more and more land became desert, and finally, in 1971, the pump was closed for eleven months. Many of the foreign nomads left In Waggeur. The Illabakan tried to put their traditional wells into working order so that they could spend the dry season away from In Waggeur.

It was too late. The rains in 1972 were so poor that the pastures had no chance to recover. Miniature deserts continued to grow around the wells, pumps, and pools of In Waggeur, Tchin-Tabaraden, and northern Niger, across a twenty-six-hundred-mile band of sahelian pastureland—wherever similar "development" programs had been introduced.

The process that created these deserts was initiated by the removal of vegetation. Without the trees that were cut down for firewood, the bushes that were burned off to clear land, or the grasses that provided fodder for the huge herds, the Azawak was vulnerable to the eroding forces of wind and water. When the brief, violent rains of 1972 and 1973 did fall, they ran off barren, baked soil or evaporated quickly. Little or none seeped down to replenish the underground water table.

Erosion continued during the dry season. Wind speeds increased along the surface of the unprotected land and blew away the fine clays and soils that had nurtured the grasses and bushes and been protected by them. These unchecked winds also carried off the seeds of wild grasses as well as those sown by farmers, and loose, plowed-up soil from the Adar farms. Ridges of sand and small dunes formed around water points and pastures and in fields that in previous years had contained millet and cotton.

The process of erosion was self-perpetuating. Wind speeds over the surface of the bare soil produced intense variations in temperature. Azawak land became warmer during the day, colder at night. These fluctuating temperatures created more local wind turbulence that stripped away more soil, added dust to the atmosphere, and suppressed rain-producing clouds. The warmer ground surfaces increased the radiation of solar energy, the surrounding atmosphere was warmed and dehumidified, and the possibility of rain lessened.

Erosion thus created a microclimate which was warmer, windier, dustier, drier, and more likely to suppress whatever monsoon clouds appeared during the summer months. It created an arid, static atmosphere which prolonged and magnified the effects of the drought.

The substandard quantity of rainfall also resulted in a series of related catastrophes throughout the sahel. Because their seasonal pools of water had vanished, wild animals made bizarre changes in their migratory patterns. Giraffes wandered into tsetse fly zones and died. Elephants in Chad, driven insane by thirst, lost their sense of direction and charged into the desert.

The wells in sedentary villages dried up and the underground water table was so low it was unable to recharge them. First single villages and then whole regions had to be abandoned. The Niger River dwindled to the lowest levels in its recorded history. Cities lost much of their electric power and river transport was interrupted. Sudden changes in the

99

ecology resulted in rare crop diseases and plagues of insects which ravaged still further the harvests of the sahel's oases and farms.

v

*D*uring the winter of 1972-1973, the remainder of Atakor's herd of animals died. This was not a unique tragedy. More than six million of Niger's animals, half of the national herd, would die before the drought was over. But the Tuareg in the northern nomadic zones suffered much greater losses. For a Tuareg tribe in the Azawak to lose from 90 to 100 percent of its animals was not unusual.

When Atakor tried to minimize these losses, he found that all of the traditional Tuareg strategies for surviving a drought were inoperative. He couldn't trade, he couldn't sell slaves in order to buy food, he couldn't raid the farmers as they were protected by the Nigerien army; he couldn't lead his few surviving animals to southern pastures since they had become farms. It was hardly worthwhile to sell his animals or trade them for millet before they died, for the terms of trade were so inequitable and the animals so thin that they were virtually worthless.

Well-digging programs, cash crops, and vaccination drives rendered his strategies useless. The Illabakan herds, marooned on eroded, shrinking pastures, were huge, so huge that when the drought became severe they destroyed remaining pasture and died almost at once. Instead of losing just a percentage of his animals, Atakor lost them all. Instead of the fittest surviving, not even they were able to find enough fodder after the weakest had died. (If twenty people were marooned on an island that could support ten, some would survive after the weaker had perished. But if there were two hundred, they might strip the island bare, turning it into a desert in which all would die.)

To remain in the bush, Atakor's family needed a minimum number of animals, enough to supply them with essential milk and food or the means to trade for them. As soon as the herd fell below this minimum

100

and he had borrowed all he could from friends and relatives, Atakor was left with two alternatives: death or migration.

When, during the soudure of 1973, Atakor first tried to kill himself and then climbed onto the truck that would take him away from In Waggeur, about a million other people throughout the sahel, farmers and nomads alike, were also fleeing from their homelands.

When Niger became independent, Atakor's bouzous, like those belonging to many Illabakan families, stayed in the Tadarast but moved away from their master's camp. They continued to work for him but they also hired themselves out to other families and Atakor and Miriam had to assume some of their lighter tasks.

In 1973 the drought succeeded in accomplishing what seventy years of laws and proclamations had not—decisively freeing these bouzous. With his animals dead, Atakor was unable to pay or even to feed them. Like bouzous across Niger, they left the nomadic zones and moved south to cities and agricultural villages. They took with them something that their masters lacked, the capacity for hard work.

Most of the Peul left the Tadarast before either the Tuareg or the bouzous. The Peul were more mobile and more familiar with the pastures in the south of the country. Unlike the Tuareg, they had no special attachment to a particular winter campsite. They considered a fixed homesite to be true homelessness. They slept under trees or lean-tos made of straw mats and settled wherever they could find the best pasture and water for their humpbacked, lyre-horned cows.

The Peul loved their cows and simply to own them and drink their milk was an end in itself. This milk was sacred and never boiled, watered down, poured out, or used to cleanse the mouth. The Peul seldom, if ever, ate their cows and their natural death at an advanced age was a prestigious sign of wealth. Sometimes the cows died of exhaustion after having been driven long distances to be shown off to friends and relatives.

Just as many Tuareg legends concern warfare, those of the Peul center on the relationship between men and cows. Cows are believed to have personalities, and to be able to choose from within families those members they prefer as herders.

For the Peul, life before the drought had pulsed with a mystical symbiosis in which human and animal rhythms were synchronized. The Peul devoted themselves to long migrations whose solitary goal was to find the choicest pastures for their animals. They played flutes to serenade their cows, and in return the cows forecast rain and sandstorms, and communicated this information to their owners by standing in different positions.

The visual climax of this symbiosis occurred during the soudure, when the Peul herders rested under trees and their cows cooled them by licking their heads. At the same time, small white "tick" birds perched on the backs of the cows and ate insects that annoyed the animals.

As drought conditions became more severe during the winter of 1972-1973, many of the Peul who had lived in the Tadarast fled to the south with their precious herds. Some fought with farmers over grazing land. Their animals trampled crops, pushed over fences, and provoked range wars. Some migrated so far south that they were searching for forage in tsetse fly zones and their animals died of disease instead of thirst or starvation. By June of 1973, instead of singing to living cows the Peul sang about their dead ones:

> When the herder walks
> without the dust of his animals
> behind him.
> When the last cow,
> who gave the last pot of milk,
> collapses.
> Then only one thing is certain,
> that his life will never be the same.
> —Peul chant heard in Niger during 1973

As the exodus of Peul, bouzou, and Tuareg grew in magnitude it came to the attention of foreign journalists and relief agencies. During the first six months of 1973 they observed the starvation and suffering. However, major international efforts to alleviate these conditions were not effective until later in the year. By then, too many animals were dead and it was too late to prevent Tuareg tribes and families from unraveling as they fled their homelands. At first, this unraveling was observed, but not prevented:

Telex to UNICEF, Office of Public Information, from the Gao-Timbuctoo line during 1973:

2000 MILE STRETCH EMBRACING ONE MILLION SQUARE KILOMETERS
MORE THAN HALF SIZE OF THE UNITED STATES
24–30 MILLION PEOPLE INVOLVED
90 PER CENT RURAL AREAS
DAKAR HAS TREBLED POPULATION IN SIX MONTHS
RUSH TO TOWNS
TENTED CAMPS SANITATION PROBLEMS TREMENDOUS
DROUGHT FOR FOUR TO FIVE YEARS
GOVERNMENTS HAVE BEEN OVERWHELMED
DESERT IS MOVING SOUTHWARD AND DRIVING THE NOMADS
INTO ARABLE AREAS AWAY FROM THE CATTLE COUNTRY
BY THE END OF OCTOBER SIX MILLION LIVES THREATENED
PROBLEM OF SURVIVAL
TUAREGS
BLUE MEN
YOUNG PEOPLE IN CITIES—A WHOLE NEW PROBLEM TO BE FACED
DROP IN REVENUE FROM CATTLE TAX-BASIS OF ECONOMY
EXPORT OF CATTLE WAS ONE OF THE MAIN SOURCES OF REVENUE
DRASTIC CHANGE IN WHOLE SAHELIAN REGION
AFFECTED REGION NEEDS 1.5 BILLION IN HELP FOR THE
DROUGHT STRICKEN REGIONS
INCLUDES WELL-DIGGING, DAMMING OF RIVERS, IRRIGATION TO
STEM THE SOUTHWARD MARCH OF DESERT
REORGANIZE RAILROAD AND RIVER TRANSPORT
INCLUDES SOME OF THE POOREST NATIONS IN THE WORLD

DESERT LINE, GAO, ZINDER, AGADEZ, TIMBUCTOO

4

Sidi

April-August 1973

Timbuctoo-Gao-Niamey

Oh my cousin, my beloved one!
Once I thought that nothing would part us.
But your companions have come back, saying you are dead far away.
I ascend the hill where my grave will be dug.
Under a heap of stones bury my heart.
I perceive your scent between my breasts.
It burns my bones.

—Tuareg poem

i

Sidi was a talented Tuareg blacksmith. Until September 1972 he had lived and worked in a nomadic center which was two days' walk northwest of Timbuctoo, a city located in Mali, Niger's western neighbor. He lived with his wife, three sons, a daughter, and a small herd of goats and sheep. His mother had been a blacksmith and most of his immediate relatives were also blacksmiths in the same region and for the same Tuareg tribe. Sidi specialized in making weapons and jewelry decorated with silver scarabs, wild animals, and the intricate Tuareg crosses. He was noted for a ring decorated with a pair of linked hearts, popular with Tuareg lovers.

"Before the drought I was a famous and skilled blacksmith, and people traveled for days to visit my forge. I made weapons and jewelry. Some blacksmiths made a sword in a single day. I copied the ancient ones so it took me days to make just one. I also made beautiful silver bracelets. I owned a book in which I drew designs for bracelets. My clients could choose from these or draw a new design themselves.

"I made knives, rings, pendants, camel saddles, and silver and leather containers for gris-gris [amulets] written by marabouts. I made wooden bowls, calabashes, and spoons, and I could repair anything made from silver or any kind of metal. But I preferred to make swords because they were courageous.

107

"My wife made articles from leather such as pillow covers, purses, and scabards for my swords and knives. She was not skilled, but my fame brought customers to her. My sister tried to teach her how to make the purses more beautiful but she refused to learn."

Sidi charged his customers five goats to make a camel saddle, two to make a sword. When the client wanted a saddle with ornaments, he charged six. When he made calabashes, the client paid by filling the new calabash with milk, Sidi then poured the milk into one of his own containers. If he made a small calabash, he received a small amount of milk.

Sidi's clients lost many of their animals during the first four years of the drought. They could no longer afford to pay for his products with either goats or milk and they reduced their purchases accordingly. Sidi's own small herd of animals also suffered. By September of 1972, he could no longer feed his family. He followed the example of his impoverished customers and fled to Timbuctoo.

The blacksmiths in Timbuctoo were jealous of Sidi. His work was more beautiful than theirs and he charged less (for the first time he was being paid in currency and he was confused about how much to charge). The blacksmiths were angry because he was a mestizo, half Tuareg vassel and half Tuareg blacksmith. It upset them that a mestizo could be such a skillful blacksmith.

They hired a powerful marabout to make an amulet that was intended to drive Sidi crazy, turn his family against him, and force him to leave Timbuctoo. When he heard about this threat he tried to engage a marabout who could write a more powerful gris-gris (amulet) that would protect him. The other marabouts were scared and they refused. There was no marabout more powerful than the one the Timbuctoo blacksmiths had already hired.

Sidi: "When my wife heard that the blacksmiths were plotting against me, she became frightened and wanted to take our children and return to her family. I begged her not to leave, but she insisted, so I demanded that my five-year-old son, Ibrahim, remain in Timbuctoo. He is my oldest and I love him the most. I also needed him to push the bellows and I wanted to teach him how to become a good blacksmith.

"My wife told me that she was going to visit her parents in Gondam

108

[a town in Mali, 60 miles west of Timbuctoo]. But the day after she left two different people told me that she and another blacksmith had taken a boat to Gao [also in Mali, 263 miles southeast of Timbuctoo]. Now I knew that I was cursed by the marabout's powerful gris-gris.

"I was lonely in Timbuctoo. If my parents had been alive I would have visited them, but both died when the drought began. The blacksmiths who were my friends in the bush had gone to find work in Algeria, Libya, or Nigeria. They did not care that I was a mestizo, and they had been my only friends.

"People think that we blacksmiths make many friends and are popular because we joke with everyone. They are wrong. We only joke with the Tuareg because they consider us so inferior that our insults mean nothing. When my Tuareg clients joked they called me the 'great blacksmith' if I was making something or the 'great repairer' if I was fixing something. Other times they laughed and called me 'good-for-nothing' and then I called them the same thing.

"There was a certain noble Tuareg who, whenever he came to my camp, said 'Here is the blacksmith who never washes, who is always filthy, and is always rich. All he can do is make things with his hands.'

"I always said to him 'You can't make things with your hands. In fact you can't even make your own living.' Then we laughed and discussed how much I would charge him. In 1972 he lost his animals and moved to a refugee camp near Timbuctoo. I gave him food but he was a noble and I was a blacksmith so we were still not friends.

"I had no friends in Timbuctoo. A marabout had cursed me and my wife had deserted me. In May 1973 I decided to journey to Gao and search for my wife."

ii

*B*efore he left Timbuctoo for Gao, Sidi bought two amulets. A marabout said they would lead him to his wife. He put one around Ibrahim's neck and added the other to the half-dozen red and black leather pouches that already dangled around his own. Sidi had similar pouches tied to his biceps. Other Koranic verses were encased in a large silver ring and in a silver cylinder strapped to the side of his turban.

Just as Islam surrounded the marabouts, magic surrounded Sidi and the blacksmith class. The amulets were symbolic of the spiritual forces dominating Tuareg life, magic, and Islam—the marabout with religious powers who wrote verses from the Koran, the blacksmith with magical powers who made containers for the verses. The monotheism of desert Islam was tempered in the sahel by the magical animism of the West African forests.

In spite of their skill and their presumed magical powers, the black-smiths were at the bottom of Tuareg society, barely higher than the bou-zous. The other Tuareg felt that their uncertain racial origins and their physical labor were demeaning.

Like most Tuareg blacksmiths, Sidi had dark skin but Semitic fea-tures. His nose was long, thin, and hooked, and his hairline was reced-ing. He had a small goatee. A front tooth was chipped from trying to open a jammed lock with his teeth. He looked wiry and wise, and he of-ten wore secondhand European clothes, especially a red turtleneck sweater.

Historians and ethnologists believe that the Tuareg blacksmiths are the descendants of early Moroccan Jews. Father Foucauld, a French missionary who lived among the Ahaggar Tuareg of southern Algeria at the turn of the century and compiled the first French-Tamashek diction-ary, identified them as "Israelites from Morocco" who had attached themselves to the North African Berber armies that invaded West Africa.

André Lhoté, another Frenchman who became familiar with the Al-gerian Tuareg during the 1950s, was told by blacksmiths that they were the descendants of North African Jews who had been driven into the de-sert by Arabs in the fifteenth century. Blacksmiths told Johannes Nico-laisen, a Danish anthropologist, that their ancestor was "Sidna Da-wud"—"Our Lord David." Sidi himself only knew that his people were different from the noble and vassal Tuareg because "we are clever with our hands and can make beautiful things. All they [the Tuareg] can do is wear them."

110

The relationship between the Tuareg and their blacksmiths was as complicated and contradictory as that between Christians and Jews in Europe during (and after) the Middle Ages. The Tuareg scorned the blacksmiths but needed them, believed the blacksmiths were inferior, yet feared them.

The blacksmiths, like the bouzous, did the dirty work. They were always squatting over a fire, pumping a bellows, pounding silver, or whittling wood. They were always covered with dust, sweat, and grime.

The Tuareg considered them treacherous. Before the French conquest the blacksmiths spied for warring Tuareg tribes. They were sometimes double or even triple agents. They also acted as intermediaries between Tuareg lovers and as advisors to Tuareg chiefs. Since blacksmiths often traveled between cities and camps, they were usually more intelligent and worldly than the noble chieftains, and many became *éminences grises*, Richelieus who gave advice, spread rumors, mediated disputes, and built their own spheres of power within those of a Tuareg leader.

The Tuareg needed the blacksmiths. In addition to making and repairing weapons, jewelry, and saddlery, the blacksmiths cut hair, pulled teeth, dressed wounds, and performed surgical operations. They played drums and guitars and sang satirical songs. Like Tuareg women, they memorized oral histories and the lineages of chiefs and heroes. In accordance with the division of labor observed throughout Tuareg society, blacksmiths' women worked only with leather and straw, making cushions, purses, saddlebags, and woven straw mats.

Until the French occupation, the blacksmiths were the Tuareg's financial experts. They collected the grain, cloth, and animals that were extorted from farmers. The French, in fact, continued to use the blacksmiths as tax collectors. But the French altered the destination of the booty and also made the blacksmiths conduct a census.

According to Digga, a Malian blacksmith interviewed by oral historians at a Niamey research center, the French "were obliged to call an old blacksmith [to take the census] because when one takes a Tuareg census it is the old blacksmith who tells the agent that so-and-so is the son of so-and-so, because a Tuareg himself would never open his mouth to pronounce the name of his father. The French know this, since they

111

have often tried to frighten the Tuareg into complying with the census, but in vain.''

One manifestation of the Tuareg's ambivalent attitude toward the blacksmiths is that the blacksmiths can beg, make jokes, and compose satirical songs about nobles and vassals. According to Digga, "Ever since the first blacksmith was created, his opinions have never been taken seriously because he is a beggar. Suppose I am sitting next to a chief for the purpose of helping him with his census and taxes. I would not have the slightest fear of him. I could put my hand into his pocket and say to him 'Give me that' and he will. He knows that I am a man of no importance. As I did this I would never worry that there could be any quarrel between us because a blacksmith is like a woman. We can joke with everyone.''

The toleration that Digga describes is reinforced by fear. The Tuareg believe that the blacksmiths command supernatural powers because they have the mysterious ability to make things and are often seen sitting next to glowing fires, molding metals, mistreating the earth, defying nature. The blacksmiths also speak Tenet, a secret Berber language unfamiliar to the Tuareg, and are half of the magical partnership that produces the amulets every Tuareg wears, and fears.

The most frightening aspect of the blacksmiths' magic, called *tisma* in Tamashek, is that neither the blacksmiths nor those against whom tisma is directed have any control over its workings. Tisma invariably harms the children and the animals of anyone who abuses the blacksmiths or fails to give them the favors they demand.

Sometimes this magic causes the blacksmiths to be blamed for sick camels, children with birth defects, even dry wells and barren pastures. A few years before the drought, a blacksmith jumped from behind a clump of bushes and demanded a sack of millet from a Tuareg who was returning from a southern market to Niger's Air Mountains. The Tuareg refused to surrender such an expensive gift, and rode on to make evening camp. That night one of his camels died, suddenly and unexpectedly. The Tuareg connected the dead camel with the blacksmith's tisma. He rode back the way he had come, found the blacksmith, and hacked him to pieces.

The blacksmiths' membership in a powerful but inferior social class

112

was especially obvious during the Tuareg conflicts that occurred before the French occupation. No Tuareg warrior wanted to kill a blacksmith and activate the magic that would avenge his death. In the larger battles, blacksmiths were grouped into phalanxes and positioned in front of the other warriors. However, their value as a human shield was diminished by the reluctance of other Tuareg to fight at their side. Since their amulets and magic could deflect enemy spears, their allies were afraid of being wounded by ricochets.

This uneasy alliance symbolizes the continuing relationship between blacksmiths and other Tuareg. The blacksmiths were undeniably useful, but no one wanted to get too close. This was why Sidi was so lonely that he went to Gao to search for his wife.

iii

*T*he Niger River dominates Gao; especially between October and February when the river rises to its highest level, its waters erode the port and foundations of the banco houses, and the city takes on the appearance of a biblical Venice. During these months, large steamboats connect Gao with Mali's other principal cities—Timbuctoo, Mopti, and Koulikoro, thirty-five miles from the capital, Bamako.

In March, when the river begins to recede, muddy beaches appear on both shores, the steamers stop running, and only the flat-bottomed pirogues, propelled by poles or weak outboard motors, can navigate the 263 miles that separate Gao and Timbuctoo. During the soudure and the summer rains, except for a twice-weekly air service and rutted dirt roads that are frequently washed out, Gao is isolated from the rest of Mali, West Africa, and the world. This isolation comes at a time when the city is least likely to have enough food.

Frequent sandstorms heighten the isolation. On the east bank of the river is Gao; on the west are enormous sand dunes. During a sandstorm these shores become invisible to one another, and Gao becomes a seaside town on the shore of a foggy, reddish-brown ocean. Only the pirogues sliding between the green islands in the middle of the river and the night sounds of frogs and bats instead of seagulls betray that the town borders a river, not a sea.

Gao has not always been so isolated. During the sixteenth century it was the capital of the Songhai State, a wealthy trading empire situated at the intersection of two great transportational arteries, the Niger River and a caravan route linking Mediterranean Europe with the gold mines of tropical Africa. Gao was often visited by caravans made up of as many as twelve thousand camels.

The Songhai kings controlled the essential raw materials of their time—copper, salt, and gold—as well as the caravan routes by which they traveled. Their wealth and power attracted scholars, teachers, lawyers, architects, and doctors from Islamic Africa and the Middle East. Their capital became a center of Islamic scholarship and a model of administrative efficiency that has yet to be equaled, either by the French or by the present independent government of Mali. The Songhai even had specific ministries in charge of finance, justice, politics, agriculture, fishing, and the "tribes of white men," Tuareg who were vassals and tributaries to the Songhai rulers.

In 1591, four thousand Moroccan soldiers defeated the Songhai army. The scholars and doctors left, the caravans shrank, and the highly developed state started to disintegrate. Economic and political power shifted to the coast, and the blacks of Gao started to pay tribute to the "white tribes," and would continue to do so until the French conquest. It was the beginning of the sahel's "dark ages."

The Songhai State was one of many trading civilizations that have flourished throughout history on semiarid "land bridges." It joined two autonomous powers, the temperate agricultural nations of Europe and the gold-producing states of West Africa.

During the sixteenth and seventeenth centuries the Arab and Mediterranean trading empires declined, and Atlantic European traders established a new sea trade with West Africa that bypassed the sahel. When the Atlantic powers, England and France, colonized West Africa during the nineteenth century, they enforced economic policies which favored the coast, destroying the inter-African trade which had benefited the hinterland and impoverishing the sahel. All of West Africa's trade

114

flowed toward the coast, and the sahel became a labor pool. Only the Tuareg refused to be integrated into this system of colonial exploitation. Until the drought they were freer than the black descendants of the Songhai empire and their culture was less compromised by European influences.

Mali's independence from France in 1960 did not alter Gao's isolation. It became the capital of Mali's sixth region, an 315,000-square-mile area, larger than France, which contained 68 percent of Mali's land area but only about 10 percent of the population, 610,000 people, less than two per square mile. There were no railroads, no paved roads (not even an all-weather dirt track), no industry, and, save for Gao and Timbuctoo, no cities. At the time of the drought Gao was the most inaccessible region in one of the most inaccessible countries in Africa. Like Timbuctoo, it became a city of starvation rather than a "city of gold."

When Sidi and Ibrahim arrived in Gao, they disembarked onto what had once been the riverbed. During the summer of 1973 water levels were at historic lows on the Niger. At Niamey the river reached only 4 percent of its average summer height. At Bamako it was so low that the city was often without electricity. The slaughterhouse refrigerators became ovens, and the carcasses of emaciated animals spoiled quickly.

To reach the city Sidi and Ibrahim walked over dry, cracked earth that looked like a gigantic jigsaw puzzle. They stepped in and out of the fossilized footprints of animals that had been driven to water at what was once the river's middle. Some animals had become stuck, and the mud had hardened around their bones. Although Ibrahim was five and could walk by himself, Sidi carried him to the shore. He worried that the boy might stumble and injure himself. He was determined to protect the last member of his family.

When they reached the shore, Sidi put Ibrahim down and began his search. A narrow canal runs inland from the Niger River to Gao's markets. Sidi followed it. Blacksmith men worked on one side of the canal, and blacksmith women on the other. He approached the women first.

They wore black cloaks and were covered with dust from the street and their labors. Surrounded by heaps of nails, scraps of leather, and broken sandals, they sat on mats pounding short nails into the sandals, sewing up leather pouches, and patching straw mats as if they were expensive cloth.

They were repairing and recycling the debris of a city in which almost everything—there was so little—had value. In Gao empty beer cans were pounded into drinking cups and funnels. Scraps of newspaper were used to wrap bits of barbecued meat or holeless doughnuts cooked in washtubs of fat. Bottles were filled and refilled with cooking oil and corked with scraps of newsprint. Used engine oil was smeared on sandals to toughen the leather or poured into open sewers to cut the odor. Inner tubes were patched until they became red-and-yellow rubber quilts. Bent and rusty nails were straightened and polished. The smallest bits of cloth and leather were used to plug holes in drafty straw huts.

The blacksmith women seldom came across an item they considered useless. If the first woman had no use for a particular scrap, she handed it to her neighbor who stroked it, pulled at it, held it to the light, and then kept it or passed it down the line until the last woman tossed it in front of a mad Tuareg woman covered by black rags. Then scrawny arms that looked and moved like a crab's inched out from under the rags, fastened on the morsel, and dragged it within.

The blacksmiths would stop working and stare as the mad woman decided either to fling the prize into the canal or add it to a hidden reservoir. If she was pleased, her bald head appeared like a periscope and she gave a grateful moan. The women whooped with delight.

No one seemed to know what she did with her collection of objects, if and when she sold them, or to whom. It was rumored that she was a witch and that when the other women left her alone at night, under her canopy of rags with the frogs and the bats, she transformed them into powerful amulets.

Less than a foot separated each of the blacksmith women. Their mats touched so that they appeared to be sitting on a long carpet of dried millet stalks. They swapped tools, cloth, and customers, news, gossip, and confidences. Since they sat along a thoroughfare joining the market and the port, they usually knew who had just arrived in Gao. As they bent toward one another, their heads swayed like stalks of grain rippling before the wind.

Sidi exchanged greetings with the woman at the end of the line and asked her if she had heard of his wife, a blacksmith woman named Fati, who had recently come to Gao. The woman answered by saying that many of her clients had gone to Niamey and that there were already too many blacksmiths in Gao. When Sidi promised that he would not work as a blacksmith, she told him that Fati had arrived a week ago. That was all she knew.

Sidi walked back toward the river, passing down the line of women, asking questions, listening to their answers. A woman near the end of the line had also come from Timbuctoo. She said that a boat from Timbuctoo had arrived a week ago with many blacksmith men and women, including Fati. They had all walked inland, into Gao's residential quarters. Sidi left Ibrahim and his suitcase with this woman and walked inland himself.

Sidi: "I was always afraid I would lose Ibrahim. When people were near us I held his hand or held him in my arms. When we were sleeping I made certain he was always touching me. When I left him in Gao I was afraid that my wife would find him and steal him."

Sidi looked for his wife in Gao's markets, residential neighborhoods, and refugee camps. While Gao's economic fortunes had changed over the past four centuries, its architecture had not. Built along a grid of symmetrical streets were one- and two-story banco houses. The streets were like wide, sandy rivers. Except for the road leading to the airport, none was paved. There was only a handful of cars, and these belonged to merchants, government agencies, and functionaries. They glided silently through the streets, the sound of their engines muffled by sand and wind.

The streets became wider as they neared the desert, the houses along them shorter and cruder, until they emptied their sand into the arid scrubland that surrounded Gao on three sides.

Sidi followed these streets methodically for two days. He walked in the narrow shade of the houses at noon, resting under a parked truck, and slept at night with Ibrahim on mats on which the blacksmiths worked during the day.

Gao had a sedentary population of nearly twenty thousand, and in any other year the Tuareg grapevine would probably have led him to his wife within a couple of hours. But in the summer of 1973 the city had

117

become a magnet for neighboring Tuareg who came hoping to find food, and money to buy new animals. The streets, markets, and open spaces were full of refugees from Mali's sixth region. Brothers and sisters, husbands, wives, and children who had separated in the bush to divide their herds into smaller units now tried to find each other. Sidi was one of thousands of refugees looking for food, work, lost family, or a way to return to the bush and survive.

Most people were too involved in their own desperate struggles to notice strangers. Some Tuareg women married anyone who could support them—bouzous, blacksmiths, Hausas, Djermas. Others became prostitutes, but there were too many of them and too few paying customers, and they only charged twenty cents. Their embarrassed husbands and brothers referred to their new profession as a "female method of survival."

Nobles who had never worked took up menial jobs, if they could find them. They carried water, unloaded sacks of grain from piroques, and made banco bricks. Weak with hunger and unaccustomed to hard work, they often tired quickly and quit or were fired. Some begged, but the drought had increased the number of beggars and decreased the givers. Blind men grasping long sticks were pulled like chariots by small children toward anyone who looked prosperous. Three or four teams were apt to converge on the same target simultaneously.

Some men tried to cultivate gardens in the sandy soil outside the town and refugee camps. But they failed to weed, protect the young plants from the wind, or water them properly. The plants died or were pulled up by hungry goats.

Men and women alike tried to sell their possessions, but there were no buyers. In the Gao tourist market, piles of bracelets, amulets, swords, purses, and knives resembled the heaps of dentures and wedding rings at a German extermination camp.

Interviews conducted by the United Nations Environmental Program with Tuareg and Peul refugees in nearby Niger showed that the refugees were extremely resourceful and tenacious. In a one-month period one refugee earned 300 CFA by begging (225 CFA equal $1); others earned CFA by selling water (500), selling wood (500), selling mats woven by their wives (1,000), pounding millet (20), making magic charms (2,100), "working at odd jobs in the village" (7,000), washing calabashes (1,000), selling their clothes (1,000), making banco bricks (500), unloading a truck (1,500), selling rope woven from the roots of trees (350), and guarding the homes of Europeans (150). The largest and most frequent sums recorded were "gifts" and "loans without interest" from family and friends.

Sidi followed Gao's symmetrical streets asking marabouts, blacks, and Tuareg refugees if they knew Fati. He learned that there was a Fati among the refugees, but she came from Menaka, a nomadic center east of Gao. There was also a Fati from Timbuctoo, but she was a bouzou. After walking through Gao for two days, Sidi began to circle it.

Before the drought, the demarcation line between the bush and sahelian towns was abrupt. There was the wall of the most recently built banco house and then flat savannah or desert. But during the drought, the tents, grass huts, and cardboard lean-tos of the refugees created a human and architectural transition zone. At first these suburbs grew without plan, the result of refugees settling in open land near the water and relief food that was the object of their migration.

Later, the government gathered the refugees into camps on the city's perimeters, which made them easier to control and lessened the danger of epidemics. In these camps the Tuareg did not have to cope with the jarring and unfamiliar rectangular architecture or with cars and trucks. Facing the desert, they could pretend they were back in the bush.

The blacksmith woman from Timbuctoo had told Sidi that the Mokhtar, the headman who administered the livestock market and collected taxes, knew the names of many of the refugees. The market was located on Gao's periphery, where it was convenient to nomads bringing their animals from the bush. It consisted of a barren rectangular space with a concrete platform and wall (the slaughterhouse), a half-dozen stunted trees which had been meeting points for buyers and sellers, and a middleman who negotiated prices between the two.

During the drought many owners slaughtered and ate their animals themselves rather than trade them, and the market was empty except for refugees, local children, and madmen. Men pointed and stared at an empty sky, and others stood near the trees, ready to bargain over imaginary animals.

119

A mad marabout who had visited Ghana sat on the curb of the slaughterhouse and gave English lessons. He screamed "Good morning" and "Nice day" at the children crouching in the sand around him. Other children buzzed around the madman, skipping, giggling, and rolling on the ground until women in black cloaks flapped after them and herded them back into the city.

The Mokhtar was a tall bouzou who wore purple robes and a white turban. He had been appointed by the government to keep order in the market and collect taxes. The ties that bound nomads, cattle, Gao middlemen, and the coastal countries may have snapped, but the Mokhtar still glided between the trees, the empty slaughterhouse, the madman, and the clusters of refugees.

In a legal-size notebook with a drawing of a French couple dancing across its red plastic cover, he recorded the names of interesting strangers. This was his hobby, and the book listed blacksmiths, Tuaregs, blacks, anyone who gave him a present or told an interesting or amusing story or took part in a memorable sale.

The Mokhtar: "Sometimes I went to the port and met Europeans who arrived on the boat from Timbuctoo. We became friends and they put their names and addresses in my notebook. I have many friends in Germany, France, and the United States. They have all promised to write me, although I am still waiting for their letters."

Sidi gave the Mokhtar a lock he had made for a client in Timbuctoo who had disappeared after making a down payment. Like other Tuareg locks it was constructed as much for beauty as for function. The key was four inches long and shaped like a narrow cross, resembling the gigantic keys that unlock medieval chests or church doors. The lock itself was rectangular, six inches long and three wide. It worked on the same principle as a padlock except that when the ornate key was inserted into a slot and moved along a groove in the top of the lock, the lock snapped open into two halves which could be closed to fasten a tin box or a door. The Mokhtar slipped the lock in his purple robes and immediately started thumbing through his notebook, looking for names that Sidi might recognize.

Sidi: "The Mokhtar helped many refugees find their families. I gave him a gift to prove that I was a skilled blacksmith, better than those

When French explorers arrived in Niger they were confronted by tall, veiled warriors fighting with medieval weapons.

The Hourst expedition en route from Timbuctoo to Niger. Like most of the French columns, it consisted primarily of African soldiers from France's coastal colonies.

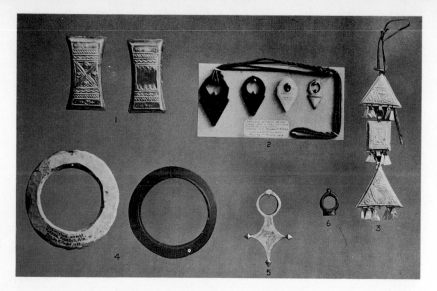

1) Silver amulets containing Koranic verses. (2) Talismen usually worn as pendants. (3) A silver ornament worn by Tuareg women. (4) Tuareg women wear these rings around their arms. (5) The Cross of Agadez. (6) Tuareg ring.

(1) Tuareg sword and sheath. (2) Leather shield. (3) A sword worn around the arm so it can be drawn quickly during a battle. (4) Tuareg daggers.

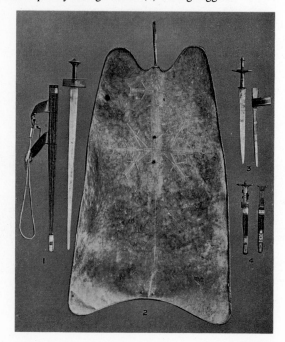

A European explorer meets a Tuareg chief in the Sahara.

The specially constructed Citroën cars of the first motor expedition to traverse the Sahara.

Atakor: "When I saw these beautiful men and animals gathered together it reminded me that we were a powerful people."

Tuareg tribesmen ride into Niamey five years before the drought to celebrate the third anniversary of Niger's independence. *Credit: Marc and Evelyne Bernheim/Woodfin Camp*

Before the drought Tuareg children played games of "raid" with camel puppets such as these. During the drought they played with homemade toys representing the Land Rovers and trucks that brought relief food. *Credit: Marc and Evelyne Bernheim/ Woodfin Camp*

A blacksmith makes the frame for a Tuareg camel saddle. At left is a completed saddle. *Credit: Marc and Evelyne Bernheim/Woodfin Camp*

Bouzou servants draw water from a traditional Tuareg well in 1968, a few months before the start of the drought. *Credit: United Nations*

Farmers and Nomads meet to trade at a weekly market located in the Adar village of Barmou. The walled banco houses and the conical graineries are constructed from mud bricks. *Credit: Marc and Evelyne Bernheim/Woodfin Camp*

This is a principal Niamey crossroads and contains one of the city's few traffic lights. Before the drought few Tuareg had ever visited Niamey and there are none visible in this predrought photograph. *Credit: Marc and Evelyne Bernheim/Woodfin Camp*

A group of Peul men at the Chadawank market. *Credit: Marc and Evelyne Bernheim/ Woodfin Camp*

The three principal forms of vehicular transportation in the sahel are lined up at this auto-station in Mali: a Peugot stationwagon, a van, and a heavy truck. *Credit: United Nations*

Piroques are the most common form of river transport in the sahel. This is similar to the one in which Sidi traveled from Timbuctoo to Goa to search for his wife. *Credit: United Nations*

A Tuareg family gathered in front of their skin tent outside Abalack. The woman at the far right is playing a single-stringed Tuareg guitar. This picture was taken in 1963, five years before the drought. *Credit: Marc and Evelyne Bernheim/Woodfin Camp*

A Tuareg refugee family in 1974.
Credit: United Nations/Gamma

During the drought people swept the bones of their dead animals into piles. *Credit: Victor Engleber/Photo Researchers*

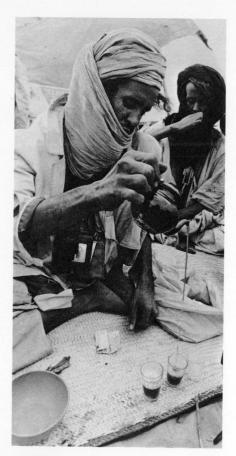

Tuareg men at the Lazaret refugee
camp near Niamey prepare tea. *Credit.
United Nations/Gamma*

A sahelian farmer ploughs his sandy
field during the drought. *Credit: United
Nations/AID/Purcell*

Peul women wait for a ration of
sorghum at a food distribution center in
Tahoua. *Credit: United Nations/CIDA/
White*

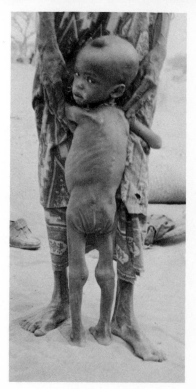

A young refugee at the Lazaret
camp. *Credit: Thomas Chambers*

A starving goat that became trapped and died as it climbed into a tree to reach the foliage on the highest branches. *Credit: United Nations/AID*

Entrepreneurs bought dead cattle in the north for their skin and bones and drove the carcasses to Niamey. They paid $2 a head; before the drought these cattle brought $200 a head. *Credit United Nations/FAO/Botts*

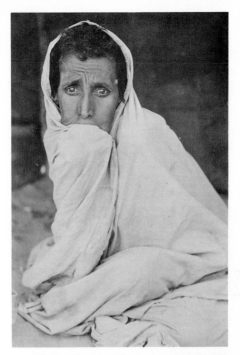

According to some relief workers and doctors, many of the Tuareg refugees died of "sadness." *Credit: United Nations/Gamma*

A Tuareg marabout at the Lazaret refugee camp. Most of the marabouts were idle during the drought because their customers could not afford to pay for their services. *Credit: Wendy Watriss/Woodfin Camp.*

A refugee woman camps in front of the Agadez mosque. *Credit: United Nations/CIDA/White*

Tuareg tribesmen distribute American sorghum. *Credit: United Nations/FOA*

Tuareg man at the Lazaret camp.
Credit: United Nations/Gamma

uareg women pound sorghum at
ee camp in Niger. Many women
ever performed strenuous tasks
s this until the drought. *Credit:
Nations/FAO*

Malien Tuareg woman and her child at the Lazaret camp. *Credit: Wendy Watriss/ Woodfin Camp*

found in Gao. Fati's name was in his book. He said that she and another woman from Timbuctoo had given him a present—not as beautiful as mine—and then left Gao to walk to Niamey. When the Mokhtar heard that I was with Ibrahim he promised to find me a job so I could afford to take a truck to Niamey and arrive before my wife. Then he arranged for me to sleep on the property of a black truck driver, Idrissa Coulibaly.''

Idrissa Coulibaly owned a walled courtyard close to the livestock market, the last walled property before the desert began. Until he could afford to build a house within these walls, he allowed the Tuareg refugees to pitch their tents inside. Sidi and Ibrahim shared the courtyard with three Tuareg families.

The largest family was Rissa's, a vassal Tuareg who had come to Gao in 1972 after his animals died and his wife divorced him. He had married another refugee and lived with his three teen-aged daughters and two younger sons, as well as his wife's two children and parents. In 1969 Hassan, Rissa's eldest son, had gone to Niamey to work and had never returned.

Rissa had sold his tent in 1972, and now he lived under a sail which had been donated to the refugees by one of the Scandinavian Red Cross societies. Along the border of the sail were colorful nautical flags, with their meanings explained in a Scandinavian language. The other families lived under a roof of grain sacks sewed together that had once contained something grown in Argentina. Sidi and Ibrahim slept on mats outside Rissa's sail.

Idrissa was enlarging the banco storeroom that adjoined his garage. He had already included Rissa in the work crew. Rissa was fifty years old, and making bricks was his first attempt at heavy labor. On his first day of work he collapsed into a pool of banco. Now Idrissa arranged for Sidi and Rissa to work on alternate days and share the wages.

Even during the drought, the residents of Gao repaired and enlarged their homes. Making mud bricks and then constructing a house from them is exhausting and poorly paid work. It was available to refugees who were willing to toil for lower wages than local workers.

On his first day of making banco, Sidi led donkeys to the banco pits outside Gao, dug up the light red clay, and shoveled it into bags slung over the backs of the animals. When he returned to the site, the men

121

working on Idrissa's storehouse dumped the clay into a pile, spread it out, and poured water into a hole dug in the middle of the mass. Then they let it sit for a few hours until the water had seeped into the clay.

To give the mixture cohesion, they threw in straw, cow dung, broken glass, and stones. They poured in more water and started to churn the banco with hoes, rolling up their trousers, hitching up their cloaks, and wading in. They struggled in the steaming puddle of mud like Mediterranean peasants treading grapes, laboring for hours in temperatures that reached 110°F.

When the clay was moist and supple, they waded out, their legs red and muddy, and scooped the stuff into wooden molds measuring six inches by twelve inches. When the clay was almost dry they removed the molds and arranged the bricks in rows to bake in the sun.

Sidi had been making bricks for two weeks. He was wading in the banco, walking at a slow, nightmare pace. The bouzou workers were naked to the waist. Sidi and the Tuareg wore their robes, but Sidi's veil hung under his chin like a bib. Suddenly the shadows of the neighboring buildings lengthened, as if time were accelerating and the afternoon were being compressed into a few moments. As the shadows enveloped the workers, they stopped walking. The banco cooled around their feet. As the moon slid in front of the sun and the darkness became total, Sidi stared at the sky. Women wailed, somewhere a drum beat slowly, and Sidi stepped out of the banco onto the cool sand.

The solar eclipse began in the Amazon jungle at sunrise on June 30, 1973. During the next six and a half hours the shadow of the moon swept across the Atlantic and then Africa before it disappeared into the Indian Ocean. It traveled 9,200 miles at a speed of 1,400 miles an hour, moving at right angles to the monsoon clouds that usually darkened the summer skies.

The heart of the moon's shadow, the "path of totality" where the moon covered the sun altogether, appeared as a black disk surrounded by a silvery halo, the solar corona. It covered an area 161 miles wide and passed over the sahel, over Gao, In Waggeur, Tchin-Tabaraden, and Agadez. At the center of this path of totality, at a point where the moon would cover the sun for seven minutes and thirty-nine seconds, a period longer than all but two solar eclipses during the last 1,433 years, was the intersection of the borders of Algeria, Mali, and Niger. At Gao, 350 miles south of this intersection, the sun disappeared for seven minutes.

Sidi: "I decided to leave Gao when the sun disappeared. It was a sign that blacksmiths should not make banco and that I should follow my wife to Niamey. I hadn't earned enough money for a truck, so Ibrahim and I walked."

Sidi returned to Rissa's sail and collected Ibrahim and his tools. Although the two men had shared the compound for two weeks, they had exchanged only formal pleasantries. Sidi said, "Because I was a blacksmith, Rissa was not pleased to share his tent. But we were both guests of Idrissa and the Mokhtar so he could not complain. When he heard that I was going to Niamey he became friendlier and wanted me to take a letter to his son."

Since 1969, Rissa's son, Hassan, had worked as a gardener for a European expatriate in Niamey. When Rissa lost most of his animals he visited his son twice but both times returned to Gao after a few weeks. Now he gave Sidi a letter written to his son in French by his sixteen-year-old daughter, Hamiyatta, the only member of the family besides Hassan who had attended school.

Hamiyatta's elegant handwriting compensated for the simple, formal French that restricted the letter's content. Each of the capital letters had ornate curls, and she had forged Rissa's name with a stylized signature that would have pleased a French banker. She had concentrated on what any Tuareg would consider the most important aspects of education, style and form.

She wrote:

> Love to you my son Hassan. I salute you many times and am sending you this letter to inform you that I am in excellent health. I ask you to tell me everything that has happened to you in Niamey. Is Abdoulye still staying with you?
>
> Houssa and Fata salute you. Akiyoya salutes you; her daughter died a few days ago. If Hadiyatta is in Niamey tell her that Azoumai'la salutes her.
>
> I have not yet found any permanent work but do not worry about me. All is well. We are still alive although we don't have any money or animals.

123

I would like to visit you again in Niamey but I don't have the money for the transport. If you would like to see your father you will have to send me the money. If you are going to stay in Niamey forever you must write and tell me so that we will not hope for your return.

So that you can send me your news I am sending you my address on the back of this letter, care of Idrissa Coulibaly, 4th quarter of Gao.

I am giving this letter to a blacksmith. He is searching for his wife and I have told him that you know many people in Niamey and will help him.

Rissa

Sidi and Ibrahim took the letter, their bag, and the money Sidi had saved. They circled Gao's outskirts until they came to the dirt track that followed the east bank of the Niger 275 miles south to Niamey. Sidi could have sold his tools and bought a place on a truck or the weekly bus, but he would have arrived in Niamey without a profession. So he and Ibrahim walked, slowly because Ibrahim tired easily and it was the hottest time of the year. The road was unshaded, and other refugees, some in groups and some alone, passed them easily.

iv

*S*idi and Ibrahim had joined a year-long caravan of 100,000 Malian Tuareg and bouzous, one sixth of the population of the sixth region and almost one half of the entire Tuareg population of Mali, who were fleeing homelands and country. Every day in 1973 an average of 300 people (and more in the hot season) left Mali and walked south, following roads, tracks, rivers, and dry riverbeds to cities and agricultural regions. Half of these 100,000 Malian Tuareg went to Algeria, Upper Volta, Nigeria, and even more distant West African countries. The rest went to Niger and of these, 20,000 stopped in Niamey, a city whose predrought population of 100,000 numbered very few Tuareg, either Malian or Nigerien.

There is little difference between the poverty of Niger and that of Mali and between the destruction caused by the drought in the nomadic regions of each country. In 1973 the per capital income in both countries was less than one hundred dollars. In health care, literacy, doctors per thousand patients, and nutritional levels, the poverty of the two countries is roughly equal.

The exodus of the Malian Tuareg can be explained in part by the geography of the sixth region, by the artificial isolation imposed on the region by the colonial boundaries and their perpetuation after independence. Niamey was much closer to the sixth region than Mali's capital, Bamako, and communications and roads between Niamey and Gao were also much better than those between Bamako and Gao. Frequent trucks and a weekly bus ran on the road that linked Niamey and Gao.

If Gao had been supplied through Niamey, it would have been 915 miles from Cotonou and 1,300 miles from Lagos, the Atlantic ports which handled most of Niger's relief supplies. Instead, supplies for Gao had to come 845 miles by road or 780 miles by river from Bamako. Bamako in turn received its supplies from Dakar over an antiquated railway. This was a total distance by road and rail of 1,580 miles, by river and rail of 1,685 miles. During the summer of 1973, when the roads were washed out and the river too low to be navigated by steamers, the only way to send large quantities of supplies to the isolated sixth region was by plane.

Other factors drove many of the sixth region's nomads to look for food and shelter outside Mali. In 1959, the year before Mali's independence, Tuareg leaders in the sixth region, with the encouragement of French army officers who hoped to form an independent Tuareg state allied with Algeria under French tutelage, petitioned France to give the Tuareg people their own nation. It was to comprise those areas of Mali, Niger, and Algeria in which the Tuareg were a majority. The Tuareg leaders and the French officers were unsuccessful, and in 1960 the Tuareg in the sixth region became citizens of Mali.

An energetic and entrepreneurial black people, the Bambara, did not, like the Tuareg, reject French education. They became the rulers of Mali. In the sixth region, Bambara functionaries enforced new regulations aimed at controlling the Tuareg's movements, cutting them off from their traditional seasonal pastures in Niger and Algeria, and integrating them into the modern state. Caravans crossing the Malian frontier were required to pay customs fees, bouzous were encouraged to

125

leave their masters, the use of currencies from Algeria and Niger was forbidden, and the livestock tax was increased 300 percent to $1.20 a head. Meanwhile, although the Tuareg represented 10 percent of the population of Mali at the time of independence, they had only two representatives to the seventy-member national assembly in Bamako.

The Tuareg resisted. They avoided government administrative centers and crossed frontiers in defiance of the new regulations. They murdered tax collectors and attacked troops sent from Bamako to protect government officials. By the end of 1963 the government had termed these skirmishes a rebellion. For the next eight months, five thousand Tuareg rebels armed with Libyan rifles and assisted by French mercenaries reenacted the raids and wars of the past. Mobida Keita, the president of Mali, sent half of the country's forty-five-hundred-man army to the sixth region to crush this revolt of "criminals" and "pillagers."

The military operation was bitter and expensive. Finally, in August of 1964, the government announced that the leaders of the rebellion had all been killed or captured. Foreign journalists reported that the Malian army had indiscriminately burned and pillaged Tuareg camps and executed suspected rebels on the spot. Many Malian Tuareg fled to Niger or Algeria.

In 1968 the Keita government was overthrown by a coup d'état engineered by the army. At many admistrative levels army officers replaced civilians. Many of these officers were the same ones who had led units against the Tuareg rebels in 1964. They were officials in Bamako, Gao, and Timbuctoo responsible in the following years for administering drought relief in the sixth region.

Throughout 1973 there were rumors in other sahelian capitals, spread by journalists, European relief workers, and the officials of the other governments, that the Malians were using the drought as a means of exterminating their Tuareg, that food donated by foreign relief organizations was being held back so that the Tuareg would die of starvation. The mildest allegations charged that some government officials in the sixth region were inefficient or callous.

A cable sent from the American Embassy in Bamako appears to give cautious support to these charges. Although this cable contained the caveat that "Information is difficult to collect due to inefficient and ill-equipped government bureaucracy, poor communications, and continuing population migration," it went on to say that "There is also evidence piling up that Government of Mali (GOM) is using grain distribution for internal political purposes." It continued thus:

Competence of GOM officials varies greatly in 6th region which is worst hit by drought. Drought relief operation in Cercle of Timbuctoo much better organized than in 6th region capital Gao (trip report of Embroff Torp of June 18, 1973). However, there is evidence piling up that GOM is hoarding grain in government warehouses at distribution points. GOM will not discuss subject but embassy believes action partly caused by GOM fear of another bad crop and early end of Niger River navigation that would stop all non-air grain shipments. Also, think GOM is doing only small amounts of food and hoarding rest to keep fiercely independent and sometimes hostile desert nomads, *i.e.* Tuaregs, under government control in towns. . . . While embassy cannot substantiate existence of anti-Tuareg policy part of GOM, fact remains that grain distribution to accessible outlying areas depending on Gao not being done (Ansongo and Menaka).

Nor was grain being distributed a year later, when conditions in the other sahelian countries had improved. During the winter of 1973 and in 1974, even though food from donor nations and the means to transport it became generally more available, the sixth region remained a disaster area. Malian Tuareg who had left for Niger in the summer of 1973, returning to Mali in 1974, found that the situation in Gao was no better, if not worse. Throughout 1974 Malian Tuareg continued to flock to Niamey in greater numbers even than in 1973. Michael Behr, an OX-FAM (a private famine relief organization based in Great Britain) representative in Niger, visited Gao in March 1974 and found that conditions in refugee camps were worse than those in Niamey.

The refugee camp that Behr visited surrounded an abandoned slaughterhouse that had become a clinic and registration center. Behr was told by the officials in charge that the camps contained 7,346 inmates, of which the majority were Tuareg. They arrived in the camp from the surrounding countryside at a rate of 400 a day.

Behr reported that the Malians seemed anxious to prevent him from wandering about freely. He was finally allowed to witness what the

127

officials described as a "special treat" for the camp's 3,500 children, a ration of eight fish chopped up and scattered over instant mashed potatoes.

Even the attitude of the refugees seemed different to him from that of the Tuareg in Niamey. He reported that in Gao there was "none of the activity that is found in the Niamey camp." Instead, there was "total resignation, and people didn't cook and make handicrafts as they did in other areas." Although there was food and medical aid in Gao, Behr looked in one of the tents at random and saw a refugee who looked "like a skeleton." He concluded that there was "something very wrong," and that "if this model camp was good, then the others must have been hell holes."

During the summer of 1973 teams of American doctors were sent to Mauritania, Upper Volta, Niger, and Gao and Timbuctoo in Mali, by the smallpox eradication program of the Atlanta Center for Disease Control, part of the United States Public Health Service under the Department of Health, Education, and Welfare. As the name of their porgram, "Nutritional Surveillance in West Africa," implies, they were sent to West Africa to survey the extent of malnutrition among the nomadic and sedentary populations of these four sahelian countries. They would try to determine if people were dying from starvation and, if so, how many.

In order to measure scientifically the extent of starvation, the Americans weighed 3,500 sahelian children on portable scales and then measured them with rulers. They compared the results to the "Scott-Meredith" standards, the median height-weight ratios of healthy American children in Boston and Iowa City. The doctors agreed that any sahelian child who fell below 80 percent of the Scott-Meredith median weight for his or her particular height would be considered "acutely malnourished." Children were chosen to indicate the condition of the rest of the population on the theory that, when food is scarce, they are the least likely to receive a proportional share.

During July 1973, just after Sidi and Ibrahim began their trek to Niamey, the American doctors weighed and measured children in Gao. Seventy percent of the nomadic and 49 percent of the sedentary children examined were below their acute malnutrition threshhold. In a survey of

10,000 inhabitants of a nomadic refugee camp in Timbuctoo, the doctors found 74.6 percent below the threshhold. (They also found that deaths at the camp were initially estimated at between 182 and 365 per 1,000 inhabitants. The 1971 United Nations demographic yearbook quotes the 1965–1970 average annual crude death rate for Mali at 26.6 per 1,000 inhabitants.)

In Europe or the United States, only 3 percent of the population would fall below this malnutrition level. During the widespread starvation in Bangladesh in May 1972, only 11.6 percent of the children surveyed by the same method were below it. In southern Niger, the area to which half the Malian Tuareg fled, the percent below was only 8 percent. In the northern nomadic regions of Niger from which Atakor fled, only 14 percent were below the threshhold. But when the doctors measured the children of newly arrived Malian refugees at the Lazaret camp in Niamey, they found that 25 percent were malnourished. This was greater than the figure for Nigerien nomads, but still a considerable improvement over the incredible 70 percent at Gao.

At the end of the study, the Americans concluded that "undernutrition in the four-country area is to be found more among the nomads than sedentary persons, and more in the north than in the south." The most severe cases of malnutrition found in the sahel were in Mali's sixth region, specifically in Timbuctoo and Gao, although conditions in isolated areas of the bush not visited by the doctors were probably worse.

Considering the quantity of rations available to the refugees, the statistics and conclusions of the American doctors are not surprising. In both the nomadic camps and the sedentary villages in the Gao region, the government distributed less than 3.5 ounces of millet a day to each person. This was less than was handed out during the siege of Stalingrad when millions died of starvation. The doctors observed that in villages near the Niger, waterlilies were being used as supplement to the diet.

The findings of the American medical team are useful for documenting the extent of the starvation that caused so many Malians to flee to countries that were statistically just as poor and drought-stricken as their own. They help to explain why Gao was a city of starving transients, why so many people chose to walk 275 miles to Niamey, and why so many were so weak and undernourished that they died along the route of

129

the exodus. Their report is useful for historians and social scientists studying the drought, for nutritionists and doctors, for anyone writing a book about the drought.

Yet, at a time when most western food aid was only "pledged," en route in ships, or blocked at West African ports; when nomadic children were dying of disease and malnutrition; when the world knew of the general magnitude of the disaster through the reports of journalists, the United Nations, and the sahelian governments themselves; when it did not take consultants or expensive studies to know that there was a need for food, medicines, and trained medical personnel; at this time the *only* major American medical exercise was a nutritional survey. In these summer months of 1973, when the need for action was critical, American doctors were sent for the express purpose of surveying the victims of malnutrition, of weighing and measuring starving children.

As was the case with the numerous other reports and studies that were conducted in the sahel during the drought, the beneficiaries of the nutritional report were often those not initially examined. The weakest became guinea pigs who were studied for the sake of perfecting plans meant to save people months hence. This was *triage* for the sake of efficiency.

By the time the nutritional report was finished and filed, the people who had needed food the most during the summer had either moved to another location or died. The final report, filed by the Center for Disease Control in the fall of 1973, was buried under other reports and studies and virtually ignored by the State Department, AID, and the United Nations.

The nutrition report was one of a multitude of reports, studies, and surveys of the sahel produced by academics and government experts during and after 1973. The justification that was usually given for this expensive cottage industry was that in the United States there was little or no information on the sahel, and that such studies were urgently needed to provide data for the efficient direction of relief and rehabilitation for the neediest regions. In truth, many of these reports duplicated each other, as well as reports already in existence but written in French.

The nutritional report was also evidence of what was to become a morbid preoccupation on the part of the donor nations with the question

130

of exactly how many people in the sahel were dying of starvation. Like welfare workers poking around a tenement flat counting razor blades and shoes, some donors wanted to be sure that no one cheated them by exaggerating the situation.

Pressure groups in the United States, sympathetic to the sahel and anxious to provide as much aid as possible, did exaggerate, claiming that six million people were starving, a figure chosen more for the impact of its historical connotations than its accuracy. By playing this body-count game, these pressure groups acceded to the rules of those who demand such a count, or similar evidence of extraordinary suffering, before they sanction aid.

Most of the figures and estimates of the number dead of starvation during the drought did not truly reflect the situation. People died in remote areas, often alone. Distinguishing between those who died of starvation and those who succumbed to disease because of malnutrition was difficult. Great distances, poor communications, and a lack of base population and mortality figures for the area with which to compare statistics gathered during the drought made mortality studies of dubious value.

The exodus of the Malian Tuareg was the largest and most concentrated of many similar migrations which occurred throughout the sahel between 1972 and 1974. Arab Moors left pastures in the western Sahara and gathered in the tiny Mauritanian cities of Nouakchott and Port-Etienne; others continued south to Dakar. Tuareg and Peul in Upper Volta fled to that country's two major cities, Ougadougou and Bobo-Dioulasso, while others, including nomads and Voltaic farmers, went on to the wealthier Ivory Coast. At the beginning of the drought, Nigerien nomads headed for the nearest towns and cities: Maradi, Zinder, Madaoua, and, in the nomadic zones, Agadez, Dakoro, and Tchin-Tabaraden. Later, many of them moved further south to Kano and other cities in Nigeria, or to Niger's capital, Niamey, where they were outnumbered by Tuareg from Mali's sixth region. Most refugees chose to flee southwards, toward the retreating monsoon clouds, remaining pastures, and cities which were closer to the roads and railways that brought food from the coastal ports.

For many, the exodus began as an attempt to save their animals by

131

finding unused pastures and water points. Then, when they failed and the animals were dead or dying and they themselves starving, they walked to the closest refugee centers. The first center they reached was often an isolated bush town that was poorly supplied. They continued south, moving from town to town, searching for the most regular and generous food distribution. Others who could have stayed in the bush joined the exodus because they became bored when their animals died and they had nothing to do, or because they were lonely. The migrations were animated by the kind of contagious panic that infects the survivors of any disaster.

The refugees walked incredible distances, especially considering their health. One fifth of those who reached Niamey came 275 miles from Gao. Another fifth came from Bourem, 330 miles away. Nine percent came originally from Timbuctoo, 540 miles from Niamey. The hardships they endured on their journeys depended not only on distance but also on the number of animals and personal possessions they could sell along the route, the state of their health, and the help offered them by others more fortunate. The lucky ones could afford to buy a place on a truck or a bus, or ride their remaining camel or donkey, but most walked.

Many who joined this sprawling, disorganized caravan never reached the refugee camps. Journalists, tourists, and government officials who traveled the migration routes by Land Rover reported seeing human bones mixed with those of cows and sheep. According to a survey taken by the United Nations among the inmates of the Lazaret camp, one out of every six Tuareg who left Mali to come to Niger—or over 8,000 people—died before they arrived. Out of a sample of 116 persons identified by friends or relatives as having perished, 49 were children under the age of five and 15 between five and ten. Forty-eight of the 116 were identified by the survivors as having died of hunger, 20 of measles, 10 of diarrhea, 9 of indigestion, 2 of pneumonia, and 24 of "no precise cause." Two were described as having been "lost."

Because of death or separation, Tuareg families unraveled. Before the drought, an average Tuareg household had between twelve and sixty-six members. Each household was usually an extended family which might include grandparents, cousins, in-laws, uncles, aunts, brothers, sisters, and all their families. The household lived in a collection of tents which were within a few yards, or at most a few miles, of one another during most of the year. Their proximity depended on the size of the family herd and the quality of surrounding pasture. At the Lazaret refugee camp, the Tuareg households averaged only between four and fifteen members.

The fortunes of the Tuareg were tied so closely to that of their herds that when the herds split up and died, so did the Tuareg. The coming apart began when families divided the original herds into small, and then still smaller, units. Each new herd was accompanied by one or more members of the family. When these small herds perished, the people with them either died too or walked to the nearest refugee center.

Men left their families to look for work in the cities and the towns. Many never returned to the bush, and those who did often found that their families had gone to a city or a refugee camp. Once people lost track of wives, husbands, and brothers, finding them again was difficult. The Tuareg were destitute, separated by immense distances, and in unfamiliar surroundings.

In 1973 and 1974 this unraveling continued. Families became even smaller as individual Tuareg left Niamey and other poor sahelian cities to look for work in the wealthier coastal countries. In the Nigerian cities of Kano, Kaduna, and Lagos, Malian and Nigerien Tuareg took menial jobs at salaries lower than those paid to local workers and became a poorly paid urban proletariat. Many stopped journeying only when they reached the Atlantic Ocean. Some now live on the beaches of Lagos, Nigeria, like European gypsies. They steal, beg from pedestrians and motorists stalled in the city's notorious traffic jams, and doze on heaps of garbage beneath the underpasses that shelter them from the monsoon rains. At night they sleep in tents pitched on the sand.

The atomization of the Tuareg family has ominous implications for the future. The survivors will have to face catastrophes without the inter- and intra-family loans and gifts that enabled many to survive the drought. Young people are learning how to beg and work at odd jobs rather than water, lead, and guard animals. Like animals caged in a zoo, the longer the Tuareg remain in cities and forget, or never learn, basic

133

nomadic skills, the less likely it becomes that they can ever return to the bush and survive.

When Sidi began his trek from Gao to Niamey, his family had already been reduced to two. His principal concerns were to find food and keep Ibrahim healthy. They walked in the cool morning and evening hours, stopping whenever Ibrahim tired. Sidi let his son eat as much as he was able of whatever food they found to share.

Sidi worked in the villages along the route, repairing cooking pots. He kept Ibrahim at his side to work the bellows and hand him his tools, and when the boy wandered out of his sight for even a moment he called his name softly but continously: "Ibrahim . . . Ibrahim . . . Ibrahim," until the child answered, "Sidi . . . Sidi."

In Ansongo, a town on the Niger sixty miles south of Gao, Sidi and Ibrahim joined a group of about ten Tuareg from Bourem, a town north of Gao, who were going to Niamey. They were led by a marabout named Moussa. Many of Moussa's "congregation" had recently emigrated to Niger, and he was hoping to gather them together in Niamey. A blacksmith from Bourem had been traveling with the group, but he had fallen ill in Gao and remained behind. Sidi was recruited as his replacement.

Moussa was famous among the people of the sixth region. In the villages south of Gao, people bought amulets from him. Sidi made the containers and they exchanged the charms for food which was divided among the party.

Moussa and his companions had also rehearsed a song to entertain townspeople and refugees along the road. Sidi and the Tuareg built a small fire, grouped themselves opposite Moussa, and began singing in a slow monotone until a crowd gathered:

> Today I am saddened by my camel, who is dead.
> Marabout Moussa, explain to me what has happened in our lives?
> Some people who were poor before the drought [the bouzous]
> Are now rich! Why?
> We were rich before and now we are poorer than these peoples.

The chorus paused and the growing audience echoed their questions, asking Moussa why they too were now poorer than their slaves, why they were heading for a strange country without their animals or their families.

Moussa closed his eyes, turning his head upwards, away from the listeners, and sang, punctuating important passages by raising his voice or pausing dramatically.

> For many years the bouzous did your work.
> Then when they were free they stole the animals of others,
> They sold them and became merchants,
> They disappeared to other countries to work, and also to steal.
> Then they returned to buy your dead animals.
> They sent their children to school,
> They learned to read and they earned money for their families.

He opened his eyes and stared over the fire at the crowd.

> Now you know nothing,
> You don't know how to work,
> You don't know how to trade.
> Now you are completely poor because you know nothing.
> Send your children to school.
> If you don't do that you will always be poor.
> The truth of what I've said is shown by the fact that
> Before independence they [the bouzous] were your slaves.
> Now your slaves who went to school learned numbers and letters.
> Now they are policemen, merchants, and important men.
> Now they are stronger than you.
> Now they give you food.

The song was clever. Bouzous in the audience were flattered and praised for their industry. The Tuareg were comforted by the fact that at the beginning of the song some of the bouzous' success was attributed to thievery. Both bouzous and Tuareg tipped Moussa and the chorus.

Moussa: "There are many reasons to pay for the services of a marabout. People would employ me to find lost animals, cure a disease, ensure good luck, persuade a beautiful woman to love them, find a husband, protect them against an enemy.

"But of all the remedies for different problems prescribed in the Ko-

135

ran, there is none against a drought. People offered to pay me for an amulet to protect them from the drought, but I had to refuse. I told them that I could not protect myself against the drought.

"I had many animals before the drought, but of course they died. Then I opened a school to teach the people of Bourem the Koran, but few could afford to pay fees. I hoped that when I arrived in Niamey I could start another school; so many people I knew from Bourem had gone there that I was certain I would be successful."

Sidi: "People always follow a marabout's instructions. If he says to take one road rather than another one they will do it. After Moussa sang this song many people agreed that when they arrived in Niamey they would send their children to school.

"Moussa could have afforded to take a truck to Niamey but he preferred to walk with the other people. He was known as a courageous man who kept his turban wrapped tightly around his face so he would see no other woman but his wife. His wife died, I don't know when, but Moussa still kept the turban tightly wrapped.

"People along the route, even other refugees, gave Moussa millet. He shared it with the people who walked with him. Sometimes we didn't have enough to eat, and once we fasted for two days. But we were not as hungry as the other people who went to Niamey. If we had not joined Moussa and the people from Bourem, we would have fasted more and I would have sold my tools."

Sidi, Ibrahim, Moussa, and the others arrived in Niamey at the end of August 1973, a month and a half after leaving Gao. The marabout and the Tuareg from Bourem joined the refugees who were gathered in the Lazaret camp about a mile north of Niamey. After spending one night in the camp with Moussa, Sidi left to deliver Rissa's letter to Hassan and to continue searching for his wife.

136

5

Atakor
June-August 1973
Abalack-Niamey

Tranquility exists in the shade of sabrés.

—Tuareg saying

i

*A*fter a six-hour, fifty-mile journey from In Waggeur, Atakor disembarked from the truck at the market town of Abalack. Like In Waggeur, Abalack had an automatic pump, but unlike In Waggeur it had a number of cement wells, a sedentary population of several hundred, and was the site of a weekly market. Before the drought nomads and farmers met at this market to exchange animals, milk, salt, and grain.

Atakor arrived in Abalack in the middle of June, 1973. People still gathered at the market but many of them had come to Abalack not to trade food but to beg for it.

Akator: "I stayed in Abalack for a week. Many people there had lost their animals. There was no work and no food, unless you could pay for it. People begged but no one could give them anything, so they begged from each other.

"I learned from a man in Abalack that my sister's husband's cousin lived at the fort in Tahoua. He was a soldier in the army. I decided to go to Tahoua and ask for his help. I left Abalack alone, since none of the other Illabakan wanted to come with me.

"I fasted while I walked to Tahoua. I stopped outside villages I had visited while taking my animals to markets. Now I waited outside until someone offered me water, food, or a place to sleep. I did not beg. One bouzou gave me sorghum. Most bouzous and Hausas gave me only water, and one man asked me to pay for it. This was the only food I ate for three days after leaving Abalack.

"While I was walking, I feared that the death of my animals had killed my hopes for the future. Often I dreamed that my animals were walking with me."

South of Abalack, Atakor crossed the border that separated pastures and farms. Villages near this border were deserted, their fields cracked and studded with the stubble of millet stalks. Next he passed villages where the only inhabitants were women and children; their men, like Atakor, had left for the south. Cotton had been the principal crop, and the few remaining people ate cotton grains boiled in water.

A week south of Abalack, Atakor passed one of the few permanent lakes in the Adar that still held water. Nearby, the bones of animals who had found water but no food had been gathered into piles as if awaiting collection or some sort of ceremony. Small waves lapped at the shore of the lake and huge white sand dunes sprouting small naked trees rose behind it. The scene was so white and bleached that it could have been a photograph of a Swiss ski slope, taken with overexposed film.

Before coming to this lake, Atakor had followed the dirt road that ran between Tahoua and Abalack. It was crowded with refugees, animals, plus the usual vehicular traffic going to or from In Gall, Agadez, and Algeria. A reporter for Niger's only newspaper traveled in this region in May 1973, a month before Atakor. He saw nomads crying over the cadavers of their animals, and the very old and very young sitting by the side of the road, too weak to walk and waiting to be helped or to die. Helping them, as foreign relief organizations in Niger were to learn, was not simple. The reporter had stopped his Land Rover next to an old man and offered him bread and water. The old man bit into the bread and handed it back. It tasted strange. He sipped the water and spilled it onto the ground. It was iced, and it hurt his teeth.

As soon as Atakor came to the lake he left the road. Too many people had begged for food and water at nearby villages. He thought he would find more hospitality away from the other refugees. Late that night he stopped to sleep under a conical granary. It sat two feet off the ground and was supported by a miniature Stonehenge of flat rocks. At daybreak he crawled out from under the granary and spent the morning propped against its side, moving with its shade and waiting for someone to bring him food and water. The outer walls of a farm village, one of many such compact islands scattered throughout the Adar, were ten yards away.

The granary was large, fifteen feet high, seven feet in diameter, and raised two feet off the ground by the rock foundation. Like the village, it was constructed of banco bricks. A thatch of dried millet stalks roofed it, and this cover could be slid aside when a villager climbed to the top on a ladder to scoop out grain.

Both granary and village were born of the same materials: red soil and dried millet stalks. After the harvest, stalks were cut from the fields and woven into straw mats; these became roofs for banco houses or granaries whose owners wore smaller but identical conical straw hats and swept dust from mud houses with millet stalks tied together with roots.

The bleached red earth was everywhere. On windy days the air was red with dust, and the earth left caste marks on foreheads that touched the ground in prayer. Red dirt was dug out of the land and molded into houses, granaries, mosques, walls, and outhouses.

People breathed it, wore it, slept in it, ate it. To escape from it farmers and nomads wore silver ornaments and dressed in brilliant, unnatural colors: dark blues, brilliant reds and pinks, bright, clean whites.

Except for the granaries scattered around the perimeter, the buildings were jammed together, giving the town the appearance of a medieval walled city without moat or ramparts. It rose starkly from the surrounding plains. Seen from a nearby hill, it was a maze of high walls, narrow passages, and rectangular one-story houses. From ground level, it seemed to have been tugged from the earth it mirrored as if by a magnet.

Like other Niger farming villages, this one was composed of *concessions,* walled enclosures containing a kitchen, bedrooms, a bathroom, small grain bins, a guestroom. The size of the buildings and the courtyard between them depended on the size of a family and its wealth. An

141

average concession held about nine people, though some had as few as one or as many as twenty.

The high concession walls offered both privacy and intimacy. Neighbors were seldom seen yet the houses were so close that it was impossible not to know what was happening, even in distant concessions. The sound of drums, babies, prayers, arguments, lovemaking, and millet-pounding carried over the six-foot walls.

Though Atakor had seen no one enter or leave the village, he knew there were people within. He knew there was food, as he could see millet scattered around the granary. He heard the rhythmic pounding as two poles rose and fell behind the wall of the closest concession, like the pistons of a primitive engine. He knew that behind the wall two women held the poles as they beat grain into a farina for the evening meal.

ii

*T*he architecture of these Adar farm villages is influenced by a fear of the bush. Farmers believe that the bush is not fit for human habitation. Its terrifying and unpredictable natural forces, violent windstorms and flash floods, threaten them. Whenever possible they build villages on high ground to escape floods, and they build narrow paths and narrow entrances to block sandstorms.

The bush harbors malevolent supernatural spirits, devils that roam at will, especially in the evening, dispensing curses that can cause insanity, poor harvests, stillborn children, and impotence. To keep the devils away, house walls are reinforced with branches from lucky trees. When mud bricks are laid, seven kinds of magical amulets, small pots or pieces of cloth, roots, herbs, grains, animal manure, and the ashes from a blacksmith's fire are entombed in the ground, encased in the walls, and suspended from the roofs at geometrically significant points. They protect the farmer's homes from the devils lurking in the dangerously open spaces of the bush.

142

In the past the bush also harbored human devils, Tuareg who taxed, robbed, enslaved, and murdered the farmers. Protection from these devils was expensive and uncertain. When it was finally achieved, it came at a high price—French colonization.

Before the French conquest, the Adar was the Belgium of Niger, a venue for the perpetual wars and raids that pitted Tuareg tribes and confederations against each other, the Peul, or the farmers themselves. Bands of Kel Gress Tuareg drifted south into the Adar from the Air Mountains at the start of the eighteenth century. They were attracted by the open pastures of the Adar, and propelled by the military superiority of rival Tuareg confederations. By the end of the century they had subjugated the farmers, enslaving some and making others into perpetual tributaries. Until the middle of the nineteenth century this Tuareg "protection racket" was tolerable, since it enabled the people of the Adar to purchase tranquility.

This stability collapsed around 1850 when the Ouillemeden Tuareg, principally the Kel Dennik from the Azawak, led herds into the Adar and raided farmers under the protection of their rivals, the Kel Gress. For the next fifty years the Adar was the scene of many battles between Kel Dennik, Kel Gress, and Kel Ferwan. Like medieval serfs on the borders of warring principalities the black farmers were caught between rival Tuareg confederations and tribes. It made no difference whom the farmers paid for protection; someone else would raid or enslave them.

This reign of terror lasted until the twentieth century, when farmers who had been driven from their lands returned under the protection of French troops. The Kel Dennik retreated into the Azawak and the Kel Gress made peace, some of them becoming farmers themselves. The modern states, first the French and then the Nigerien, strengthened the farmers' economic and political power at the expense of the Tuareg. As early as 1907 it was clear to a French officer in Tahoua that "under our rule the blacks have gained a great deal and lost nothing. The Tuareg have lost, and gained nothing."

The farmers remembered the reign of terror long after it ended. Their oral histories, like those of the Tuareg, made the past seem vivid and current. The Tuareg's bouzous, who had been farmers themselves be-

143

fore their enslavement, wore veils and spoke Tamashek; they were an ever-present reminder to other blacks of the victimization of their people.

The shifting border between pastures and farms never satisfactorily separated farmer from herder. When a drought unbalanced the delicate symbiosis that bound them together, the resulting clashes could be fierce. In good years Adar farmers often encouraged Tuareg and Peul animals to graze in their fields between the fall harvest and the late spring planting. This gave the nomads access to virgin pastures at precisely that time when their own were barren. The farmers, in turn, had their fields fertilized for free. But if the rains in the Azawak were poor, the nomads might arrive in the Adar before the harvest, allowing their animals to eat the ripening grain.

The Tuareg's belief in their own racial superiority was based on a contempt for anyone who had to work with his hands, and this also caused friction. Tuareg oral histories are rich with incidents reminding them of past victories and keeping alive their conviction that blacks are cowards.

"The Hausa and Djerma are like sheep," said Atakor. "They are afraid to fight us. If we wanted we could defeat their soldiers in a day. They would run like sheep. Baa . . . baa!"

A Tuareg from Agadez was certain that his tribesmen could overcome the garrison in Agadez with their swords and old rifles because "The blacks would never fight. They know that we are more courageous than they are and they are still terrified of us." Despite the fact that most young Tuareg have rarely, if ever, used their ancient swords and rifles in anger, their history has convinced them, and many black farmers as well, that they are invincible.

Considering the history of relations between Tuareg and blacks in Niger, the treatment accorded Tuareg refugees by farmers who themselves were suffering almost equal deprivations was generous. Two out of every three families interviewed at the Lazaret camp in Niamey said that they had been "well received" by farmers. They told of farmers who gave food to nomadic children and cloth to their parents in which to wrap their dead for burial.

This charity toward their former oppressors is not surprising. Both nomads and farmers were Moslems, and the Djerma in particular have a tradition of forgiveness and generosity toward a defeated enemy. Throughout all of West Africa, black Nigeriens are known as an exceptionally gentle and humane people.

Some Tuareg who were not treated generously returned to thievery, which they preferred to think of as "raiding." They stole from each other around the water points of the Azawak. When they reached the Adar, some Tuareg, for the first time in decades, crept into villages, drew swords, and made off with food and animals—the "Huns" returning for a last, desperate raid. [']

⋯

*A*t noon, Atakor sat upright, his back flat against the wall of the granary. The sun was overhead and shade was scarce. Still no one had left the village or approached him with food, water, or welcome.

The two poles continued rising and falling hypnotically, pounding grain he could not see but could imagine. Suddenly one pole stopped in mid-journey, wavered, and fell against the wall. The human machine had stopped. The beat of drums replaced the beat of the poles. Shadows swept out from the walls of the village granary and a cold wave of darkness rolled over Atakor.

White tick birds that had been roosting on the backs of emaciated cows in a nearby field flapped away to take up their night positions in trees. Against the darkening sky they looked like tufts of white cotton blown by the Harmattan and snagged by thorny branches. The cows stopped nuzzling the ground and walked toward the village. A bouzou guard, the first man Atakor had seen all day, ran out from a hidden resting place to chase them. The sand around Atakor cooled. He knew nothing of the eclipse and, his eyesight becoming dim as the light changed, he believed at first that his blindness was returning.

145

He pulled his possessions and his father's ancient sword from where he had hidden them under the granary. He touched the scabbard lightly, gingerly, as if it might scorch his fingertips. He grasped the hilt with his right hand, drew out the sword, and ran his fingers up and down the blade, sensuously, stroking it. He touched close friends, Miriam, a beautiful camel, other treasures, in the same fashion, exploring them as if his fingers were the most perceptive and pleasurable of all senses, as if only they could find hidden sources of delight.

Akator: "I was glad that I did not sell my sword at Abalack. It was so old and beautiful that before the drought a man offered to buy it for twenty camels. But at Abalack I was offered only 5,000 CFA [$25] and I was later told I was fortunate to have found anyone who could afford to pay anything. I kept it and exchanged my purse and tobacco for food. I liked my sword so much that I would have liked to have bought another because they were so cheap during the drought.

"My father's father gave the sword to him and he gave it to me. His father won it from an enemy after a battle and afterwards he used it himself many times. My father said that the sword was so powerful that if it cut anyone and drew blood then that person would surely die. My grandfather had once wounded thirty blacks and they all died because they had been touched by the sword. After this battle he was rewarded for his bravery with a herd of camels. Some of the camels that I lost during the drought were the descendants of those.

"I met many people in Abalack, Tahoua, and Niamey who said they wanted to have new animals so they could live as before, so that the young women could see them riding their camels and admire their herds. They wanted good pastures, good trees, and full ponds. I wanted these things too but I also wished that we could live as we had before the French, when people were courageous and fought with swords.

"Before the French we were not afraid of anything. But before the drought I was afraid of the government because I knew that it was stronger than I. If I fought or stole animals from the blacks, the government would punish me and take away my animals.

"But because of the drought I had no more animals and I became

146

more afraid of hunger. I learned that hunger was more powerful than the government and I knew that if I was going to live and see Miriam again I should fear hunger more."

The eclipse was total. The moon slipped in front of the sun for seven minutes. A silvery solar corona sparkled around the moon's circumference. This perfect symmetry of moon, sun, and earth created an unusual shade of darkness, one unlike night. The darkness had a luminescence, an undertone of light like that in the sky a moment before the first light of sunrise, or when the dark clouds of an afternoon thundershower turn day to night. For seven minutes the eclipse strung together these split seconds of half-light.

Atakor rose from behind the granary and, the fingers of his left hand caressing the sword he held in his right, walked toward a narrow opening between the walls of two concessions. It led to the center of the village.

The raids by the Kel Dennik against other nomads and farmers were conducted in secrecy. There was always the danger that a rival Tuareg confederation to whom the farmers had paid tribute might intervene. Later, the raiders also worried about French patrols. Lieutenant Hourst, a French military explorer who witnessed some of these raids in 1896, compared them to European "hunting expeditions":

What I may call these hunting expeditions are greatly facilitated, if not altogether necessitated, by the very nature of a nomad life. The preparations are made with the greatest secrecy, and only the sturdiest walkers and the best horsemen are allowed to take part in them. The party, never very large, numbering at the most a hundred, if the way is long, as it often is, starts preceded by the guides, who lead the razzia (raiding party) by the least frequented route. The most important point to be kept in view is the position of the various wells by the way, for on a knowledge of this essential detail success chiefly depends.

Gliding silently between the encampments of the enemy the Tuaregs are always on the alert, for their exposed situation makes them watchful. . . . The greatest skill is needed to take the enemy unawares, and

147

sometimes all the precautions are in vain, for those attacked have had warning beforehand, but not in time to send couriers out to summon their friends to their aid.

The men then all take to flight, but the women remain, for though the men who resist are slain, no Tuareg would stain his hands with the blood of a defenceless woman.

As the moon slid away from the face of the sun and the eclipse continued its fourteen-hundred-mile-an-hour journey across Africa, Atakor wandered between the village concessions. Only a few had tin doors and locks, and most of the doorways were open.

Atakor: "I went to the house where the women had been pounding millet but there was no one there. I went inside and saw they had been pounding not the millet but cram-cram [a wild nettle]. I visited other houses in that village but saw no one. I knocked on walls with my sword and tried to push open doors that were locked. Behind some of them I heard people talking. I looked for food but I saw only cram-cram. I kept my sword unsheathed until the sun reappeared."

In 1895 a black inhabitant of Timbuctoo described to Felix Dubois, a French traveler, the injustices that the sedentary black people suffered at the hands of the Tuareg:

Thou hast seen those veiled men in sombre garments, with chest and back covered with red and yellow talismans as though by cuirasses. When they come to us now they are modest, but before the French arrived they walked insolently through the streets, carrying iron spears. Every year we paid them tribute in gold or kind, corn, salt, garments, and turbans, etc. Their chiefs with their retinues were well lodged when they came here. The caravans bound for this town paid them toll in the desert, and they exacted toll upon the river also, from the fleets going to Kabara. This did not suffice them; these were the least of our evils. From one end of the year to the other they treated us as captives of war, as slaves. They were constantly arriving in groups and dispersing through the town. All doors were closed as soon as they appeared, but they beat upon the doors, and thou canst see the traces of the heavy blows from their lances everywhere. We were forced to open to them, and without paying the least attention to the master of the house or his family, they would install themselves in the best rooms, taking all the cushions and couches, insolently demanding food and drink, and insisting upon having sugar, honey, and meat. On departing to rejoin their camp the only acknowledgement they made was to steal something from the house and spit upon their host.

Atakor: "I expected to find food in the village. I saw some women and a few children, but they ran away and hid when they saw me. When the sun returned I followed them and found them and other women and children sitting in the concession of a marabout.

"I told the marabout that I had only drunk water for a number of days and asked him for food. He said they only had food for themselves since all their men had already left. He told me to go away because the women were frightened. When he said this I became angry and picked up some grains of fornio [wild grass] that I saw scattered on the ground of his concession and said 'How can I buy food or animals when I have nothing? You have animals outside in the fields and so much fornio that you scatter it on the ground.'

"After this the marabout agreed to give me some fornio and water if I would leave. He gave me enough fornio to last for two days but I ate it all at once. Then we talked about the drought until I left to continue my walk to Tahoua."

(Two years later Atakor was ambiguous about what had occurred in the village during the eclipse. "I would never steal food," he said, "even if I was hungry. I would ask for it. This is why I went into the village when the sun disappeared." Later he said, "If I had taken food from that village it would have been a raid. I stopped when I saw that there were only women and old men."

Before the French pacification, the Tuareg had always distinguished between pillaging, which they considered a noble pursuit, and pure theft, which they abhorred. During the drought, this distinction became confused.)

*   *   *

iv

*M*any other Tuareg refugees walking through the Adar found villages that were abandoned or filled with people as desperate as they. Farmers too joined the nomadic exodus to cities and towns where the government distributed food donated by the relief organizations. This common fate was proof that, despite their racial, historical, and occupational differences, the nomads and the farmers of Niger were linked by a crucial common denominator—their reliance on the monsoon rains.

A hundred years ago most black Nigeriens were traders, herders, and gatherers. There were only half a million of them, and there was ample wild game and food. As a result, they did not have a long tradition of farming. During the twentieth century they practiced a crude agriculture that involved clearing land, weeding, digging a row of shallow holes, dropping in a random number of seeds, weeding again, and then waiting for a harvest.

The farmers, like the nomads, need specific quantities of rain at specific intervals during the germination of their crops. Because of the variability of the rains, farmers often plant a number of times each year to ensure at least one harvest. The first planting usually occurs at the end of the soudure, when the huge Gao trees grow new leaves and other trees bear fruit, signs that the monsoon is imminent. Farmers suck the fruit and foretell from the hardness the start of the rain. They stick their arms in holes dug in the ground to measure the depth of moisture.

When the rains become regular, they plant. This is a crucial decision, since once the young plants sprout there must be rain again within a week. If the farmers plant too soon, before the main thrust of the monsoon, the plants sprout and die, and they must sow a second time. This time insects may eat the seeds or windstorms blow them away. They plant again, and this time there may be too much rain, producing floods that wash away the young plants.

Throughout July, August, and, if they are desperate, in September, the farmers continue to plant until the rains are sufficient to produce a harvest, or their seeds are exhausted, or there is no longer hope for even

150

a meager crop. The longer they wait, the greater the risk that the monsoon will retreat south before crops have matured. When seeds are gone and the rains end, only then are they totally defeated.

In economies scarcely more advanced than Niger's, it is said that herders try to accommodate themselves to nature, adjusting their migrations and herd size to available resources, while farmers try to fight nature; to transform it through technology by means of irrigating, fertilizing, weeding, and crop rotation. In Niger, the growing season is so brief and the agricultural techniques so primitive that except for the farmers' six or seven courageous replantings, this distinction is minor.

Nigerien farmers only weed once before planting and once afterwards. They do not irrigate or use the most rudimentary tools. Were they to plough their land even once during their many sowings, nutrients would be released that would promote a better harvest.

In 1972 Niger's harvest was so poor that there were few seeds available in the spring of 1973 to provide for the farmers' hit-and-miss sowing practices. In a Hausa agricultural village in southern Niger, studied by American anthropologist Ralph Faulkingham, 17.4 inches of rain fell in 1969 and only 7.1 in 1973. The harvest declined accordingly; in 1969 there were 271 pounds of crops harvested per capita, in 1970 there were 97, in 1971 there were 120, in 1972 the number of pounds decreased to 84, and in 1973 they dropped to 10 pounds. The same pattern was repeated in different degrees in most Nigerien villages.

The spacing of the rains that inundated this village was as poor as their quantity. In 1972 there was no rain at all between the tenth and twentieth of July, and between the first and the tenth of September. In 1973 the situation was worse. There was no rain until July 1, and then only 1.4 inches during the entire month. During another crucial period of time, the last ten days of August, there were only 1.6 inches. Farmers who had had enough seeds to plant a second and third time harvested nothing. Many of them could not even plant a first or second time, having no reserves from the poor 1972 crop. Some had been forced to eat what seeds they had to survive the soudure. Others who did plant became so hungry that they harvested their millet prematurely. The underage grain turned into black dust when rubbed between the fingers.

151

In Gouré, a farming village in eastern Niger, there was in 1973 only 5.1 inches of rain instead of 15.6 as usual. The farmers planted five times, and each time nothing grew. Ninety percent of the villagers were anemic, half the village herd died, and millet which had fetched twelve CFA a kilo in 1972 brought fifty-five in 1973. Nevertheless, nomads in past years had come to consider the village a "granary," and flocked there during the drought to look for food.

For many farmers 1973 had been their last chance. To survive the previous disastrous harvests they had already eaten their reserves and sold their possessions. When the rains of 1973 were worse than those of the preceding year, they were stranded in their villages with neither food nor the prospect of a better harvest in the fall. They left their homelands and walked to the cities to look for work, or to other villages where they had friends and relatives.

Not all the farmers joined the exodus. A few had surpluses of grain in their storehouses, or their fields had received enough rain. Others who anticipated a harvest, who had planted but not yet harvested their crops, stayed in their villages and mortgaged future harvests to traders in return for food and seeds. When they had harvested the grain they had used as collateral, they put it in their own storehouses. Since some or all of it belonged to a trader, they were obliged to pay the trader or mortgage a future crop if they wanted to eat it. The trader never had to harvest, transport, or store the grain himself.

Even during normal years, many of Niger's farmers needed an exceptionally good harvest to pay off debts and build up reserves. The drought increased this rural indebtedness, lowering their standard of living even more, and promoted a major redistribution of income between farmer and trader. The farmers became even poorer and the traders richer, although these latter were rarely wealthy by the standards of most other countries.

When Tuareg who had led their animals south failed to find enough pasture for them, they sold them to traders (or farmers) who could afford to purchase feed. Many of these same Tuareg were then hired as wage laborers to tend what had once been their own animals. Food and/or wages were often milk from these very animals.

152

In the summer of 1973 some Algerian merchants drove across the desert to Niger in empty trucks, bought herds of starving cattle for a few pennies a head, loaded them into the trucks, and drove them to feeding points they had already stocked and prepared.

A Canadian entrepreneur, with the connivance of government functionaries, also bought starving animals cheaply, planning to transport them on government barges to a secret feeding station on an island in the Niger River south of Niamey, and fatten them on imported grain. The scheme failed. The entrepreneurs discovered that the herders insisted on setting a different price for each animal, according to its condition. The bargaining process took so long that it was impossible to obtain enough animals.

Though many farmers had to leave their villages and join the nomadic exodus, their futures were not as bleak as those of the Tuareg. They were not fleeing to live among a foreign people in a strange environment, and the social and cultural dislocations they experienced were not as extreme. Many had already made seasonal migrations to the large villages and cities of West Africa. After a harvest, a third of the young men of many villages customarily went to Niamey, Maradi, Kano, and coastal cities like Lagos and Abidjan and took unskilled, seasonal jobs. They returned in April to prepare for the planting. Their wages helped pay taxes, buy luxuries like radios, and procure food that enabled them to survive the soudure. They were familiar with modes of transportation, ways of finding employment, and they were more likely than the nomads to have friends and relatives in the cities.

v

*T*ahoua is a dusty, almost treeless, market town with modest relics from three quarters of a century of colonial modernization: a few paved streets lined with concrete bunkers called "villas" built for government functionaries and European doctors and experts; a handful of two- and three-story government buildings and banks; some service stations —Mobil, BP, Texaco—with signs and pumps like those found on American highways; a traffic island in front of the bank four feet in diameter with weeds growing in its center; a small hospital staffed by foreign doctors; and the hotel, an unsightly concrete structure with a cracked asphalt tennis court. The rest of Tahoua is, as it has always been, a trading center of banco houses and grass huts, on the border of Niger's nomadic and agricultural regions.

During 1973 it became a way station for refugees, a smaller version of Gao. Some stayed and worked, begged, or survived on a distribution of relief food more regular and generous than in Gao. Others continued south.

Most Nigerien Tuareg who passed through Tahoua walked on to refugee areas in closer southern cities such as Maradi, Birni-n'Konni, and Dosso. During the summer of 1973 there were 7,500 refugees in Tahoua, but in November the government suddenly stopped giving away food and the number fell to 1,200. Most of the others went south to camps near Maradi. Not many Nigerien Tuareg went to Niamey, which was 350 miles from Tahoua and closer to the homelands of the Malian Tuareg.

Atakor arrived in Tahoua in the middle of July and was housed and fed by his distant "cousin." In August this cousin was transferred with his regiment to Niamey. Before he left he gave Atakor food, paid for his truck passage to Niamey, and promised to find him work when he arrived. Atakor said, "He was an Illabakan and a relative, so of course he helped me."

(Atakor was neither the first nor the last fellow tribesman helped by his cousin. During the drought, the handful of Tuareg who had adopted sedentary occupations and earned a regular wage, as well as any farmers who held salaried jobs in Tahoua, Zinder, Niamey, and other cities, were suddenly inundated with relatives, friends, and even people they didn't know but who came from their village or tribe; people whom custom and humanity demanded that they aid. They seldom refused. These wage earners were poor themselves—porters, janitors, cooks, housecleaners, small merchants, taxi drivers, and beggars. To help the refugees, they liquidated savings, abandoned educational goals for their children, and sold possessions that were the triumph of years of industry and thrift.)

For two days and 350 miles, Atakor sat on top of a cargo truck. Once it started down the paved road that led south from Tahoua to Birnin'Konni, then west to Niamey, he was in foreign territory. It was the first time he had ever seen a paved road, and he passed more traffic and a greater variety of vehicles than he had seen in In Waggeur.

There were small pickup trucks and station wagons bound for Nigeria, and *rapides,* large white tin trucks that looked as if they had once been bread vans. All had wooden benches built inside and parcels and luggage piled on top. They sped down one-lane macadam roads with their rear doors open and people hanging on as if they had just caught a moving trolley. They were so overloaded with people and cargo that they swayed as if buffeted by a hurricane. When these vehicles met head-on, one or both had to move onto the gravelly shoulder of the road, kicking up of sand that choked passengers and stones that shattered windshields.

Occasionally, the *rapides* crashed head-on or rolled off the road because of a blowout. People and cargo spilled out like fruit falling from a market lady's overloaded basket. Fifteen to twenty people could be killed or injured in a single collision. Orphans were adopted by nearby villagers; survivors walked to their destinations or, if they had money enough to pay another fare, flagged down another *rapide.* Burnt-out trucks and sparkling little heaps of shattered glass marked the shoulders of Nigerien roads with the regularity of mileposts.

Ninety-four miles south of Tahoua, Atakor's truck turned west toward Niamey on the National Route One. More people and more villages were visible from Route One, and the effects of the drought were not as severe. Human ligaments, lines of people on foot walking along the sides of the road, connected market towns, fields, and distant villages. For ten miles on either side of a market there were women with piles of firewood, baskets of onions, and milk-filled calabashes on their heads. Little girls and boys balancing bales of grass on their heads looked like walking birds' nests. Men and boys rode or drove cows and

155

goats whose grazing had created desert corridors for yards on either side of the road.

Atakor's truck arrived in Niamey at night and he crawled underneath to sleep until morning. For Tuareg refugees like Atakor, Niamey was a strange and sometimes hostile place. Niamey's workers feared, justifiably, that the refugees would steal their menial jobs. Government officials worried that Malian Tuareg would create political difficulties between Niger and Mali and consume relief supplies that otherwise might go to Nigeriens. They were also nervous about the influx of Nigerien Tuareg, and feared that these Tuareg might fight with the farmers and foreign Tuareg.

Since 80 percent of the Tuareg refugees in Niamey came from Mali (90 percent of those in the Lazaret camp), Atakor was a minority within a larger Tuareg minority. He was from the Kel Dennik confederation of the eastern Ouillemeden Tuareg; Sidi, Ibrahim, Moussa, and Rissa's son, Hassan, were from the Kel Attram of the western Ouillemeden. These two Ouillemeden branches, the eastern located primarily in Niger and the western in Mali, had been enemies since the eighteenth century, when the Kel Dennik split from the western Ouillemeden and wandered into the eastern Azawak.

During the anarchy of the late nineteenth century, these two factions fought frequent wars. The last and most decisive battle occurred in 1872 at Werzey, a well fifty kilometers northeast of In Waggeur. Although the oral histories of both people concede the bravery of their enemy, each claims Werzey as a victory.

Full-scale battles such as Werzey were fought with a strategy and chivalry that intrigued the European observers. After witnessing one Ouillemeden battle, Lieutenant Hourst wrote in his diary that

Everything is in fact so settled by tradition amongst the Tuaregs that even a battle is more like a set of quadrilles than anything else.

To begin with there is generally a palaver, and when all attempts to patch up the quarrel have failed resort is had to arms. The disputants separate, having fixed a time for their meeting, and on the day and at the place agreed upon the two armies or "attabu" are drawn up as in a medieval tournament.

The forces advance in closely serried battalions. Sometimes the Tuareg fights on horseback but as a rule he prefers to meet his foe on foot. The combatants hurl defiance at each other and rush shouting to the fray. Spears are flung at a distance of some fifty feet, but they are pretty well always caught on the shields of those at whom they are hurled.

Meanwhile the confusion rapidly increases; the chiefs now begin to challenge each other to single combat and it is not an unusual thing for the two armies to cease hostilities with one accord to watch the issue of the struggle between the leaders. Spears, no longer of any use, are flung aside, the dagger and sword taking their place, and gleaming in the sunshine as they are raised against the foe. Blood begins to flow copiously on either side. Here two warriors are holding each other at bay at arms' length, each trying to pierce his adversary's heart with his sword; there are two locked in a murderous embrace, stabbing at each other with their daggers, or trying to crack each other's skulls with the stone amulet. . . .

At last one side wavers, inferior in strength or in numbers to the other. The warriors begin to flee, and the victors shout, "Ah! ah! there will be no violins for you!" And this sarcasm, which means that their wives will be angry and scorn them, often so stings the fugitives that they rally and go back to the struggle, eager to win the praises of their women on their return to their tents.

The Battle of Werzey was preceded by numerous minor raids and skirmishes. While most of the Kel Dennik warriors were attending the Cure Salée, the Kel Attram attacked a Kel Dennik camp at Derkatin, a well fifty-five kilometers northwest of In Waggeur, and stole slaves and animals.

When the chief of the Kel Dennik, Mus ag Boda, heard of the Derkatin raid, he sent a blacksmith diplomat to Inebeg, the Kel Attram chief. The emissary told Inebeg that Musa Boda was in agreement that his raiders had stolen the animals fairly but was upset that they had violated the rules of chivalry by carrying off the wives of the black Iklan N'egef. These Iklan, or black slaves, were in a special category. Known as "captives of the dunes," they lived in their own villages and fought as spear-carrying auxiliaries in Kel Dennik armies. The Kel Dennik believed that for the purposes of chivalry they had the status of freemen. While it was acceptable to carry off the wives of slaves, the wives of the

Iklan N'egef were not to be kidnaped. Musa demanded that the Kel Attram treat the Iklan women as if they were free and return them to their husbands.

Inebeg refused. Musa's blacksmiths beat the war drum and Kel Dennik assembled on camel, horseback, and foot, ready to fight to avenge the black women and uphold the rules of warfare.

Musa's brother, El Kumati, hid his blacksmith and slave foot soldiers in a forest of thorn trees near the anticipated battlefield. When the Kel Attram arrived, Kel Dennik horsemen engaged them briefly and then galloped into the woods as if retreating. The Kel Attram pursued, only to find themselves in the woods and encircled at close quarters. Foot soldiers sprang from the trees behind them and the retreating Kel Dennik horsemen turned to face them. The Kel Attram fled, abandoning animals and captive women taken during the disputed Derkatin raid.

This was the first in a series of raids between the two armies. Each resulted in deaths, alleged injustices, and departures from chivalry. All spurred further reprisals and revenge. During one engagement two famous Kel Attram warriors, Azekor and the brother of Firhoun, were killed. (Firhoun was later to lead a rebellion against the French.) Their deaths called for a special level of vengeance. The Kel Attram expeditionary force returned to the Kel Attram homeland surrounding Menaka (now a village in Mali 170 miles north of Niamey and just across the Mali-Niger frontier), assembled a larger army, and returned to make camp at Werzey and prepare for what they hoped would be the final and decisive engagement.

El Kumati, who became chief of the Kel Dennik following the natural death of his brother Musa, sent blacksmith emissaries to the other eastern Tuareg confederations, the Kel Gress and the Kel Oui, inviting them to forge a temporary alliance to dislodge the "common enemy," the Kel Attram, from their temporary camp at Werzey.

Fearing that they would be outnumbered by this new alliance, the Kel Attram built a wooden fortress of stakes bound together with skin ropes, called an *arafag* in Tamashek. They gathered inside it with their animals and slaves to await the attack of the eastern Tuareg alliance. When El Kumati arrived at Werzey, he offered the Kel Attram the opportunity to surrender their booty and return to Menaka. To encourage their compliance, he sent Elsinar, the Kel Attram chief, a message promising that if his army had to breach the *arafag,* it would "not leave even a bird alive within."

Elsinar refused to surrender. A battle followed, lasting seven days. On the seventh, the Kel Dennik army cut the cords that held the enclosure together and recaptured their animals and slaves. The Kel Attram fled, abandoning their women. Despite El Kumati's warning, the rules of chivalry were observed and these women sent back to Menaka unharmed. They were even provided with animals for food and transport.

Only one Kel Attram warrior, Ghalisun, refused to surrender or flee. He had built his own personal *arafag* within the larger one and remained inside with his camel, repelling with sword and knife any Kel Dennik who tried to breach it. At one point Ghalisun's camel gave a sharp, piercing cry. "Do you know what he said?" Ghalisum shouted to the Kel Dennik. "He said he would never leave toward the east" (as he would if captured).

El Kumati was so impressed with this bravery that he ordered his warriors to leave Werzey. When they rode away, Ghalisun and his camel stood alone, still within the small *arafag.*

After Werzey, contacts between the eastern and western Ouillemeden, the Kel Dennik and the Kel Attram, diminished. A hundred years later, the descendants of El Kumati (Atakor) and those of Ghalisum (Sidi, Ibrahim, and Moussa) were reassembling, not on an Azawak battleground but in the city of Niamey. This time it was a Kel Dennik warrior, Atakor, who stood alone. This time they were all members of a defeated army.

6

The Donors
1972-1974
Niger

Give to your brother despite the fact that he has given nothing to you.
God will give you whatever he does not give you back.

—Tuareg saying

*f*ifty-two experts flew over the sahel in an American Air Force jet, more followed in the supersonic Anglo-French Concorde. Hundreds of foreigners peered into telescopes on cruise liners off the Senegal-Mauritania coast. On the ground, technicians anchored expensive equipment in the sand. Arab laborers erected villages of tents in the remote Mauritanian desert. In Niger, grass huts with cooking and toilet facilities were built on a plain outside Agadez.

Many of the technicians were astronomers. The expeditions were scientific, representing twenty-eight nations. The planes and boats were crammed with tourists who never disembarked and whose view was obscured by sandstorms. According to a representative of the Catholic Relief Service who visited Agadez in June, "Next to the distribution center [for relief food] was a large area, fenced by wiring, which I first took to be a camp for the Tuaregs. There were a number of small huts made out of straw in the local style. It turned out that this was a camp constructed by the government for the foreigners coming to see the eclipse at the end of the month."

On the morning of June 30, 1973, Farley Winson, a Rhodesian pilot-for-hire, and his wife and young children were crossing the Sahara in a Land Rover. They were returning to southern Africa from a mission in the Middle East. When the sun disappeared they were a day's drive from Agadez.

As it had Atakor and Sidi, the eclipse caught Farley Winson unawares. Immediately before the sudden darkness, he had been talking about the uncertainty and the impermanence of his varied life. The eclipse began as he was analyzing his well-traveled past and promising his wife that they would buy a plantation and settle in Rhodesia. Farley believed that his penitent conversation and the eclipse were a coincidence with religious import. He pulled the Land Rover off the road and, though he was not a religious man, led his family in prayer.

When the Winsons arrived in Agadez that evening, Farley searched for a garage to repair a tire. Since he couldn't speak French, he enlisted the aid of a French-speaking American missionary, a member of the fundamentalist Sudan Interior Mission. Once the tire was repaired, the missionary invited the Winsons to dinner. Farley described his conversion on the Agadez road.

That evening, at the Agadez campground, Farley was unable to sleep. In the middle of the night he returned to the missionary's house and asked to be baptized. His wife and children were baptized the next morning. Because of the circumstances of his conversion, Farley decided that it was his "calling" to remain in Niger and help its people survive the drought. He traveled to Niamey to confer with other missionaries and decide what form his calling should take.

Farley worked at first as a pilot for the Nigerien Peanut Cooperative and marketing board, SONARA. He was not a pilot for long. He was an attractive and extremely persuasive man who soon became as friendly with Nigerien officials and foreign relief experts as he was with the missionaries. The most important among them was the African expert from the American Lilly Endowment who gave him a quarter of a million dollars of Lilly's funds to build an experimental irrigation project in southern Niger at the village of Tara.

Farley hired African laborers to dig canals and ditches and to flood fields. By 1975 they had produced a modest but extremely expensive peanut harvest; according to a SONARA executive, the harvest was the

164

most costly per peanut in Niger's history. In the meantime, Farley had acquired two private airplanes, a hangar, and a paved landing strip with two runways—all in all, probably the best airport in the entire country after Niamey. He had also become the owner of a forty-yard-long, Tudor-style plantation house on the edge of the Niger River.

When Farley visited the United States during the drought, the media hailed him as a savior of the sahel. He was featured in a Public Broadcasting Service documentary. A meeting with President Ford was scheduled but canceled at the last minute. The Methodist Bishop of Alabama pledged bulldozers and tractors for his plantation, and the Lilly African expert was collaborating with a Hollywood scriptwriter on a television movie fictionalizing Farley's conversion and subsequent accomplishments.

For two years Farley Winson was the most successful of the many disaster entrepreneurs who came to Niger after 1973. Intentionally, miraculously, or by chance, they profited or tried to profit from the money suddenly available for relief and development. English businessmen from Lagos and Accra tried to sell the Nigerien government surplus World War II transport planes. One who was unsuccessful returned to try again with a truck full of crop-spraying equipment. An American proposed that Niamey, a city in which most people ate or resold garbage, invest in a fleet of modern garbage trucks.

The entrepreneurs arrived in Niamey at the same time as the administrative representatives and disaster specialists employed by an acronym soup of private, government, and multinational relief and development agencies. Collectively, they were called "the donors." Some were new to Niger; others, veterans of the country, were increasing their in-country staffs and financial commitments.

Among them were private organizations, such as the British OXFAM, the Catholic CARITAS and CRS (Catholic Relief Services), SIM (Sudan Interior Mission), CWS (American Protestant Church World Services), CARE, AFRICARE, and the War on Want. There were the relief agencies of individual foreign governments: AID, United States; FED, European Common Market; DKW, Germany; FAC, France;

165

CIDA, Canada; and SIDA, Sweden. And there were the United Nations entries: FAO, Food and Agricultural Agency; WFP, World Food Program; UNDP, United Nations Development Program; and OSRO, the Office of Special Sahelian Services, a special UN agency created to coordinate sahelian famine relief.

The employees of these agencies, and those who came to Niger on their own in one-man or one-woman rescue teams, had diverse skills and motivations. For every scalawag with broken crop-sprayers there was a European student leading a food convoy across the Sahara in 140-degree summer heat at his own expense or a missionary spending his life savings to feed people. For every administrator for whom a posting to Niger was part of a careful career strategy, there were others willing to dispense with bureaucratic routine in order to transport relief food to those in need.

The speed with which this relief reached the sahel was crucial to Atakor, Miriam, and Sidi, to every nomad who joined the exodus. If animal feed had been shipped to In Waggeur and stored in sufficient quantity between 1969 and 1972, it is likely that Atakor could have saved enough of his animals to remain in the bush until the monsoon rains returned. In the sixth region, Sidi's clients could have saved enough animals so he could have continued to work in the bush and keep his family together. The disastrous migrations that took place in 1973 and 1974 would have been smaller, and in the end, less relief food would have been required.

Although the foreigners who arrived in Niger during 1973 and 1974 were unlike in nationality, skills, and even sincerity, they did have one thing in common: they were in many respects too late. They were too late to save many people weakened by malnutrition from dying of disease; too late to save others isolated and abandoned in remote areas of the bush; too late to save the herds of animals that had bound together the Tuareg's families and culture and enabled them to survive.

They arrived with money, food, and development plans in time to save lives but not in time to save what made these lives worth living. They were in time to save many individual Tuareg but not the Tuareg people, to save them from dying of hunger but not from dying of sadness.

ii

*f*amines were common in Niger in the nineteenth and twentieth centuries, and they were given special names which expressed their unique horrors. Before the colonial occupation there was a famine, noted for killing many children, called "the wind that carried away our children." Following it was the "famine so severe that it was necessary to pound up the calabashes."

The French colonization of Niger did not end the famines; French policies made them, if anything, more severe. The names of famines continued to convey horrors. That of 1942 was named "withdraw and separate from the wife," for in that time, in order to survive, men had to think of themselves and unburden themselves of their wives.

The worst twentieth-century famines occurred in 1913–1914 and 1931–1932. After heavy rains fell prematurely in May 1930, Nigerien farmers planted their seeds. In June these rains suddenly ceased, and were followed by dark clouds of locusts instead of moisture. Young millet stalks dried up under the soudure sun or were cut and eaten. The farmers planted again in July and August. The rains were excellent, but the locusts reappeared in the autumn and devoured the harvest.

Boubou Hama, the president of Niger's National Assembly after independence, remembers that "the locusts flew in from the east. On many days in Niamey the sky was covered by a cloud of locusts. Ditches were dug to prevent their larvae from crossing the road, but all efforts to stop them were in vain. The locusts ravaged all the harvests and left our people abandoned to their own resources."

"Their own resources" were all the Nigeriens had. The French gave them practically nothing, and after people exhausted their reserves, they starved. At least fifty thousand people, a tenth of the entire population

167

of Niamey, Dosso, and Tillaberry in western Niger, died in the vicinity of Niamey, the new colonial capital. Because it cut down so many people, the famine was named *"coupe-coupe,"* or "cut-cut."

The colonial administrators not only did nothing to save the thousands of starving farmers who gathered in Niamey; they even reduced the already meager 1930 harvest by requisitioning food and demanding that taxes be paid. Their principal concern was to prevent the famine from interrupting the orderly economic functions of the colony.

To pay their taxes, farmers sold animals and thereby further reduced possible sources of food. Many colonial officials were of the opinion that the peasants had brought this disaster on themselves because of their "fatalism" (men who walked five hundred miles to the Gold Coast for seasonal labor) and "inactivity" (farmers who planted seven or eight times a year before reaping a single harvest).

By 1931 great numbers of starving farmers had left their villages. They slept in Niamey's streets and stormed the hospital and food warehouses. The government waited until the summer of 1931 before issuing a few cautious decrees. On June 25 the rations of horses and prisoners were reduced and the exportation of food from the colony was forbidden. No food was imported, and Niger continued to fend for itself.

Between May and September 1931 the French distributed thirty-five tons of relief supplies in Niamey. The rest of the surpluses in the capital remained in warehouses, and the money stayed in the treasury. The lieutenant governor was reluctant to distribute more. He argued that the budget prevented him from making any humanitarian gestures. He also feared upsetting the local grain market and encouraging dependence and laziness among the "natives." He said, "If we feed part of the population today, we would be giving them a mentality that would harm the future production of the whole colony."

The French were not unique. Other colonial powers had the same priorities: tax collection and the harvesting and processing of cash crops. Large-scale, direct aid from other foreign governments during the colonial period was rare. If France chose to allow its subjects to starve, then other sovereign nations felt they had neither the right nor the duty to offer assistance.

168

In 1931 the colonial government contributed 35 tons of food. By the end of 1974, foreign donors had sent more than 230,000 tons to Niger. The difference lay in the fact that forty-three years after "coupe-coupe" Niger was independent, and the rich countries of the world now had the wealth and the technical ability to alleviate famine wherever and whenever it occurred. It was possible to send food anywhere with greater speed. Better communications meant that the rich countries could be aware of potential famines sooner. A country like Niger, independent and a member of the United Nations, could accept relief from any donor. Some donor countries also considered famine relief the price of keeping friendly regimes in power in poor countries.

In a world both richer and smaller than that of 1930, there was also a growing consensus among its citizens and governments that the rich nations had a responsibility to prevent people from dying of hunger. Widespread belief in a duty to feed the starving is recent. The first, and still the most successful, famine rescue occurred during the 1966–1967 Bihar famine in India, where a generous and timely response by the donors prevented famine. Next was the Biafran war; and in 1970, a cyclone and flood in Bangladesh brought the relief agencies back to the Asian continent.

While the drought in the sahel was developing, and the attention of the donors was focused on Bangladesh and Biafra, the standards of performance to which the public, the media, and the politicians would hold donor agencies responsible were shifting. What was considered a timely, efficient, and generous response ten years ago now seemed to border on neglect.

The drought in the sahel began with the poor rains of 1968. Yet during the next four years there were few indications that by 1973 it would have accounted for unprecedented animal deaths, human migrations, and ecological changes.

In 1970, 1971, and 1972, the United Nations World Food Program (WFP) sent grain to supplement the consecutively poor sahelian harvests. By the spring of 1972 the WFP was considering a proposal by the United Nations Food and Agriculture Organization that because of the drought's unusual duration, special emergency food assistance be granted. The proposal was discussed within the United Nations bureaucracy. There were none of 1973's dramatic announcements of six million people close to death, either by the United Nations, the other donors, or the countries themselves.

So many people already live so close to absolute poverty in the sahel that a disaster such as a drought does not result in a sudden cataclysm. It is not like an earthquake or a flood in a developed country that suddenly turns a prosperous middle class into temporary wards of the state or private charities. Instead, an already disastrous situation is made even more disastrous.

Between the autumn of 1968 and 1972 the famine and suffering resulting from the drought were camouflaged by the usual poverty of the sahel's people, and by the temporary success of their traditional techniques for surviving hardship.

Niger is a perpetual disaster area. It is ranked by the United Nations as one of the twenty countries in the world most severely affected by inflation and the rise in oil prices, as one of the sixteen least developed, and as one of the ten most prone to disaster. In the understated language of an AID report, Niger's development "constraints" are "extreme poverty, rising population, a small resource base, and poor overall economic prospects."

Niger has both more land and more poor land than any other country in the sahel. Four fifths of it is desert; of the remaining fifth, only seventy-seven thousand acres are irrigated and invulnerable to yearly fluctuations in rainfall.

Niger is also one of the most inaccessible and isolated of the independent African nations. It is one of thirteen landlocked African countries and one of only six countries on the entire continent without a railroad. The French had once planned to connect Niamey with Abidjan on the Ivory Coast by a so-called Niger Railway, but the line never reached beyond Ougadougou in Upper Volta. The only relic of this plan is Niamey's Hotel Terminus, built on the site of the envisioned railway station.

Air Niger, the national airline, owns two elderly DC-4's and a DC-3

170

piloted and serviced by French crews. They make twice-weekly trips between Niamey, Maradi, Zinder, Tahoua, Agadez, and the Arlit mines. When they break down, as they often do, they are sometimes out of service for weeks.

Living in this vast, isolated country at the time of the drought were between 4 and 4.8 million people (depending on the statistics consulted). Whatever the population, it was growing at one of the highest rates in the world, 2.7 percent a year. In 1972 government services for these people were provided by a budget of only $47 million (about one twentieth of the municipal budget of Washington, D.C.). The greatest proportion of this money was spent on modern services that benefited Niamey and Niger's elite; the total budget represented a $10 per capita expenditure for health, education, defense, and all government services (as compared with $1,700 in the United States).

Medical facilities in Niger are not simply primitive; they are barely existent. Malaria, tuberculosis, leprosy, dysentery, schistosomiasis, and measles are common diseases. In 1973 there were only sixty-one doctors to treat the entire country. There were regions the size of Massachusetts in the bush where three hundred thousand people were under the care of a single physician. Life expectancy at birth is thirty-seven years, but one out of five children dies before reaching the age of five. At the age of thirty most people appear to be fifty.

Those who manage to visit a hospital or dispensary receive little. They stand in line for hours for aspirin and antimalarials. Wounds are stitched up with unsanitary needles and patients develop serious infections. Vaccinations strike nerves and cause paralysis. In the bush, if a critically ill or injured person needs an ambulance to take him to a hospital, he must pay for the gasoline in advance.

The education system is of like quality. In 1973 fewer than nine thousand children were enrolled in secondary schools. Only 5 percent of the population is literate. The illiteracy rate of Niger's adult population, 99.1 percent, is the highest in the world.

A study of Niger's schools by the University of Montreal concluded that they are doing the country more harm than good, since they fail to educate students in the management of the agricultural and livestock

171

sectors so crucial to the economy. Instead, the schools produce a semi-educated, frustrated urban proletariat, trained for jobs that do not exist and disdainful of jobs that do. Among the handful of students who completed their studies abroad, only 22 of 342 were studying the veterinary sciences and agriculture.

Before the drought Niger had been becoming poorer. Since 1965 the gross national product had been rising an average of less than 1 percent a year, the population at 2.7 percent, turning a tiny economic advance into a deficit.

Niger has no nuclear reactors, fleets of Mercedes and Cadillacs, or huge mansions. The obscene discrepancy between wealth and poverty found in many poor countries is absent. What passes for an elite—government functionaries and traders—is small, and its material comforts and pleasures are modest. Many live in houses that would cost less than $50,000 in a suburban subdivision in the United States. Besides a few out-of-date shopworn goods in Niamey stores, opportunities for consumption are limited. A big night at the home of a middle-level bureaucrat usually involves sitting in canvas chairs on the rough concrete patio of a small rectangular house, drinking whiskey and listening to the radio. Government ministers often complain that prices in Dakar and Abidjan are so high and their budgets so small that when they visit these cities on official business they must stay in seedy hotels.

iii

By autumn of 1972 Niger's customary poverty and the stamina of its peoples could no longer disguise the disaster. The harvests of food and cash crops was the poorest yet. Malnutrition had become starvation.

Desert crossers arriving in Niamey reported seeing groups of nomads walking beside roads, begging for food, water, and transportation. A party of tourists who stopped to picnic at what appeared to be a deserted stretch of bush between In Gall and In Waggeur were instantly surrounded by a circle of silent, hungry people. Like statues, they stood without moving or talking, watching the tourists eat and then climb into their Land Rover to continue their journey. Only when they thought the car was out of sight did they scramble forward to tear at the remains of the meal.

During the autumn of 1972 this and other stories circulated in Niamey, Washington, European capitals, and the United Nations. Niger's representative to the United States, Ambassador Diallo, made many private requests for aid from the American government and the United Nations. He was hampered by his government's failure to declare openly that it was menaced by famine and to solicit assistance.

Even so, these overtures, as well as reports from their own ambassadors and representatives in the sahel, made it clear to the donors that the region was in grave trouble. In November, an American Drought Emergency Task Force, comprised of members of AID, the State Department, and the Department of Agriculture, evaluated the informal requests for assistance from the sahel governments. The task force recommended an extra 108,000 metric tons of American grain, less than the sahel countries had requested and an amount that failed to take into account the problems of transportation and spoilage that might reduce the amount delivered.

In February the FAO chartered an interdepartmental sahel working group, and on the nineteenth of the month the United Nations Economic Commission for Africa urged the sahelian countries to declare an emergency and request relief. But not until the end of March did the sahelian governments admit officially that their economies were in ruins, their lands devastated, and their people starving.

The delay between October 1972 and March 1973 was to be crucial. During the winter months the donors could have been stockpiling feed and food, enabling Atakor and his remaining animals to survive. Niger waited because statistics were so scarce and so chaotic that not until late in 1972 did the numbers reflect the tragedy building in the bush. Like the FAO's ineffectual Famine Early Warning system, Niger's statistics were a country-wide average and not broken down into regions. This made it impossible to identify the districts in which there had been virtually no harvest. There were also no figures to show how many animals had died.

In Niamey, where most of the government functionaries lived, not only was there little statistical evidence, but photographic or written documentation of the drought was scarce. Throughout the fall of 1972 Niger's newspaper, *Le Temps du Niger,* chronicled the arrival of foreign dignitaries—the president of Senegal, a Dahomian minister of development, King Faisal, the Mayor of Hamburg. It reported the travels of the president of Niger, Hamani Diori, to African and European capitals—he opened an African arts exhibition in Paris, stopped in Algiers, returned to receive the Soviet ambassador's credentials, made a state visit to Dahomey.

On the front page there were articles about the Olympic Games, the Common Market, the Organization of American States, numerous impotent West African political alliances, customs unions, and the travels of their accredited representatives. Little about Niger was to be found. Every day the temperatures in other African capitals were listed on the second or third page, never local temperatures or rainfall.

Stories about the drought were rare. In a September interview, the minister for finance, nomadic, and Saharan affairs referred to the "degradation of the conditions of life in the nomadic zone." A month later, Tuareg north of Niamey were said to have "mentioned the disappearance of their pasturelands" to the subprefect in Tillaberry.

In November the only drought headline told of a "Disquieting Cereal Situation in Mali." At the end of December an article reported that the Council of Ministers had called on all Nigerien resources to be mobilized to combat the effects of the drought. Then there was almost nothing until late February, when the FAO meeting was reported, with a foreign dateline and, as if it had little local importance, no editorial comment. Not until May 1973, two months after Niger declared a disaster, did *Le Temps du Niger* publish its first drought photograph, a cow's carcass lying on a cracked riverbed.

Niger also waited to ask for foreign help during these crucial six months because of pride. Since independence, Niger's elite had depended on foreign charity, primarily French, to subsidize their government's budget and to import their food, their furniture, and even their clothes. The pride of the Nigerien elite was pride in a nation state whose boundaries were created by France, a pride anchored in European nationalism. For the elite that ran this fragile state, to declare an emergency and ask for aid was an admission of what had always been true but unspoken, that their survival depended on European charity.

The question of Nigerien pride and French aid was never as thorny and complicated as in 1972. In January of that year President Diori asked France for more economic independence, including the right to trade and solicit help from other donors, a reduction of French advisors and teachers, and greater revenues from the uranium mines at Arlit.

Throughout the year there were incidents and misunderstandings. The French ambassador visited his sick wife in France and Diori announced that he was not welcome to return. The French retaliated by claiming that only the ambassador could sign aid agreements. For weeks assistance was stalled until the French backed down. The deterioration of Nigerien-French relations was punctuated by a ripe tomato that hit President Pompidou on the shoulder during a motorcade in Niamey in November. (These differences may also explain some of the reluctance of the French to give Niger emergency food aid.)

Niger also waited because the government perceived that an announcement of disaster and need would lead to a humiliating loss of sovereignty. In Niger, the dispenser of charity gains power over its recipients. A wealthy person who feeds a hundred people is more powerful than one who feeds only fifty. Nigeriens knew about the power of charity, and they feared it.

(Their fears were realized as soon as the country requested assistance. Niger had to confer with donors, particularly the United States, over such internal matters as how much donated grain the government could sell and at what price. Some of the donated grain was distributed free, and the rest was sold at a reduced price or released onto the open market. The monies from the sale of donated grain were kept by the government, supposedly to be applied against the costs of the free distribution. Thus the government had an incentive to sell as much as possible. Since

175

records were poor, some donors suspected the government was selling too much grain and making a profit exceeding distribution expenses.

The government's sensitivity to encroachment on its sovereignty was not confined to the sale of food. In response to a government request, a unit of the Dutch army was relieved of NATO duties and sent to Niger to distribute food. When the soldiers arrived, they were refused permission to enter the country because they were armed and unwilling to operate without their rifles. The Dutch failed to understand that the officials of a poor country can be touchy about its sovereignty and they accused the Nigeriens of being ungrateful.

This same misunderstanding kept an unarmed Canadian logistical unit from participating in the distribution of food. After the Dutch incident, the Canadians withdrew an offer to send a similar unit. They thought it would be unseemly to participate after the troops of a fellow NATO member had been rejected.)

At a meeting of the foreign ministers of Mali, Mauritania, Senegal, Upper Volta, and Niger, held at Ougadougou at the end of March 1973, the sahel countries finally appealed publicly to the United Nations and other national and private donor agencies for food to save their peoples.

During the spring of 1973 the donors met, organized, and created special organizations. Prestigious emissaries were sent to the sahel to assess the crisis. The most important mission was that of Raymond Scheyven, a former Belgian minister. Scheyven believed the situation was so dire that he sent telegrams from each of his stops to FAO headquarters in Rome urging that famine relief begin immediately. But a strike had paralyzed Italian postal services, so his cables didn't reach FAO until he himself had returned from the sahel.

Scheyven concluded that the sahelian people were closer to mass starvation than their governments realized. He recommended sending more food than they had initially requested, and he urged a massive airlift.

Donor agencies assume that requests for food from poor countries are exaggerated. Yet in the sahel the opposite proved true. "You will probably be surprised," said Scheyven, "as we were, at the considerable discrepancy between the aid initially requested and the amount that still has to be sent. How can this wide gap be explained? Apparently the interested governments were themselves unaware of the proportions of the catastrophe; they therefore underestimated its impact and only became aware of the gravity of the situation as the nomad and farm populations fled into the cities, the misery growing hand in hand with the widening famine and the decimation of the livestock.

"The painful experience of the last few months has proven the low efficiency of the various national services. Most of them are understaffed. But more often it is the sometimes total lack of financial means that paralyzes their functioning. For instance, if agricultural engineering services or hydraulic works, stockraising and agricultural services had vehicles, pumps, trucks, water tanks, reconnaissance aircraft, vaccines, thermos bottles, etc., many of the currently difficult situations might have been avoided."

iv

For the United States, Niger's reluctance to request aid was initially convenient. If a formal request had been made months earlier, the American response would have been embarrassing. Two thirds of the disaster relief funds appropriated by Congress for the 1973 fiscal year (July 1, 1972 to June 30, 1973) were already allocated for Vietnam. Also, because of drought around the globe, total world food production had declined in 1972 by 1 percent. Since the world population was growing at 2 percent, there was a 3 percent decline in available food per capita. To compensate, the United States increased its grain exports by 30 percent. American and world surpluses fell by 40 percent, and wheat reserves in the exporting countries fell to four weeks of world consumption.

Poor rains also caused substandard harvests in India, East Africa,

Central America, the Soviet Union, and China, creating a famine belt that circled the world. In 1972 they were all competing for dwindling American surpluses. The Russians were the most successful.

After its own disastrous harvest, the Soviet Union purchased American wheat for its citizens and feed for its animals. Previously, to compensate for grain shortages, Russian farmers had slaughtered their livestock. But by 1972 Soviet citizens had become accustomed to a better diet containing more meat, and the government wanted to avoid a massive slaughter which would decimate the national herd. By June 1972 it had contracted to purchase 20 percent of America's grain reserves. When this grain was needed for the sahel in 1973, it was already being loaded into ships destined for Soviet ports.

Besides having less available grain and money, the United States also had few economic or political ties to the sahel. All six sahelian countries were considered to be French responsibilities.

This sentiment had been reinforced by a 1967 State Department "Review of Development Policies and Programs in Africa," conducted by Edward Korry, then the American ambassador to Ethiopia. Because of the Korry Report, the United States not only did virtually nothing to develop the sahel between 1968 and 1973 but remained uninformed about sahel conditions. The report recommended that "the United States should continue to concentrate its major economic assistance in those key African countries where the United States has major economic development or political and security interests."

Since none of the sahel countries qualified for assistance under these criteria, AID field staffs were withdrawn from all capitals except Dakar and Niamey. The reductions were disguised by an allocation of American aid on a "regional" basis, whereby the favored countries and those losing aid were lumped into a single region, making it appear to the American Congress that some regions were actually receiving more assistance than before.

After March 1973 American policy changed dramatically. Within a year the United States had replaced France as the sahel's largest external donor, and by the end of 1973 it was supplying 40 percent of all food and monetary aid and promising huge grants to rehabilitate the region and make it "drought-proof." During the 1973 fiscal year (FY), America sent 156,000 metric tons of grain to the sahel; in FY 1974, 350,000 tons. By the end of FY 1973, American nonfood aid—medicine, airlifts, transportation—subsidies amounted to $4.7 million. By FY 1974 this sum was $25 million, and in June 1974 Congress voted an additional $63 million for short- and medium-range programs expected to show results within from three to five years: road repair, building of storage facilities, irrigation of land, and reclamation of pastures.

This change of policy came about because of successful lobbying for more aid to the sahel by AID officials, American black groups, and private donors. Among the Congressmen most receptive to this lobbying were Senators Kennedy, Brooke, and Javits, and Representative Diggs.

Press coverage helped the sahel lobby. During June and July, the *Washington Post* and *The New York Times* each carried seventeen articles about the drought. According to one AID official, "The press was extremely helpful, even though it was annoying at times, such as their 'sing-song' that we were letting 25 million people starve to death. It put the whole problem into people's living rooms. Prior to that, people had not heard of the place or the names of the countries. This coverage led to public support. . . . The public got ahead of the administration and of Congress."

Support from the American public for famine relief in the sahel was greater than anticipated. In July 1973 AID was receiving an unprecedented amount of mail, as many as three hundred letters a day, urging greater assistance. This response made a tremendous impression on agency officials and Congressmen, who also received many letters, and was reported to Secretary of State Kissinger. The CARE representative in Niger attributed a 70 percent increase in donations in 1974 to a sudden emotional giving tied to the press coverage of the sahelian drought.

There were many motives for this sudden American generosity. These included guilt about Vietnam; an internal momentum within AID to find both new positions and a new cause for personnel made redundant by the cessation of American aid in Vietnam, Cambodia, and Laos; and the romantic appeal of desert countries that had been unknown to the United States except through Foreign Legion films. Most of all,

American generosity was motivated by the maturing of a belief among the citizens of wealthy countries that they had a moral responsibility, not just to alleviate famine but to prevent it from occurring. The letters to Congressmen, donations to private agencies and churches, outrage in the press over delays and inefficiency in administering relief—these were the signs of the new sentiment.

This new concern was not always translated into prompt, efficient action in the sahel. There were six sahelian countries, unique in many respects, and dozens of donor agencies, many of which disagreed about philosophy and technique, responsible for the relief effort. In comparison with these other agencies, AID's performance in Niger was good. In fact, some of the representatives of these agencies in Niger, who admitted to having been critical of AID in the past, conceded that its operation was probably the most effective. Still, it was not until 1974 that AID had the personnel, supplies, and an understanding of the situation to enable it to operate effectively.

Even when food arrived in great quantities, too often it was administered tardily and inefficiently by the government. The relief supplies took so long to have any impact in the bush that a year later, during the summer of 1974, Tuareg were streaming into cities and refugee camps in even greater numbers than in 1973.

υ

In 1973, four thousand Europeans, mostly French (although to the Nigeriens, North Americans as well were regarded as "Europeans"), lived in Niamey. After 1960, colonial administrators were renamed advisors, and they were joined by other French technical experts and teachers. Many of these were "co-operants," young Frenchmen who worked in Niger and other ex-colonies for several years instead of serving in the French military.

During the drought, the French were joined by a polyglot group of foreign administrators, advisors, and specialists employed by the donors and the expanded foreign missions. Some were sent as the resident representatives of their organizations for two- and three-year periods; others came for a few months to do a specific job—fix trucks, seed clouds, study grasshoppers.

These Europeans stayed in Niger for a shorter period of time, were younger and more liberal than the traditional French residents, and were more likely to criticize what they found. According to an American livestock specialist who spent years in Niger as a Peace Corps teacher and returned during the drought as a consultant, "If there had been any members of the elite stranded in the bush who mattered, reporting on the drought, they would have found out about the magnitude of the drought much sooner in Niamey. Instead, the elite in Niger is a new tribe with its own unique social code. Its homeland is not the bush, but Niamey. Their survival depends on Europeans to provide money, technical advice, everything they need to make their tribe work. If the Europeans left, their tribe would be destroyed, but the traditional life in the bush would be largely unaffected."

The Niamey representative of a private charity was more blunt. "Progress for these people [the elite] is to become western in the most vulgar way. Few of them want to face the fact that they are the citizens of a very poor country, not of France."

These statements are representative of the lack of sympathy that the new Europeans had for the dilemma of the elite—a class of people suspended between their African heritage and their European educations and life-styles.

Other rivalries complicated the relief effort. In the former French possessions of West and North Africa, many of the French were convinced, sometimes correctly, that the United States wanted to replace them and become the dominant economic power. Many French now living in Africa also once served or lived in Algeria, and were still bitter over the Kennedy administration's support of the Algerian rebels. There were also rivalries and conflicts too numerous to list between the different relief organizations and the individuals in charge, to manage more and better projects and to have better entrées with the government.

181

Many foreigners who came to Niamey were consultants and "inspectors" who stayed for only a few days or weeks. The inspectors were from the donors' home offices; the consultants were from universities, and their studies, usually concerned with some aspect of the sahel and the drought, were for the most part financed by grants from the UN, AID, or a foundation. AID signed a $2-million contract with MIT's Center for Policy Alternatives to study the causes of the drought and make recommendations for projects that would reduce the sahel's vulnerability to future disasters. According to AID's representatives in Niger, the results of this study were unsatisfactory.

The donor representatives in Niamey are unanimous in condemning the study. Sandy Rotival, the UNDP representative in Niger, calls it an "insult" to the Nigeriens and says, "At the same time that this country [Niger] was fighting for its survival, MIT was carrying out a $2-million planning exercise and telling them how to organize themselves. The government officials resented it, but considered it part of the price they would have to pay for American aid. The graduate students MIT sent to Niger knew almost nothing about the country, and since they couldn't speak French very well, they knew little more by the time they left. American AID personnel, for whose benefit and enlightenment the study was supposedly being written, had to take them around and interpret for them."

Laura MacPhearson, one of those AID employees, says that "A lot of bright-eyed, overpaid graduate students and young professors came to Niger to learn about the drought from people—us—who had only arrived in the country a few months earlier. We had to waste a tremendous amount of time talking to them and interpreting for them. Somehow, their computers had forgotten to impress on them that the officials here spoke French. In most cases their French wasn't good enough to allow them to interview the Nigeriens themselves."

The head of AID's agriculture program in Niger, Jim Livingston, says, "The project must have been a vehicle for a graduate thesis. It didn't come close to fulfilling the contract, and at least a dozen glaring errors rendered it useless. AID instructed me to throw away the preliminary report and not to consult it."

182

The Nigerien officials also resented the inspectors and consultants. The inspectors reminded them of their humiliation, and the consultants consumed relief and development funds. President Diori told an American relief volunteer, "A donor announces a $500,000 development project and then later it turns out that half of this is going to be spent to pay the salaries and transportation for staff and consultants and to begin a cautious experimental project. So we never see much of this money. It goes back into the American economy, not ours. The excuse that the donors don't have enough information about our country is nonsense. People have been doing studies and plans here ever since independence. Our ministries have plans and projects for almost every region, but the donors keep commissioning new ones."

Among the most effective and useful of the foreigners was a cadre of ex-Peace Corps volunteers who had already spent years working in the bush in Niger or other West African countries, and who spoke the African languages as well as French. AID and other American volunteer agencies wisely hired them to administer and develop programs.

In the months following the declaration of a national emergency Niamey was inundated with foreign administrators, technical experts, academic consultants, free-lance volunteers, journalists, and disaster entrepreneurs with schemes to make arid lands bloom, rescue animals, and feed thousands quickly and cheaply.

Many of these foreigners and the agencies that they represented worked heroically to save lives and alleviate suffering. However, there was also competition, waste, and inefficiency which marred the relief effort.

An "at risk" population team was sent from the United States to study the refugees. But they arrived late in 1974 when there were fewer "at risk" people and the government had lost patience with these studies. The AID representative who took them around remembers that one man was ecstatic when he found a malnourished baby.

The Womens' Benevolent Association of a church in Pennsylvania sent crates with travel-size toothbrushes, Crest toothpaste, and a motel-size bar of Ivory soap, all wrapped in a white washcloth and tied with a red ribbon. A card was attached to each package that said "To the Tuaregs from Mrs.————."

A Dutch woman made several plane trips to Niamey with large suitcases filled with complicated mechanical toys that she handed out to Tuareg children.

An American doctor and his wife came to Niamey with automatic vaccination guns called ped-o-jets, and statistics to prove how many thousands of Nigeriens a day the ped-o-jets could vaccinate. They wandered between government ministries asking to be supplied with vehicles and gasoline so they could head into the bush and begin vaccinating. But the government, which ran its own modest program, was insulted and refused their requests. People in or near the cities had already been vaccinated and Niger's population (in the bush) is so scattered that it is absurd to imagine that thousands of people could be rounded up in order to make the program worthwhile.

The Carnation Milk company sent a hundred cases of a discontinued instant chocolate-flavor, nonfat powder. "Just add water. Makes one quart." Brown milk scared the Tuareg and they refused it. The farmers in the south were less discriminating; they ate the powder raw and became ill. Finally it was given to Peace Corps volunteers.

In Niamey the sudden influx of foreigners and money was highly visible. The donors, particularly UNICEF, scattered Land Rovers among government ministries. Hotels were filled to capacity. The construction business flourished, concrete villas went up in a few months, and the wealthy Plateau neighborhood expanded. New French restaurants and boutiques opened. In 1971 there were 39,927 air passenger arrivals; in 1973, there were 65,937. Niamey had become a famine boomtown.

7

Miriam
July 1973-April 1974
In Waqqeur – Tchin-Tabaraden

The hand that holds the brand will never be burned by the fire.
　　　　　　　　　　　　　　　　　　—Tuareg saying

*A*s soon as the taillights of the truck taking Atakor from In Waggeur to Abalack had disappeared, Miriam tied her infant daughter to her back and started walking toward Tchin-Salatin, another pumping station and well situated among strands of dead sand dunes about fifty miles to the west. (Atakor's two sons remained at In Waggeur.) Miriam's parents and her brothers and sisters were camped nearby. As she walked, she composed a poem describing how Atakor had tried to save himself in the bush. She would recite it when she arrived.

Since Miriam had given most of their remaining food to Atakor when he boarded the truck, she was forced to depend on the meager hospitality of Illabakan camps that lay between the two pumping stations. If the camps were deserted, she picked leaves and weeds and boiled them. If there was no water, she ate them raw.

She arrived at her parents' camp toward the end of June. For the next two months she watched small storms explode on the horizon. Banks of black clouds darkened the eastern skies, passed overhead, filled pools to the west or sprinkled the camp, and retreated east. To the south they washed out the Tahoua road.

Where grass grew, there was no water. The pump at Tchin-Salatin brought up water where there was no grass. There was no grain. At

187

Tchin-Salatin there was a little millet in the storehouses but Miriam had nothing to trade. She had sold her jewelry months earlier and her animals would have been worth little had they lived.

There were no cows. Without rain or pasture they died. People swept their bones into piles but were too weak to drag the carcasses away. Vultures picked at them and people ate them and became sick.

There were no herds of goats or sheep, only a few sickly survivors. Their udders were dry. Their owners killed them to prevent them from being stolen.

There were few men. They left during the soudure to search for pasture for their surviving animals or food and work for themselves. Many disappeared, and it was unclear whether they had died, committed suicide, or intentionally deserted their families. Some said later that they had left to avoid watching their families suffer.

Most of the men who remained were useless. They compared misfortunes and pushed themselves into hysterias of grief. They exaggerated their losses, doubling and tripling the size of their herds in the telling. They wandered, cried, slept, became catatonic. Men who were accustomed to physical hardship were unable to cope with mental anguish.

The women were stronger. Anchored around Miriam were her aunt, her aunt's two teen-aged sons, her sister and her sister's children. Miriam and the boys began to do some of the work traditionally performed by the bouzous. Camped nearby were other families who came to the pumping station hoping to find food and water. There were Peul, Arabs, and Tuareg from other tribes, maraboutique and vassal. Some had wandered across the border from Mali.

Miriam: "I worried that Atakor would stop loving me because I was not drinking milk and was becoming thin and ugly.

"At Tchin-Salatin we talked about the animals we lost, how we would eat, if we would live, when our husbands would return. We worried that the children would become sick and die, that our clothes would tear and leave us naked.

"Although I was with my family, I was lonely without Atakor. I wanted to join him but couldn't pay for a truck and was afraid that if I walked I would die. After I arrived at Tchin-Salatin he sent me news from Tahoua: He was staying with another Illabakan man. But later I heard nothing. I hoped that he'd send me money to join him or that he might return himself. Often I worried that I would never see him again.''

Miriam's family survived on the charity of friends and relatives who still owned something that could be exchanged for food. The Illabakan were accustomed to charity. Animals were often lent to destitute friends, who could drink their milk but not sell them, and were obligated to surrender any offspring to the original owner.

By the end of the summer of 1973 the reserves of even the more fortunate families had been exhausted and the people at Tchin-Salatin were destitute. They depended on sacks of grain that arrived from Tahoua by way of Tchin-Tabaraden. The trucks came infrequently, and brought only enough food to support each family for a few days. When the storms washed out the roads, nothing arrived for weeks.

The boys took wooden spears and hunted desert rats. Miriam skinned and cooked their catch. She broke up cracked gourds and pounded them into a paste. She cut strips of leather from the tent and boiled them.

She considered this work so shameful that she worked at night when no one could see her. However, she refused to do the most physically demanding job, pounding and cooking sorghum or millet. Instead, like other Illabakan women, she hired one of the few remaining bouzous. The bouzou charged a percentage of what he prepared, resold it, and saved enough to pay the drivers of the relief truck to take him south.

At the beginning of October, Miriam and her family followed the bouzou and walked ten miles to Tchin-Tabaraden, a larger pumping station and the administrative capital of the arrondissement. Tchin-Tabaraden, the "House of Beautiful Girls" in Tamashek, attracted nomads from all over the Azawak. They came to trade, pay taxes, visit the dispensary, and water their herds at rows of basins that the automatic pump filled with clean, cold water.

Tchin-Tabaraden's small sedentary population is made up of government officials, their servants, salaried workers, and traders who sell tea, sugar, onions, garlic, pimentos, salt, dates, millet, and sorghum from small mud-walled shops and open-air stalls. The officials are Hausa and Djerma living in banco houses built inside walled courtyards. The larg-

189

est cement house belongs to the subprefect, the senior official responsible for all the arrondissement's government services. Most of the other inhabitants live in small banco concessions or straw huts.

The town also has a modern water pump, a school doubling as a granary, and offices and houses for OFEDES—the government well-diggers, Water and Forests, the National Gendarmes, and OPVN, the official grain-marketing board charged with distributing relief supplies.

While Miriam was at Tchin-Tabaraden, there were four European residents. Two were American Peace Corps volunteers assigned to a nearby government reforestation project, one was a Frenchman, André Marty, working for the government to reconstitute Tchin-Tabaraden's pastures, and the last, Marty's wife who ran the dispensary.

Tchin-Tabaraden is dominated by sand. The town is sunk into a sandy, sloping plain ringed with waves of dead sand dunes which, unlike the shifting dunes to the north, theoretically stay in the same position year after year. Clumps of grass and small trees appear to grow directly out of the sand and dot the flat places between the dunes.

The dunes are immobile, but the sand on their surfaces is loose. Winds whirl it around like snow, piling it into drifts, burying grass, covering the windows of the subprefect's office. People sweep it from tents and huts with straw hand-brooms.

Sand dunes 300 feet high guard the dirt track running south 100 miles to Tahoua, the capital of the department. Eighty- to 100-feet-high dunes also ring the town to the north and east, and some buildings, including the water pump and the prefect's house, are anchored on their lower slopes.

ïï

When Miriam arrived at Tchin-Tabaraden, eight thousand sick and malnourished nomads were camped on the far side of the dunes, hidden from the village and the administrative buildings. By December 1973 almost a third of Niger's nomadic population was gathered in similar concentrations on the outskirts of cities, towns, and administrative centers. These concentrations were called refugee camps, but they were usually unplanned and lacked adequate health, housing, or sanitary facilities. They were more the result of people collecting where they hoped to be fed.

The government believed that it was easier to feed large groups of nomads rather than small ones scattered in villages and isolated camps, and encouraged the trend toward camps. In the final months of 1973, many refugees were heading for Niger's southern cities—Zinder, Maradi, and Niamey—hoping to better their chances of receiving regular rations. Those reluctant to embark on such a long migration were left behind in towns like Tchin-Tabaraden, where food supplies were intermittent and inadequate.

By the fall of 1973, forty thousand metric tons of food had been given to Niger by the United States alone. The drought had received widespread publicity, but food was still scarce at Tchin-Tabaraden and many other refugee camps. When food did come the refugees gorged themselves, eating a week's ration in two days.

In Tchin-Tabaraden, as in other parts of Niger, even if there was no free food, there was always some for sale, sometimes at a subsidized price. The traders, officials, and Europeans could afford it. The refugees on the far side of the sand dunes could not. There was hardly enough free food to prevent starvation, much less malnourishment and disease. Children and adults died of measles, tuberculosis, dysentery, pneumonia, and, as the nights became chillier, colds.

Between the second and sixth of October, while Miriam was moving from Tchin-Salatin to Tchin-Tabaraden, representatives of the foreign donors met with Nigerien officials in Niamey to determine how much relief food would be needed during the coming year to prevent starvation. They agreed that half of the population would need free or subsidized food for the next twelve months. But they disagreed as to how much they needed.

The United Nations computed that the average Nigerien required 2,250 calories daily (in 1965 the average Tuareg caloric intake was 2,600), and that, since this diet had a high cereal content, each person had to be supplied with 425 pounds of cereals a year, the highest figure

191

for any sahelian country. The Nigerien government complained that this estimate contained no margin for error and asked for 550 pounds per person. But these "consulatations" were between a government that had admitted its inability to feed its people and the foreign donors who were feeding them. The donors' figure prevailed.

In October 1973 Niger's real problem was not persuading the donors to send more food, but distributing the food they already had to people like the refugees at Tchin-Tabaraden.

The obstacles to delivering this food were official corruption, geographic isolation, poor roads, not enough vehicles, and inefficient use of what vehicles were available. Miriam and the refugees at Tchin-Tabaraden were at the wrong end of one of the least developed and most inefficient and expensive transportational systems in Africa.

The people of Tchin-Tabaraden needed fifty tons of food a day. Every day, between sixteen and eighteen three-ton trucks should have carried this food over the 100-mile rutted and sand-covered one-lane track between Tahoua and Tchin-Tabaraden. During October 1973 nothing approaching this tonnage was delivered to Tchin-Tabaraden.

Cotonou, in Dahomey, was the port closest to Niamey. Food and material unloaded in Cotonou had to be hauled over 640 miles of dirt and poorly paved asphalt roads to Niamey. The alternative was to consign the freight to Dahomey's ancient railway. Then it traveled 260 miles by train to Parakou and was transferred to trucks for the remainder of the journey.

The theoretical capacity of the Dahomey railroad is 1,050 tons a day; the actual capacity is 500, and because of outdated equipment and poor maintenance, only about 200 tons a day can actually be handled. (Perhaps the most that can be said for this railway is that before it was built in 1934, goods for Niamey had to be carried by porter and the trip took an average of seventy days.) Not all of this tonnage is food, and not all of it is destined for Niger. Some is consigned to Parakou or northern Dahomey. Thus the Parakou railway, Niger's most direct, convenient, and best all-weather link to the Atlantic, was only just capable of transporting the 50 tons of food a day needed solely for the refugees at Tchin-Tabaraden, not to mention the rest of the country.

Niger's other supply routes run 720 miles by rail or road from Lagos,

Nigeria, to Kano, and then another 165 by road to Zinder in the east of Niger or 140 to Maradi. Limited supplies can also be sent from Lomé, Togo, or Abidjan on the Ivory Coast. But all of these ports, particularly Cotonou and Lagos, the most important of them, are crippled by frequent strikes, bureaucratic inefficiency, and inadequate storage facilities.

Blaming Niger's inaccessibility entirely on its distance from the sea is misleading. There are no natural barriers, mountains or deserts, between Niger and the sea, only distance. The difficulties are really political and economic: absurd colonial boundaries hardened into unrealistic international frontiers and nationalist squabbles between coastal countries and their sahelian neighbors over port fees, customs duties, and access to docks.

Even after donated food was delivered to a Nigerien city, distributing it in the bush created even greater problems. At the end of 1972, Niger had only 4,400 miles of "roads," of which only 350 miles were paved and 49 miles two-lane. Most of the 350 paved miles were poorly maintained one-lane strips, lacking grading and drainage and constructed to accommodate light trucks hauling agricultural products, not heavy ones delivering relief food.

In all of eastern Niger, an area as large as Pennsylvania, there were in 1973 only seventy government vehicles, including small pickups and Land Rovers. There were also few competent mechanics, spare parts, or garages. Trucks that broke down in remote areas were parked on roadsides for weeks and sometimes months until a part and a mechanic arrived from Niamey, Maradi, or Zinder.

Like food, gasoline had to be brought up from the coast and then hauled over Niger's abysmal local roads. Niger has very few gasoline pumps; these are often dry for weeks, and when gasoline is available it is very expensive. The 1973 war in the Middle East and the oil embargo made gasoline even more expensive and scarce. By December of 1973 its price had risen 50 percent, and the cost of bringing fifty tons of cereals from Cotonou to Niamey and then to Tchin-Tabaraden was three times that of the cereals themselves.

After his inspection of the sahel in April 1973, Raymond Scheyven recommended that, since only a few weeks remained to stockpile food

193

before the rainy season made roads impassable, the donors should organize a massive airlift of food to Gao, Agadez, and Timbuctoo. The FAO issued a formal appeal for planes. Belgium, Canada, and the United States volunteered a total of twenty-one, less than half the fifty-one the FAO considered the bare minimum necessary, and the massive airlift never materialized. Of course, the individual donors had thousands of airplanes at their disposal, individually and collectively, through NATO. Yet, despite a request to that organization for planes from the EEC economic development agency, none were forthcoming.

At the end of July, at a meeting of the major donors in Abidjan, it was determined that because of short runways, a lack of maintenance and fuel storage facilities, the price and unavailability of fuel, the absence of night landing facilities, and frequent sandstorms, it was more efficient to use a small number of small planes than to mount the airlift the FAO had requested in the spring. This assessment, however, was formulated in hindsight. When a massive airlift was thought necessary, it was refused. The obstacles to an airlift cited by the donors at Abidjan could have been overcome easily by the sophisticated logistical skills of the donors' armies.

On October 29, 1973, a party of young Frenchmen left Abidjan in 50 Citroën cars for a 4,490-mile road rally, the first "Raid Afrique." Their route lay through Upper Volta and then to Niamey, Tahoua, the Ténéré desert, and north across the Sahara to Tunis. The rally was organized by Citroën (a French automobile manufacturing company that also made trucks) and the Total gasoline company (with stations in Niger) that was under the patronage of the French Secretary of State for Youth and Sport. The rally arrived on November 2, and the following day the cars raced on through Tahoua, In Waggeur, and Agadez. A chartered plane patrolled the route, reporting to mechanics and support vehicles whenever a car broke down or needed replacement parts.

Even when grain was delivered to Niger's regional centers, there was still a chance that it would never reach its intended recipients. It rotted in warehouses, or was hoarded, stolen, or sold on the open market.

Some grain was hauled in trucks owned by government ministers or their relatives, which may have accounted for the reluctance of the civilian government to allow the army to haul relief supplies. A portion of the cargo on these trucks was sometimes delivered to private warehouses and later sold. OPVN, the government grain-marketing board, was entrusted with the responsibility for selling and distributing relief food during the drought. Because OPVN had no representatives in Cotonou, no one in Niamey knew how much grain had been offloaded at the docks.

Even if the truckers were honest, OPVN's lack of control made it tempting for officials who received the grain to divert some into their own storerooms and give it to their relatives or villages.

Honest officials could show so little initiative and had so much respect for bureaucratic rules and procedures instilled by French training that the result of their decisions was often the same as if they had been corrupt: Those who needed food did not get it. During October 1973 Niger's star reporter, Amadou Ousmane, traveled through the southeast of the country. In one subprefecture he discovered that twelve tons of sorghum had been sitting in a warehouse for weeks. Meanwhile, people from the region had gathered around the building and kept vigil there, waiting for the sorghum to be distributed. When Ousmane asked the subprefect for an explanation he was told: "I am waiting for clearance from OPVN in Niamey before I release the food."

In another bush center, Ousmane saw people who had walked twenty-five miles or more from villages where there was no food to a distribution center where there was food. Yet he noticed that vehicles belonging to another government agency, one which had no official responsibility for distributing food, were idle. When he asked the subprefect in the town why he didn't use these cars and trucks to take food to people stranded in the bush, the reply was, "The idea never occurred to me."

In the village of Goudoumaria, also in the east of Niger, there had been substandard harvests for five years. Yet, according to Ousmane, because the village was geographically within the southern part of Niger, its people were ineligible for food because of an OPVN decision that in the south food could be sold at a reduced price but not given away.

When Ousmane's articles were published in Niamey's *Le Temps du Niger*, he was arrested and, according to him, confined and tortured by the police. Eight days later he was released and permitted to return to the newspaper.

The misuse and abuse of modern charity by some of Niger's civilian officials contrasts with the success of the traditional forms of charity among villagers, families, and tribesmen that saved so many Nigeriens from starvation. (Sometimes, what is seen as corruption by the modern state is really traditional charity: caring for one's own family and people first. Officials who seemed to be callous or corrupt from the prospective of relief organized on a national level could be extraordinarily generous on a traditional level.)

Peter Marshall, a young British mechanic who traveled throughout Niger servicing the Bedford trucks donated by the British government, witnessed many astonishing acts of traditional charity, of people starving themselves and endangering their lives by sharing their food with others: "In one village only four animals were left alive and all were owned by the same man. Although he was very thin and undernourished, he fed his animals well and they looked quite reasonable. Everyone else in the village was drinking their milk, and he wasn't taking any more than anyone else.

"At a nomadic camp I saw a sixty-year-old man, the leader, who was so weak from hunger he could hardly walk. But since he was the leader he had to share whatever he got. He did. He could have survived in comfort but he shared with his people and suffered with them. Would I have done the same thing? I doubt it."

Instead of building on this charity, the nation state superimposed an alien philanthropy of bureaucratic regulations. Some Nigerien functionaries found it difficult even to understand a charity that was administered on a national and international basis. One subprefect told an AID administrator that, although he was thankful for the American sorghum, he couldn't understand why it had been given to Niger and said, "If you (United States) were suffering from a drought we wouldn't help you."

* * *

iii

Miriam: "We were hungry at Tchin-Tabaraden. The trucks arrived with sorghum and we ate for a day. Then we waited for the next truck.

"When the food arrived it was like the Cure Salée. There was no Cure Salée that year and we pretended we were at In Gall. We sang, clapped our hands, and danced.

"If there had been more food at Tchin-Tabaraden, it would have been like a continuous Cure Salée since there were so many people camped together, and when we were given sorghum we had something to celebrate."

A Belgian woman who edits Niger's weekly newsmagazine remembers that in the Agadez refugee camp she "couldn't believe it. I expected to see people quiet and suffering, but the day I arrived there was a distribution of food followed by singing and even dancing. But as the people became hungry again the celebrations dropped off."

When modern relief failed and there was no free sorghum to sing about, Miriam relied on traditional charity again. "We lived because we shared whatever we had, because we harvested fornio, and because Mohammed and Khamed Moussa gave us food. When there was no food we fasted and prayed."

When the French reorganized the nomadic tribes of the Azawak into seven groups after the 1917 uprising, they placed the Illabakan in the third group, led by the Kel Nan noble tribe. The chief of this group was Mohammed El Khorer, son of the El Khorer who died near Agadez during the 1916 rebellion. Mohammed El Khorer complained that the French tribal system had reduced him to a man concerned only with "taxes, pastures, and the quarrels of women."

Before the drought Mohammed was the richest man in the Tchin-Tabaraden arrondissement. His herds were so large that he claimed to have no idea of their numbers. Many were entrusted to the care of shepherds who led them to pastures in Algeria and Libya.

During 1973 his animals died (a few camels and cows sent to pastures

197

south of Tahoua survived). According to Khamed Moussa, the Illabakan who had been a deputy and was now a government official in Tchin-
Tabaraden, Mohammed lost 3,000 cows, 4,000 sheep and goats, and
hundreds of camels.

In July, after suffering his worst losses, Mohammed decided to shift
his camp from Dembouten, fourteen miles from Tchin-Tabaraden, to a
location only three and one-half miles away. Because his pack animals
had died he mortgaged his house in Niamey, bought a used Land Rover,
and moved his belongings, sick animals, family, and other tribesmen.
After he finished, Khamed Moussa used the car to deliver food to isolated camps in the north of the arrondissement and to transport the sick and
starving to Tchin-Tabaraden.

Khamed Moussa: "Compared to the refugees in the bush, the ones at
Tchin-Tabaraden were lucky. In Tchin-Tabaraden they died of diseases,
but in the bush they died of starvation. During my trips I often came
across the bodies of animals and people.

"Some waited until their last animals died and then were trapped in
the bush without food, water, or a way to escape. I drove many of them
to Tchin-Tabaraden, but some didn't want to leave the bush and insisted
on staying."

The Illabakan were accustomed to eating wild grass, berries, and
melons as a supplement to their diet of millet and milk. No labor was
more strenuous than gathering, pounding, sifting, and cooking fornio,
the collective name given to edible wild grasses. (Many of these grasses
are considered weeds in other countries.) To produce a single meal
could require two days of work; to fill a single bowl, scouring acres of
land was necessary.

During the late fall and winter, bouzou women rode into the bush on
donkeys to harvest fornio. A few days or a week later they returned,
their baskets bulging with crabgrass-like grasses, hard red juju berries,
acidic white melons, and sharp nettles. Even after the bouzous were
liberated, they continued harvesting fornio, and the Illabakan paid them
to collect what was free.

When Miriam joined one of the numerous female expeditions that left
Tchin-Tabaraden in November to harvest fornio, it was for the first

time. An old bouzou, Takalafa, organized the women and accompanied them. They walked for a day before finding enough fornio to make a harvest worthwhile. What few grasses had flourished near the camp had been eaten or trampled by the animals.

There were many species of fornio. Each was harvested in an order of preference determined by taste, availability, need, and the labor required for preparation. The most difficult to gather was a nettle called cram-cram, which looks like a burr but, unlike a burr, breaks up into dozens of tiny prickles, each as sharp as a needle and so fine it can hardly be seen. These prickles stick on the hoofs of animals and fall off around water points and migratory routes. They also pierce human skin and stick to clothing.

The Illabakan were afraid of cram-cram. They knew that cows and sheep could be blinded by it and feared that its prickles might land in their own eyes during the winnowing and beating. This fear, and the exceptionally long and arduous labor needed to harvest it, made cram-cram a food of last resort. Bouzous gathered it in large quantities only when other grasses and grain were scarce.

During the 1919 famine, when grasshoppers ravaged the Adar and the Azawak, the Tuareg also harvested a cram-cram called "agerouf" in Tamashek:

> O daughters of our tribe!
> Of Temina, of Iqqadi and Assassa
> And those of Douroum and Assakafa,
> And of the dune of Amoulas,
> And of Ataya, Amanr'is and Takouba,
> Of Werzey and Tilia
> And of D'Ajmelli and the dune of Agoda.
>
> Leave your chores!
> Leave chasing after the camels and kissing them!
> Look up to the sky
> Where the invasion of grasshoppers is coming.
> Not a husk has been stored
> That they have not found and devoured.
> They have ransacked Kalfou and pillaged Terimma,
> Plundered Gougoufema and Arewa

And the Kingdom of Tahoua.
They have attacked Barmou so it no longer exists!

This year the famine is moving toward us,
This year the grasshoppers are moving in a formation,
They carry rifles and swords,
They are leaving only the bitter gourd behind them.
This year the Calabash spoon is empty,
We have drunk the last of the milk,
Now that even the bitter gourd and jujube are exhausted,
The agerouf is king, all-powerful, our last food.
We foolishly threw it away last summer,
Now we harvest and eat it as we lie
Next to those who are telling of
Hunger, exhaustion, and starvation.

Takalafa waded through patches of cram-cram. She banged the
weedy stalks with a long stick and nettles fell to the ground. Miriam and
the other women followed, crawling forward on hands and knees. They
carried hand-brooms, hard, dried weeds tied together with roots, with
which they brushed the nettles into piles. Hunched-over black forms
moving in and out of the small puffs of dust raised by their passing, they
swept up sun-bleached nettles, broken stalks, and discarded pebbles,
scouring the land for its final resources. When they had denuded one
area, they scooped the piles into straw baskets and dumped the nettles
from the baskets into a blanket.

After three days of work, they tied full baskets to the donkeys and returned to Tchin-Tabaraden. When they passed an anthill, Takalafa
swept away the top with her stick and dug out deposits of wild seeds,
storing them in a knotted cloth. She pulled up roots which could be sold
as cords or fashioned into sieves to winnow cram-cram. She collected
firewood, some to sell, some to use for cooking.

At Tchin-Tabaraden they poured the nettles onto a mat and Takalafa
beat them with a long, curved stick. Before the drought the bouzou men
had done the pounding. When Takalafa tired, Miriam took her place;
imitating her movements, she bent over the mat and separated grain
from sand, pebbles, stalks, and other impurities. She shoveled what remained into a basket and tossed it in the air. The lightest powder blew

200

away in the wind and the grain fell back into the basket. She stopped to pull prickles from her fingers. She looked away, to protect her eyes and to see who was watching.

The grain was poured into a hollow tree trunk and pounded with a club. Miriam pounded, sifted, pounded again, and winnowed one last time. The grain, reduced to a farina, required hours of boiling before it was edible. Miriam, Takalafa, and other women who had gone on the expedition shared the hot meal. Miriam mixed her portion with water and gave her family and dependents, who now numbered ten, one large bowl of porridge.

iv

*W*hile American food sent months earlier seldom arrived at Tchin-Tabaraden, American technology watched from above as Miriam gathered cram-cram. Every eighteen days, the Earth Resources Technology Satellite (ERTS), part of a program designed to chart the earth's topography, passed over Tchin-Tabaraden, taking color photographs. Each represented an area one hundred miles square. When the photographs were assembled in sequence, they showed Niger's fossilized valleys, the Air Mountains, and the dark laterite plateaus around In Waggeur. Visible as usual on the pictures of November 22 and December 10, 1973, were the lines of dead sand dunes around Tchin-Tabaraden.

When ERTS took another sequence of pictures of Tchin-Tabaraden on December 27, image E-1523-29331 showed pronounced lines, 150 miles in length and up to 2 miles wide, running from east to west, almost perpendicular to the normal direction of the dead dunes. The stationary coating of iron oxides gave the dunes their usual reddish-yellow color. But the new lines were beige, dusted by white quartz sand from eroded soil which, before the drought, had been protected by vegetation.

In May 1973, a month before Atakor and Miriam left In Waggeur, a drought analysis laboratory had been established at the Goddard Space

Flight Center in Greenbelt, Maryland. It was supervised by Norman MacLeod, a professional agronomist. MacLeod identified the new lines as moving sand streams, an alarming extension of the kind of living sand dunes ordinarily found much further north. The streams were extensive and fast-moving; in only eighteen days they had suddenly appeared on the Tchin-Tabaraden photographs.

Live dunes were forming where there had been forests thirty years before, grazing lands three years earlier, and dead dunes just three weeks previous. The dunes were covering rangeland and marginal cropland, and trapping the Tchin-Tabaraden refugees in a dust bowl. According to MacLeod, "The kind of erosion we observed around Tchin-Tabaraden is the real end point of the desertification process. It means that soil is being removed and is not just deteriorating. . . . This is what happened in the midwestern dust bowl during the 1930s." (The ERTS pictures also showed up a mysterious green polygon near the Niger-Mali border in a region of fixed sand dunes and little surface water.

MacLeod made inquiries at the Nigerien Embassy in Washington and at the State Department. No one could identify the strange anomaly. He went to Niger to investigate. Ministers and even President Diori appeared ignorant or vague. Finally, MacLeod chartered a helicopter and flew over the polygon. It was the Ekrafane Ranch, financed by French interests and controlled partially by Madame Aissa Diori, the president's wife.

Access to the ranch was controlled by guards, and there was a fence around its perimeter. Inside, wells had been carefully spaced and the number of cattle regulated. Even during the drought, these animals were healthy.)

Since MacLeod became known as the drought's "space expert," he was chosen to brief the Skylab Three astronauts at NASA headquarters in Houston in August 1973. In an hour he summarized the causes of the drought and told them what to look for—dust and cloud movements, vegetal patterns, the color and distribution of surface water—when their spacecraft passed over Africa.

Skylab circled the earth every ninety minutes. The Himalayas, the Mediterranean, and a piebald African continent with a "white" Sahara were visible in their entirety. A "bland" sahel was blanketed by brown, dusty clouds.

On January 22, 1974, dust storms obscured Tchin-Tabaraden, Niger, and the sahel to the Skylab observers. The pilot described the view to Mission Control: "I've noticed it now for two days running, and this is a pervasive and extensive cirrus development which extends off the coast of Somalia and the southern end of the Arabian peninsula out into the Indian ocean for 1,500 to 2,000 miles. As far as you can see. The particular character of the cirrus clouds is that they are dirty-looking, and appear much darker than other clouds in the same area."

He observed the same phenomenon over West Africa: "The cirrus clouds I saw today at Sokoto, Nigeria [fifty-seven miles from the Niger-Nigeria frontier] had the same appearance. They had a striated texture of a cirrus cloud, but were dirty. It looked like a jet-stream path. It didn't seem to be associated in any way morphologically with the lower clouds that were in the area."

Just south of the sahel, in the regions not obscured by dust storms, the astronauts could see one source of these dusty clouds: firelines ignited by farmers practicing slash-and-burn agriculture and hunters flushing game from the underbrush. These fires blazed across Nigeria, the Cameroons, and the Central African Republic. At night the fires burned brightly; during the day their dark plumes of smoke blanketed the landscape.

The astronauts were seeing Stone-Age images flickering across a giant rounded map of Africa, like globes in movies that burst into flame to identify wars and native uprisings. This time the fires were real, a desperate, ages-old technique practiced by a people destroying their land in order to survive.

They saw clouds heavy with dirt and dust stripped from new deserts, kicked up by herds of starving animals, and joined by the small clouds raised by Miriam and her companions as they swept for cram-cram. The winds carrying these dusts swept across a land as foreign to the white shirts, glowing dials, and computers of Mission Control as Mars, transporting the delayed consequences of seventy years of disastrous development.

203

v

*D*uring December and January relief trucks from Tahoua continued to arrive at Tchin-Tabaraden infrequently and sporadically. Yet without what little food that did arrive, Khamed Moussa believes that "no one in the arrondissement would have survived the first six months of 1974."

Refugees continued to arrive throughout the winter. Pat McDuffie, one of the American Peace Corps foresters who watched the accumulation, said, "I'd go to sleep and wake up the next day to find the camp had moved a hundred yards overnight and now contained three or four hundred more people. People were always coming. There was a lot of coming but very little going. By February 1974 we had about 13,000 refugees camped in the dunes outside Tchin-Tabaraden. By July there were 40,000."

The astronauts and the ERTS photographs from an altitude of five hundred miles were forerunners of a sudden outside interest in the Tchin-Tabaraden refugges. On February 4, President Diori left Niamey for a tour of the Tahoua department. He stopped en route at Birni-n'Konni for the inauguration, with President Gowon of Nigeria, of a newly paved fifty-seven-mile road from Birni-n' Konni to Sokoto, Nigeria. He continued to Tahoua, where, to the dismay of his chief of staff, Lieutenant-Colonel Kountché, he failed to reprimand the Tahoua prefect for inefficiency and neglect that had become notorious.

News of the president's visit had already circulated among the refugees at Tchin-Tabaraden. In the week preceding his arrival they moved closer to the town, crowding into a smaller area and causing sanitary problems. On the morning that the president was scheduled to arrive, a few Tuareg mounted camels and waited five hours along the airport track. The nomads blamed the subprefect and other lower-level officials for their troubles. President Diori was still popular.

Accompanied by the subprefect and an entourage, Diori inspected Tchin-Tabaraden. He waded through sand separating rows of tents and mats and saw thin, sick, malnourished women and children. Under one tent he found a six-year-old Tuareg boy so emaciated that his mother held him between her hands as if he were a feather. Diori asked if the child was sick.

"No," answered the woman, "only hungry."

Diori turned to the subprefect and said, "I want you personally responsible for seeing that this child is always fed."

As he walked past Peul with only skin loincloths to protect them from the Azawak nights—temperatures often dropped into the low thirties— he demanded to know why no one had told him the situation was so desperate. The subprefect replied that he had written, but his letters must have been lost or intercepted.

He might have spoken the truth. Officials in Niamey tried to keep bad news to themselves. Some were afraid it would reflect poorly on the competence of their ministries. Others did not want to "bother" the president. They knew Diori preferred to concentrate on pan-African and world affairs. Shielding him from the horrors of the refugee camps was not difficult.

However, someone had written. A month earlier, Khamed Moussa had sent a letter describing the conditions at Tchin-Tabaraden. Diori said that he had never received it.

Diori was a compassionate man. At Tchin-Tabaraden he was confronted suddenly and dramatically with the failures of his government. He telephoned Niamey and demanded that food be sent immediately. He was unaware that over a thousand tons of food were already sitting in government warehouses in Tahoua, only a hundred miles away. Unable to sleep, he woke the subprefect at 1:30 A.M. and made him open the OPVN warehouse that held food marked for sale at a reduced price. Diori paid for and distributed it himself. He also bought mats and clothing and carried them to the shivering Peul.

To prevent the refugees from eating a week's ration in a single day, Diori ordered a daily rather than a biweekly or weekly distribution of food. He sent Khamed Moussa into the bush to open distribution centers. (According to Khamed Moussa, Diori was sobbing so much that his instructions were hard to understand.) He sent vitamins and clothing when he returned to Niamey. His wife flew to Tchin-Tabaraden with a delegation of Nigerien women bringing blankets and supplies. The government announced a special emergency program for stricken nomadic

zones. Articles about the camp appeared in *Le Temps du Niger.*
Diori gave speeches in Niamey. He said, "I survived the great famine of 1931. But since that time I have never seen a spectacle so poignant as that which exists presently in Tchin-Tabaraden. . . . In addition to famine and sickness, the wretched refugees live outdoors exposed to a drying wind and nights much colder than those known in Niamey."

This activity was similar to the sudden explosion of concern that followed Diori's visit to Agadez in 1973. It was as if the drought were only serious when and where the president himself witnessed its devastating effects. And, as had happened at Agadez, as soon as he publicized the plight of the refugees, chartered planes and Land Rovers started arriving in Tchin-Tabaraden. Their cargo was an assortment of Nigerien and European visitors, some necessary but others, for want of a better word, "tourists."

The first wave of planes brought the most necessary visitors, the resident representatives of the relief organizations, the veterans of Biafra, Bangladesh, Vietnam, and other disasters. They wrote reports and sent cables to Rome, Paris, New York, and Washington, cables containing the words "urgent" and "desperate." They were followed a month or two later by the people to whom the cables had been addressed—supervisors, trustees, consultants, and representatives from universities and newspapers. Stories datelined Tchin-Tabaraden started to appear in newspapers in Europe and the United States.

Miriam: "I was afraid of Europeans. When I was a small girl some French soldiers came to our camp in trucks. The children who attended the school went for rides in the trucks. Since our parents kept us away from the school, most of them were bouzous. We hid because we had been told the Europeans would eat us. I hid under a blanket, but lifted it to watch the bouzous riding in the trucks. This was the first time I saw trucks or Europeans.

"Europeans [tourists] often drove through In Waggeur but I never saw them up close. Before the drought a Frenchman and his wife visited the camp. Until I came to Tchin-Tabaraden they were the only Europeans I had been next to."

Miriam had more contact with Europeans than most of the other refugees. There were Tuareg at Lazaret who, until the drought, had never seen a European or an automobile. There were Peul north of Dakoro who, according to a Peace Corps volunteer, "believed that Europeans were immortal, were never born, never died, and dropped from the sky like parachutists." On the rare occasions when they saw a European, it was always an adult—a volunteer, a soldier, or a technical supervisor. Since they never saw a child or an old person, they concluded that they did not exist.

Mark Neukirk had been an IBM executive in the Netherlands before the drought. He resigned to become the OXFAM representative in Niger. Neukirk drove a Land Rover to Tchin-Tabaraden shortly after President Diori's visit. He had planned the trip earlier, in January, after hearing rumors that conditions at Tchin-Tabaraden were grim.

According to Neukirk, "When I arrived at Tchin-Tabaraden, the relief supplies were inadequate and there was a measles epidemic. Many of the people were sick with dysentery and pneumonia.

"While I was there some OPVN trucks arrived with sorghum, and I was impressed with the dignity of the people. There was none of the pushing I had witnessed at the other camps. The people who distributed the food went down the lines of tents and scooped the sorghum out of sacks into people's bowls. One man walked behind the sack with a notebook recording the names of the families and the amounts they were given. The people who received the food were very quiet.

"When I first arrived the people had not received food for a number of days. They were exhausted, and one thing that impressed me about the camp was its silence. Most of the time the refugees were too tired to move or make noise. They sat in the open or gathered firewood when they had something to cook. Of course, this was very difficult since there were very few trees or bushes left.

"While I was visiting the camp there was a sandstorm. You couldn't hear the people but you could hear the wind. Many were living and sleeping in the open with no protection, and they sat with their backs to the wind. Drifts of sand built up behind them and ridges of sand formed in their eyebrows. They looked like sand statues. As I walked through the camp there was so lttle visibility that I couldn't see from one island of sand statues to another. Since I couldn't see any end to the camp, I had the feeling that these islands of suffering people continued endlessly into the desert.''

Many visitors to Tchin-Tabaraden blamed the subprefect for conditions at the camp. Neukirk was generally impatient with the mentality of many Nigerien bureaucrats. He said, ''Some of the officials really live in a different country from the rest of the people here. It's hard for them to face the poverty when they don't have to.'' But he was sympathetic to the plight of the subprefect. ''There was nothing the subprefect could do. He never received enough food. He was tired, harassed, and couldn't cope with the situation. I don't think he was an evil or corrupt man; he was just overwhelmed.''

The refugees at Tchin-Tabaraden that Neukirk describes appear to have been either resigned to their fate or extremely disciplined. Peter Marshall, the British mechanic, witnessed a more common reaction to the arrival of the grain trucks. He said, ''There seemed to be four or five hundred people lying on the sand with shreds of clothes and little bits of things, their possessions. Some had been lying in the sand for weeks, waiting for our trucks to arrive with food. Then as soon as the trucks stopped they got up from the sand and rushed us. Some even tried to climb into the trucks. In fact, even after we unloaded the sacks of grain, people jumped into the empty trucks and swept them out to collect grain that had fallen out of the sacks. Others got into the trucks and wanted to stay, to go anywhere, anywhere we were going.''

When Terry Lambacher, a young AID administrator and former Green Beret in Vietnam, visited Tchin-Tabaraden, he was surprised that it seemed to be deserted. He had just come from a highly visible camp of 6,000 people gathered around the Abalack pump. He approached Tchin-Tabaraden from the east, driving the last three hundred yards over loose sand dunes. When he arrived, he saw only ''the government buildings, the pump, and about seventy-five banco and a few cement houses. The first thing I asked the subprefect was 'Where are all the people?' He said 'Walk over the hill' and he pointed to one of the dunes.''

Lambacher struggled through the loose sand and, when he got to the top of the hill, saw a "tent city of about 10,000 people stretched out in front of me. 'Holy cow,' I thought. 'Now I know how Custer felt.'

"Most of the refugees were Tuareg women and children. There was no sanitation and some of the children had bloated bellies. All were gaunt. I saw very few skin tents. Many refugees, I was told, had sold or eaten their camel skins. Most people lived under straw mats or in the open."

Lambacher arrived in Niamey in January 1974 with the authority to give two-and-a-half million AID dollars to Nigerien government agencies for "high-risk" relief and rehabilitation projects that would show rapid results. He invested the money in reforestation, animal health, the construction of warehouses in food deficit areas, and the repair and enlargement of Niger's small fleet of vehicles.

He visited Tchin-Tabaraden to see how this money could help refugees stranded in nomadic areas. Like most of the visitors, he went to the dispensary and talked with Madame Marty. He learned that in a camp of 13,000 people, many of whom were undernourished children, there was only one bottle of vitamin A and only a few of Nivaquine, an anti-malaria drug.

Between February and May 1974, when European visitors to Tchin-Tabaraden were increasing, the refugees, whose resistance to disease was dangerously low because of malnutrition, continued to die.

Traditional Tuareg burials are quick and unelaborate. The body is washed, wrapped in a white sheet, and buried. At the grave a marabout reads verses from the Koran. Family and friends mourn, then slaughter an animal and eat it.

At Tchin-Tabaraden the dead were placed in shallow holes dug by relatives and friends. In the winter of 1973-1974 Pat McDuffie often rode his camel past small, lone groups of refugees who had walked a mile or two from the camp. He soon discovered that they were burying their families.

As people became too weak to dig holes, small mounds began to appear around the camp. Bushes were piled on top to keep animals from the bodies. When six or seven people died at once they were laid in a mass grave at the foot of a tree that had escaped the search for firewood.

The tree was felled so that it covered the grave and protected it from wild dogs. When the trees were gone, graves were planted with a weed that grew quickly during the dry season. It was too milky and full of latex to tempt the remaining goats. Soon the only clumps of grass near Tchin-Tabaraden were those growing over these burial mounds.

There was a fenced-off tree nursery a few miles outside town. It was part of a reforestation program that continued during the drought under the direction of the Nigerien Office of Water and Forests. After President Diori's visit, the subprefect became sensitive about conditions at the camp. He finally forbade the foresters to remove the sand that accumulated inside the nursery during the frequent windstorms. (He was afraid that it would be dumped outside the town and mistaken by visiting dignitaries for burial mounds.)

Madame Marty—and two Nigerien paramedics who could give injections, deliver babies, and sew stitches—operated the Tchin-Tabaraden dispensary. They were responsible not only for the 13,000 refugees but also for the 100,000 people in the arrondissement.

The dispensary buildings contained a storeroom, an office, a treatment room, a laboratory, and beds. Madame Marty and the paramedics worked sixteen-hour days attending the mothers and sick children who formed long lines around the buildings. They were too busy to visit the patients in the camp. The remedy for most sick refugees was a gruel of salt, millet, milk, and other foods purchased by the Martys at the market with their own money. A European who visited the camp a number of times said that for every month she worked in the dispensary, Madame Marty aged a year.

One of the biggest killers at Tchin-Tabaraden was measles. There was a government vaccine program but it was hampered by a shortage of vaccine and vaccinators. The Peace Corps volunteers were asked to help, but at least one, after seeing the condition of the children, refused: "I wanted to help Madame Marty vaccinate the children, but once I saw them close up I knew I couldn't do it. They were so thin you just couldn't find any meat on their bones. I'd already noticed that many of the Tuareg children had been paralyzed from shots that struck nerves, so I was afraid of crippling them."

Sandy Rotival, an American, was the senior United Nations official in Niger during the drought. He was also the resident representative of the United Nations Development Program (UNDP) in that country. Rotival is a blunt and dynamic man; an economist, a career civil servant, a professional with years of experience in the sahel, he has seen starvation during tours of duty with both the UNDP and AID.

Rotival flew to Tchin-Tabaraden in March 1974. He now says the situation there was the most desperate he had ever witnessed anywhere: "There were constant sandstorms while we were at Tchin-Tabaraden. It was a windy day with a yellow horizon, and I remember walking over that hill and seeing endless rows of tents and mats set up as wind breaks. There was only a distance of a few feet between the refugees' shelters.

"Many didn't have any shelters at all, and I remember a group of Peul lying prostrate on the ground. Most of the men were either very young or very old and the children were the most desperate of all . . . I didn't visit a single tent in which someone was not prostrate, just too weak to move.

"The people moved very slowly, erect, and no one begged. While I was walking through the camp I witnessed the arrival of a caravan of several donkeys. One person walked, the rest rode, and three people were tied to the donkeys' backs. One of these was a woman who looked like a skeleton. She was unconscious or dead. Her eyes were open and you could see that some vitamin deficiency had caused them to become very milky.

"I was so shocked by what I saw at Tchin-Tabaraden that I felt like crawling into the sand and disappearing."

As if in a grainy, slow-moving nightmare, visitors to Tchin-Tabaraden waded over sand dunes, through sandstorms, expecting to find a refugee camp. What they found more nearly resembled a concentration camp.

Like a concentration camp, Tchin-Tabaraden had a façade of life-sustaining services: a hospital, an administrative presence, and a periodic distribution of food. Also like a concentration camp, the hospital was understaffed and undersupplied, the administrative structure worried about burial mounds and pleasing the official visitors, and the food was insufficient to sustain the health of the inmates.

Unlike a concentration camp, the refugees gathered at Tchin-Tabaraden freely. They were not dissuaded from leaving by machine guns and barbed wire but rather by their most likely alternative, starvation.

An optimist might consider Tchin-Tabaraden an anomaly, the result of famine and drought striking a poor people in a poor country; a pessimist, as the precursor of an institution that may become common in an increasingly hungry world.

Miriam: "A European woman visited us at Tchin-Tabaraden. I put my arm next to hers so we touched. Before the Europeans came to Tchin-Tabaraden I had thought I was white.

"Some people said that the Europeans had come to replace the bouzous. Now that the bouzous had left, the Europeans had come to serve us. I didn't agree. They were white, and although they brought sorghum and millet, they did not pound or cook it for us."

Some relief workers called the Tuareg "lazy," and certainly the evidence to support this judgment was widespread. In the Dakoro camp, a group of Tuareg men who had gone without food for days refused to help unload sorghum from an OPVN truck and then ridiculed those who did. At the Lazaret camp, others gave a portion of their rations to bouzous to induce them to draw water, collect firewood, sweep their tents, and prepare their food.

An article in Niger's weekly magazine, *Sahel Hebdo,* reported that some Tuareg were demanding servants to pound millet and act as houseboys, and that they were even asking the government to supply sunglasses. It concluded that the "victims are no longer in need if one judges them by their comportment . . . with each passing day these people are becoming too demanding toward those who help them within the framework of African brotherhood."

Attempts by the donors to turn nomadic Tuareg suddenly impoverished by the drought into farmers had failed because farm work was felt to be demeaning. In a government project near Niamey, Tuareg refu-

212

gees subcontracted their new farm plots to Djermas who agreed to work them as sharecroppers, thus avoiding work as they had when they owned animals by paying blacks with income generated by their capital.

A Red Cross medical and nutritional team came to the Tchin-Tabaraden camp to teach the women sanitary education, preventive medicine, and nutrition. As part of the nutritional program they demonstrated how to concoct a nourishing porridge of millet, red palm oil, and fishmeal, an exercise which the Tunisian in charge of the United Nations Food and Agriculture Agency in Niger believes was futile, since "after the expatriates had left, the women had neither the inclination nor the ingredients to make these special foodstuffs."

Before the Red Cross team could demonstrate how to mix the porridge, they needed some women from the camp to pound millet as one of the ingredients. When volunteers were called for from the audience, none stepped forward. A small group of women were approached and told that if they prepared the millet they would be given the porridge after the demonstration. The women refused to help unless they were paid. Finally the Red Cross team had to agree.

Miriam was not at Tchin-Tabaraden when the Red Cross came. But she thinks the women probably refused to pound the millet because it was hard work and because it was demeaning to do it in front of an audience. "The first time I tried to prepare millet, I didn't pound or cook it enough," she said. "We ate it anyway and everyone was sick. The next time I spent the whole day pounding, sifting, and cooking, and I spoiled it again. It took a long time for me to learn. Pounding sorghum is even more difficult. Besides, if it was the Europeans who wanted the millet pounded and not the women, why shouldn't they pay?"

Other Europeans left Tchin-Tabaraden with the impression that the refugees were lazy. According to one, the "Tuareg were lazy and had an exalted opinion of themselves. Very simply, they were not about to do any manual labor. They were just as willing to accept death."

"Lazy" is an inappropriate word to describe the actions of a people who, in some cases, preferred to starve rather than work. Death was familiar; work was not. Many Tuareg were prisoners of a culture which had enshrined an antiwork ethic, and it would take time for them to adapt to new circumstances.

213

The Tuareg were also called "fatalistic." But what was perceived as fatalism was more likely to be stoicism and patience, transferred from survival in the bush to a newer challenge, survival in the camps. Tuareg lives were conditioned by unpredictability, by the impossibility of planning ahead, and by the daily search for food and pasture. To live from hour to hour was normal, from day to day a luxury. But away from the bush the virtue of nomadic flexibility became a vice.

There were, even at the start of the drought, exceptions to the "lazy" and "fatalistic" Tuareg. One family camped along a route frequented by Malian refugees. They bought emaciated and dying animals for as little as twenty-five cents a head, slaughtered them on the spot, and resold them at a profit to the refugees. When this story reached Niamey, the enterprising butchers were criticized for profiting from the misery of their own people.

Hundreds of "disaster tourists" visited Niger and the other sahelian countries during the drought. They filled local hotels and they bounced off in Land Rovers on inspections, duplicating those made by the permanent representatives of the relief organizations. They came to see what made their paperwork and bureaucratic routine more humane than that of other bureaucrats. They followed the tendency of home offices to check up on the field staff. They came for adventure and travel.

The same romantic myths and promises of adventure that had drawn Caillié to Timbuctoo and young French officers to Agadez, and that prompted Europeans to paint "Sahara Trek" on the doors of their Land Rovers and set out to cross the desert, now brought attention, money, and food to the sahel. They were also factors in persuading inspectors and consultants of every nationality that they should inspect their organizations' operations personally.

Important visitors were pictured in *Le Temps du Niger* sitting with a smiling Diori on his colorful couch or standing in front of new trucks, boxes of food, or mounds of clothing. Sometimes they posed handing a check to a Nigerien official, each holding an edge, smiling as though they were sharing a lottery prize. The value of their donations was sometimes small, their airfares and expenses often large.

Tours were organized. Scarce vehicles and expensive gasoline were requisitioned to take visitors to refugee camps and development projects, and some busy officials became permanent tour guides. Since most visitors only stopped for a few days, their tours were restricted to sights within a few hours' drive from Niamey. The standard tour included the Lazaret camp, a Chinese rice-paddy project, an agricultural school, a visit with a government minister, and cocktail and dinner parties given in the visitors' honor. They took notes and pictures, bought Tuareg swords as souvenirs, and flew on to the next sahelian capital.

After February 1974 many of these tourists, if they had access to an airplane, included Tchin-Tabaraden in their itineraries. Some never made it, for sandstorms often obscured the camp and made landing treacherous. When the visitors did land they followed another routine itinerary: a talk with the subprefect, a visit to the camp at feeding time, a chat with Madame Marty at the dispensary. If they were staying overnight, the subprefect, who, like most Nigeriens, was hospitable, gave a *mechoui* in their honor.

A *mechoui* is a feast. A goat or sheep is split open, propped against two crossed sticks, and cooked slowly over a fire. It is served with couscous, rice, and condiments. At Tchin-Tabaraden, the subprefect served it with Coke, Fanta, and Johnnie Walker Red Label whiskey.

One of the many visitors to the camp was a Swedish princess, the honorary president of her country's Red Cross. She arrived at 5 P.M. and was given a rapid tour of the camp. Then the subprefect presented her with a Tuareg saddlebag and played host at a *mechoui* in the walled courtyard of his house.

During the *mechoui*, the subprefect's house guard attacked the sheep while it was still cooking. He ripped off a joint, thrust it under his cloak, and ran off into the night. After the guests ate, the leftovers were given to the rest of the servants. Then Tuareg and Peul from the camp entertained the guests with traditional songs and dances.

During March and April the subprefect's feasts became more frequent. People from the village and the camp were attracted by the noises, the smells, and the exotic Europeans. They gathered outside the walls of the house, often jumping up to peer over the walls to glimpse the party. One of the guests at the princess's party remembers that during the feast and the entertainment, veiled heads and women's faces were continually bobbing over the high courtyard wall.

Miriam said that the refugees were "happy to have so many Europeans visit us. We talked about them, what they wore, what they looked like, and what they did when they were in Tchin-Tabaraden."

Pat McDuffie agrees. "I think that the refugees enjoyed seeing the Europeans. They were a free show, a source of gossip and amusement. I remember one day a bishop arrived who weighed three hundred pounds. All day long people talked about him and said, 'That European has been eating a lot of biscuits.'"

The three-hundred-pound bishop, the Swedish princess, Rotival, Neukirk, and Lambacher were all on one edge of a chasm, Miriam and the refugees across from them on the other. Satellites and astronauts on one side, camels and cram-cram on the other. They represented two tribes, those who eat and those who don't.

The Europeans in Tchin-Tabaraden stood close to the edge of their side of the gulf, coming near hunger, observing but never experiencing it. Even among the starving they could never be hungry. Feasts would always follow them.

Europeans in Niger who tried to cross the chasm risked falling in. A Belgian nurse gave away her clothes, her money, everything she had. She wore Tuareg robes and ate sorghum, and became sick. She broke down, cried uncontrollably, and had to be evacuated.

Most of the visitors adjusted. As the CARE representative said, "It won't help anyone here if I go on a diet of rice and sauce." The situation made some of the privileged uncomfortable, but there seemed to be no alternative. In Niamey they had the same, if not a better, material standard of living than what they were accustomed to in their own countries.

Comfortable Nigeriens experienced the same dilemma. Miriama Keita is known as "Niger's liberated woman." She is a well-known personality, an announcer for the country's only radio station, "The Voice of the Sahel," was a delegate to the United Nation's women's conference in Mexico City. She was with Madame Diori's delegation of women who distributed blankets to the refugees at Tchin-Tabaraden.

She said, "When the president's wife saw the condition of the people at the camp she was appalled. She promised them that she would try to have the government buy them new animals.

"The women at the camp were doing all the work. Obviously the drought had forced the Tuareg women to take on new responsibilities and spend long hours cooking and preparing food. Before the drought they never did this.

"What moved me the most was that many of the women were almost naked. They wore no jewelry and hardly any clothes at all. I know how much clothes meant to them. All they were eating was a little cram-cram. Whan I saw how sick and hungry they were I couldn't bear to eat. I only drank water while I was at Tchin-Tabaraden. I felt it was an insult to eat when they were suffering so much."

When OXFAM's Neukirk returned to Tchin-Tabaraden in early April, he found that the Martys and the subprefect were totally exhausted. They complained that the demands occasioned by the visitors were so great that they were left with little time to care for the refugees. Neukirk also saw that, despite the visitors and the attention and the promises, conditions at the camp were scarcely better. Food was arriving with greater regularity but it was not enough. People were still sick and undernourished, and more refugees arrived every day. The basic problems were the same: inadequate transportation and official neglect, particularly on the part of the Tahoua prefect.

After President Diori's visit, France, Belgium, and Germany, acting through FED, the development arm of the European Common Market, flew sixty tons of powdered milk to the Tahoua department aboard transport planes belonging to the Belgian air force. Ten tons of this milk was consigned to Tchin-Tabaraden. It arrived at the Tahoua airport between March 19 and 21; ten days later it was still there, stored neatly under tarpaulins.

Claude Sanz is one of the two resident FED representatives in Niamey, a slight man who wears wire-rimmed spectacles and talks with the precision of a French academician. When he was told that the "emergency" milk shipment to Tchin-Tabaraden was being held up, he visited Tahoua to find out why.

He arrived at the airport on April 2 and found that all the milk, with

217

the exception of three and a half tons which had been handed out in Tahoua itself, was still under tarpaulins next to the runway. He went next to the OPVN warehouse and saw 1,300 tons of relief supplies that had been there for as long as six months. More than half was American sorghum; the rest was millet, powdered milk, CARE civil defense biscuits, and Red Cross semolina.

The director of OPVN and the Tahoua prefect claimed that they did not have enough trucks to move the supplies to the distribution centers in the bush. OPVN in Tahoua had only two seven-ton trucks of its own, and three ten- to twenty-ton rented vehicles. Another five private trucks were available, but their owners were prone to return to Niamey, 350 miles away, on the slightest pretext. Others truckers feared getting stuck in the sands of the Tchin-Tabaraden track and refused to make any trips at all unless the government promised to compensate them for any accidents or delays they might suffer while delivering relief food.

There were other vehicles in Tahoua under government control—Land Rovers and lorries belonging to the army, trucks from other government agencies such as OFEDES, Water and Forests, Rural Development, Posts and Telegraphs—but none of them had been requisitioned to move food. The Tahoua prefect's most generous critics charged him with a lack of initiative.

In Tchin-Tabaraden, the subprefect complained to Sanz that he had only three trucks with which to pick up food in Tahoua and supply the rest of the arrondissement. Some 120 miles north in Tassara, a trip few of the earlier visitors made, Sanz found people even more desperate than those at Tchin-Tabaraden. No food at all had arrived for ten days. The chief of the post was absent and there were numerous untreated cases of diarrhea, dysentery, and measles. The refugees were so thin and weak that Sanz was convinced they would die without immediate medical attention. "We left these people" he said, "with sadness and a feeling of impotence before the disaster of starvation."

8

Niamey
September 1973 - April 1974

When a man does things that were unknown to his father, he will see things
that his father never saw.

> —Tuareg saying (whose sense is that any-
> thing innovative is dangerous).

i

*T*hroughout 1973 and the first six months of 1974, Atakor, Sidi, Ibrahim, Moussa, and twenty to thirty thousand other refugees from Niger and Mali—nobles, vassals, marabouts, bouzous, and black-smiths; the remnants of a disintegrating people—descended on Niamey as it was becoming a famine boomtown.

Niamey is a fragmented city; like Niger itself, a collection but not an integration of many disparate people:

> A French hostess plans a gala Christmas dinner complete with roast suckling pig. At the last minute she tells her African servant to "put parsley in the ears." When he brings the pig in to dinner sprigs of parsley are sticking out of his own ears.

> Because of the drought, the consumer price index for low-income families in Niamey rose 9.7 percent in 1972 and 11.7 percent in 1973. (The largest jump was in food prices, which increased 16.4 percent in 1972 and 17.1 percent in 1973.) The price index for high-income families in Niamey rose only 3.8 percent in 1972 and 4.3 percent the following year. Since 70 percent of the articles in their index were imported, one would have expected that their index would rise at a rate somewhat similar to, rather than strikingly less than, that of French inflation. Instead, price controls on imported goods were applied rigorously by the government. This protected the elite and subsidized their food and luxuries.

221

Some French technicians and Nigerien officials meet for an aperitif. Hands cross and recross the table in a pattern of formal handshakes resembling a throughway interchange. The French is exquisitely spoken, the greetings formal. A bottle of Johnnie Walker and glasses are brought by the waiter. The French continue to exchange pleasantries. The Nigeriens are suddenly silent, staring fixedly at the measuring bulb on top of the bottle, making sure the waiter allows it to refill completely before tipping an expensive measure into their glasses.

The Djerma consider certain green lizards to be a jinx and they beat them to death with sticks. Tuareg nobles think these same lizards contain the spirits of ancestors. They wear their heads as amulets to protect them from vipers and scorpions and grind their parts into love potions.

During 1973 and 1974 the Tuareg refugees became scattered among Niamey's different fragmented communities. Many congregated at an enormous refugee camp where the population at the beginning of 1974 reached 20,000, a fifth as large as that of Niamey. Others stayed at the camp when they first arrived but then settled elsewhere, wherever there was food, shelter, and work. They found these among the educated Nigerien elite and a European community which had been enlarged and diversified by the drought.

Unlike Gao, Timbuctoo, or Agadez, Niamey was never an ancient trading city or the center of a wealthy African empire. It was a European creation. Until 1926, when the French moved their colonial capital there from Zinder, it had been a small, unimportant village of Djerma fishermen and farmers on the east bank of the Niger River.

The most popular of the many stories which explained its selection as Niger's capital is that it was chosen by the French governor's wife. In the course of a boat trip on the river, she was impressed by the high plateau that rises steeply over the Niger at Niamey and remarked that it would be a splendid site for a city.

Her husband agreed. Although Niamey is in the southwest corner of the country, its road and telegraph connections to Dakar, the ex-capital of French West Africa, are superior to Zinder's. The river also connects it to Gao and Timbuctoo in the north, and Nigeria and the Atlantic to the south.

The French built their capital on the high plateau. Homes, government ministries, army forts, and a governor's palace were constructed in a French adaptation of the sahel's cool, thick, white-walled architecture. Wide, straight avenues connected the forts and met at dusty traffic circles. After World War II, French trading companies built block-long arcades in the same style. The arcades contained offices and shops which sold imported goods to the growing French community and to the educated Nigerien elite. Most of the members of this elite worked for the colonial administration and had learned to prefer education, food, furniture, and clothes imported from France.

Niamey's greatest growth came between 1945, when the city had a population of only 3,500, and 1973, when it reached 100,000. As Niamey became Niger's most important trading center, the small fishing village also grew in area and population. People emigrated from the Nigerien countryside and from France's coastal colonies to work as clerks and domestics, and to fill other positions created by the concentration of Europeans and educated Nigeriens.

Niamey is known in West Africa as one of the most authentically African of the capital cities. The reason is that with the exception of a tiny elite, the life-style—clothes, food, and homes—of the people approximates that of the bush. Camels, donkeys, and goats roam through the streets. Most people live in banco houses, and even some grass huts can be found scattered throughout the city's quarters. In Niamey, the bush is not just close at hand but is part of the city itself to a greater extent than in Ougadougou or Bamako, the capitals of Upper Volta and Mali, neighboring and equally poor sahelian countries.

Yet Niamey is also considered the most French of the landlocked sahelian capitals. In 1960, at the time of Niger's independence, very few Nigeriens had been trained to replace the French administrators and technicians. Many French remained after independence, to operate the country's post office, electric works, and industries, and to advise Nigeriens. Hundreds of French taught at every level of the country's educational system. Still others worked as advisors to the country's most senior officials.

Thirteen years after independence, the French still carved fancy cuts of meat in Niamey's butcher shops, baked croissants and pastries, wrote airline tickets and insurance policies, and supervised cash registers in markets. French pilots flew the planes of Air Niger, and French mechanics repaired them. French couples owned the city's restaurants and hotels or managed them for a government company. Many middle-level jobs as clerks and secretaries, unappealing to the French, were filled by educated Africans from Togo and Dahomey.

Late every afternoon, just before dusk, Niamey's different societies and peoples meet. At 5:30 policemen climb onto umbrella-shaded pedestals at crucial crossroads and circles. At first they are merely spectators, watching men driving goats across the street, children returning from school with books balanced on their heads, or men lying on mats playing a game with stones and twigs on a board scratched into the dust on the street. At street corners the agents of bicycle and motorbike repairmen start canvassing the traffic, listening for dragging mufflers and loose drive chains and looking for flat tires.

At six, government offices, embassies, stores, banks, and factories begin closing. Niamey's people begin to crowd the streets, moving together in distinctive and unsynchronized rhythms. Wealthy traders and functionaries race the engines of their secondhand French cars at crossroads. The police, or one of the half-dozen traffic lights, signal them on and they jostle for position with clerks on motorbikes and sputtering taxis crammed with market women and driven by slight young men with tribal scars. The taxis jump over rutted side streets of dirt and buckled asphalt, and kerchiefed heads bob in the rear windows like ducks in a shooting gallery.

Boys on old bicycles pick up crippled lepers from the choicest locations: hotels, banks, and the huge ant castle by the entrance to the post office. They tie them onto the fenders, strap them into baskets, and chauffeur them home or to a choice evening location near a cinema. Other beggars scuttle along the roadsides like crabs, their hands jammed into sandals, their crippled legs tucked under their arms like swagger sticks.

Bush trucks, muddy in summer, dusty in winter, packed with bowls, bags, and animals, sway into the market after ten-hour trips, police

224

checks, flat tires, and fights. Passengers leap out, broad-jump over open sewers, hail taxis, or, bowls and suitcases tottering on their heads, join the crowds of pedestrians.

A few minutes before sunset, the traffic slackens and slows. Dusty whirlwinds race down side streets, and sun, cars, camels, and pedestrians disappear into a darkening red haze, a seamless union of dust stirred from the streets and dust, once sand and soil from farms and pastures, now blown into the atmosphere by the Harmattan and reddened by a vanishing sun.

In 1973 a new people who walked with a new cadence joined Niamey's evening ritual. Hungry, bewildered, and exhausted, as many as two hundred Tuareg refugees arrived daily.

The men were more assured and walked with long bush strides, their hands clasped behind their backs or holding the hand of another man, tightly when they first arrived and then more loosely until connected by a single finger. In the markets they stood an inch or two taller than the black Africans. Veiled, visible, moving at a different pace, they could easily be picked out of the dust and turmoil of dusk.

The women were tentative, terrified. At the sound of a horn or a noisy engine, they darted like rabbits away from the road, into a ditch, behind a building. Or, unpredictably, they ran straight ahead until they found a side street down which to escape.

ii

*H*assan: "When I was a schoolboy in Gao I spent afternoons standing in front of the Hotel Atlantide. When the European tourists [who came to Gao on, or to catch, the Timbuctoo riverboat] left the hotel, I followed them, trying to imitate the way they walked. I thought that if I walked as they did and wore their kind of clothing that I would learn the secrets of their magic. Later I came to Niamey, worked for Europeans, and wore their clothes, but I never learned their secrets."

225

Between 1969 when he left Rissa and the rest of his family in Mali and 1973 when the Malian Tuareg refugees began to arrive in Niamey, Hassan was employed by three different families, always as a gardener and always at the same house. With the parrot and the rattan furniture, he and the housecleaners, the cooks, and the guards were passed from one European family to the next.

When he was interviewed by his original employer, Hassan said that he preferred guarding the house to tending its garden, a job that required him to dig, weed, water, and plant. But he was only fourteen in 1969, too young and too slight to be a guard. Instead, his gentle appearance, curly brown hair, freckles, and huge brown eyes, convinced the European family that he could be trusted as a children's babysitter.

When his wages as gardener and babysitter were combined, he sometimes made more than $50 a month, a stunning salary in a country where the average yearly earnings of an entire Tuareg household were only $80. Of this $80 only about $10 was a cash income, the rest was barter. Until 1972 Hassan sent most of this money to Gao where it bought food and clothing for his father, Rissa, and the gradually expanding group of brothers, sisters, and relatives gathered around him.

He spent the rest on food, tobacco, tea, and secondhand European clothes. This was an expense in keeping with the Tuareg's traditional fondness for clothing and ornaments. Before the drought, the average household spent 26 percent of its yearly budget on trousers, cloaks, sandals, leather pouches, amulets, jewelry, and veils. A swath of Kano lithiam, the blue-dyed material which gave blue tint to the skin and was favored as a veil, cost $40.

When Hassan was a student in Gao, he wore blue gym shorts and a blue cotton shirt. He put on his veil, baggy white trousers, and blue poncho shirt during infrequent visits to his parents' camp. In Niamey he dressed only in European clothes. His favorites, which he slipped on after work, were a blue polo shirt with a tiny sailboat on the pocket and blue-and-red-checked double-knit trousers, once part of a leisure suit. Even when he was in the garden he wore a heavy brass identification bracelet that said "Herve," a gift from the son of a French diplomat.

Secondhand clothing was America's largest export to Niger, the cornerstone of economic relations between the two countries before the drought. The clothes were collected by American churches, the Salvation Army, and various private charities. Middlemen in New York and Philadelphia bought, cleaned, pressed, and fastened them with metal straps so that they resembled bales of cotton, and shipped them to West Africa. Trucks and trains hauled them to Niamey and other Nigerien cities.

Merchants in Niamey, Agadez, Maradi, and Zinder bought the bales by weight and stacked them in open markets or behind shops. They sat on them, slept on them, and built stalls out of them. When their inventory became low they snapped open a new one, releasing a sharp odor of cheap laundry detergent and mold which had formed on clothes pressed together before they were dry. Each bale was a surprise package containing university sweat shirts, dinner jackets, tweed jackets, underwear, school uniforms, dresses, and work shirts whose stains and colors had been burned away by the powerful bleaches. The merchants pawed through them, sorting them by size and style and hanging the treasures—Muhammed Ali and James Brown T-shirts—on coat hangers over their stalls and throwing the disappointments—ripped bathing suits and torn underwear—into a discount pile.

The garments were as colorful as, but cheaper than, the robes and shirts made by local tailors. In Niamey's main market, an open plaza as large as a city block held only old-clothing merchants. Those who sold cloth, and the tailors who sewed it into robes and shirts, gathered in a smaller area.

For the Americans who lived in Niger, the clothes had eerie echoes. A servant mopped floors in an Elvis sweater, and another did the laundry in a "Virginia Is for Lovers" T-shirt. A legless leper was the "Property of the Tulane Athletic Department." Tuareg urchins were New York Mets' fans, a bouzou watered flowers in a dinner jacket and white ducks, and a withered bicycle repairman's Cub Scout shirt sported rows of gold and white merit badges.

After buying his secondhand clothes and food, Hassan put some money aside and sent the rest of his wages to his father. As the drought continued through the early 1970s and more of his father's relatives mi-

227

grated to Gao, Hassan sometimes had to borrow from his employer to support them. By 1972 his generosity had convinced Rissa that his son was fabulously wealthy. Twice during 1972 he siphoned off some of Hassan's donations and came to Niamey to visit him.

When he visited Niamey the first time Rissa told Hassan it embarrassed him to accept a monthly dole. He wanted to support his family himself. Hassan gave him $50 from his own savings so that he could return to Gao, buy some inventory, and become a trader.

This was a profession that appealed to many Tuareg because it seemed to be lucrative without being strenuous. Unlike blacksmiths, farmers, or laborers, traders didn't appear to work with their hands. Trading involved unwrapping popular items so that the quantities offered for sale corresponded to local demand and budgets. As the drought reduced the size of these budgets, it also reduced the amount of inventory and the capital necessary to become a trader.

Rissa returned to Gao and bought a wooden table, blue boxes of sugar cubes, plastic bags of hard candies, and cartons of cigarettes and gum. He opened the cartons, boxes, and bags. He tried to sell the cigarettes and gum by the pack, the sugar cubes by the dozen, and the candies by the handful. Within a month he was selling individual cigarettes, sticks of gum, and sugar cubes. His profits couldn't feed his family, and within two months he had eaten or sold his entire inventory without saving any money to purchase new supplies.

Again he came to Niamey. He told Hassan that his failure was the fault of black children who robbed him during his afternoon nap. Hassan gave him another $50 and suggested that he trade in something more familiar. He returned to Gao and bought herds of emaciated goats in the animal market. He tried to resell them immediately for a slightly higher price without spending money for feed. His margin was too small; if only one or two died or became ill, he lost his week's profits. Soon he was bankrupt.

Throughout 1973 Hassan was terrified that his father would return to Niamey. In September, when Sidi appeared at the Belgian's with a letter from Gao, he feared the worst.

Hassan: "I wanted to become a teacher or work for the government.

228

Being a gardener is not the work for a man who has attended school. I hoped that I could save enough money to return to school but I had to send my pay to my family.

"During the drought my older sister and her husband went to Kano. Her husband earned a salary by guarding the lottery booths. Until 1973 she too sent money to Gao but she had children and her husband's family to support so she sent less than I did. During that year my brother-in-law fell asleep and lost his job. They left Kano and since then I have not heard from them.

"When the blacksmith gave me the letter I was afraid that my father was coming to visit me again. When I read it I understood that he had not yet saved enough money to come. After I gave him money to buy goats, I decided that I would send him less, enough to allow him to buy food but not to come to Niamey."

Since Sidi had brought Rissa's letter, Hassan felt responsible and arranged for him and Ibrahim to sleep outside the Belgian's. Sidi, however, unlike Rissa, could support himself since he was a talented blacksmith. He built a small forge at the side of the street and made jewelry for first the Belgian and then, as his reputation spread, for Europeans and Nigeriens living in Niamey's Plateau and Terminus quarters.

Although Sidi made enough money to buy food and replenish his materials, he was not satisfied. He wanted to buy new tools. His present anvil was too small. He wanted to rent a house for the winter. The weather was warm when he arrived in Niamey but he knew the evenings would soon become colder. He wanted to follow his wife to Kano. A Niamey blacksmith had told him that she and her paramour had gone there. In order to earn more money, he joined the cooperative of skilled blacksmiths who worked at Niamey's national museum.

Most blacksmith refugees in Niamey turned out inexpensive knives, swords, jewelry, and purses, and spent long hours just hawking these wares, competing with nobles and vassals who were trying to sell their own knives and swords. Anyone who walked around Niamey and appeared to be prosperous attracted men holding up spears, knives, leather pouches, and red boxes made from dyed camel leather.

Blacksmiths stood in front of the huge glass windows of the favorite

229

European cafés pulling swords out of sheaths, opening boxes, and sometimes gesturing at their mouths with thumb and forefinger. They followed Europeans from bar to market to bank until they made a sale or saw another potential customer. Their asking prices were absurdly high, their final ones absurdly low: a few dollars, some food. Often the closing price was "anything"—any amount of food or money. A loaf of bread could buy a beautiful sword.

Finely crafted silver Agadez crosses which could be worn as pendants around the neck normally cost around $5. But during the drought Tuareg women sold them for less than $2. Antique jewelry that had survived generations was sold and melted down for its silver content. Antiquities dealers from Europe and the coast came to Niamey and left with suit cases filled with Tuareg jewelry.

Many Tuareg women wore a large triangular pendant with five smaller triangles hanging from its bottom. It was like a miniature mobile, and when the women walked or were buffeted by gusts of wind the triangles tinkled like prayer bells. Women hated to part with this ornament so much that they often detached the little triangles of silver and sold them one by one, replacing each with a triangle of identical shape and design cut out of empty sardine tins pounded flat.

Sidi eliminated the problem of selling his products by working at the National Museum. The museum is Niamey's only tourist attraction. Located adjacent to the commercial quarter, it is a conglomeration of folklore "attractions" and animals scattered across an enclosed park that slopes down to the Niger River. The museum has giraffes, ostriches, giant land turtles, and wiry, wolfish predators, animals that are, or, before the drought, were, indigenous to Niger.

The museum also has exhibits of Hausa and Djerma villages, Peul and Tuareg encampments, each with unlit fires, unpounded grain, and the appropriate cooking and household utensils, beds, chests, brooms, cradles, all neatly arranged in front of or within the huts.

On the rise of a hill overlooking the villages, the animals, and a handicrafts store is a square, whitewashed Hausa building, cool and quiet, a mausoleum containing the traditional clothes of the inhabitants of the deserted villages. Inside, spotlighted male and female mannequins wearing Hausa, Djerma, Peul, and Tuareg clothes rotate mechanically in glass cases. During feasts, people from the villages near Niamey, villages almost identical to those at the museum, dress in their finest clothes and visit Niamey. Sometimes they stand inside the clothing museum, transfixed by a revolving mannequin identically clothed.

The liveliest building at the museum is a long, grass-roofed, open-air shed in which Niamey's most talented blacksmiths pound out jewelry and other souvenirs which are sold in the gift shop. Since prices at the gift shop are relatively high, working in the museum shed is a coveted position. Yet, despite the advantages, Sidi quit in November after less than two months.

Sidi: "I was unhappy and lonely at the museum. Ibrahim stayed with Hassan at the Belgian's and I never had a chance to joke with my clients or discuss what I made. Small boys at the museum stole my hammer, a pair of tongs, and a ring. None of the other blacksmiths stopped them. I think they were jealous of my talents.

"After I left the museum I returned to the Plateau and continued working for Europeans and functionaries. As before, I lived outside the Belgian's house. I made less money but I could talk with my clients, and Ibrahim pushed the bellows and handed me my tools. One of the Europeans gave me a chair [a tattered, canvas deck chair] and I encouraged my clients to sit and talk while I worked. If I was making something for them, I insisted that they visit me at least two times so I could be sure they would be pleased when I finished. They became my friends and never patronized other blacksmiths.

"Hausas, Djermas, and bouzous from other quarters as well as the Europeans came to me. I became their friend and they sent me their friends as clients. After I left the museum I also began to work again for Tuareg clients who wanted knives and swords. I liked making these things because the blacksmith who makes a famous sword is remembered and celebrated. This is how I became friends with Atakor. He owned a beautiful ancient sword and he wanted me to copy it."

* * *

iii

*D*uring a dusty November evening, Hassan's mother, Fadimatta, arrived in Niamey. She neither joined the traffic nor, like the other
Tuareg women, scurried away from it. She was unconscious, tied to a
donkey, and led through the red dusk by two relatives who asked directions to the road that led to the Plateau and Hassan.

Fadimatta often told friends that she had always disliked Hassan's father, Rissa, and that she had been sick with fever when she married
him. She blamed Rissa for the quarrel which led to Hassan's being sent
to school, and she was not surprised when Rissa lost his animals. She
was convinced that she was not only more intelligent than he but also
wealthier and better bred. Rissa's parents had both been vassals, while
her father had been a noble.

Fadimatta's herd of animals—eleven camels, twenty-two cows, and
three hundred goats—was almost twice the size of Rissa's. After the
poor 1968 rains, she shrewdly divided them, and the animals belonging
to Hassan by inheritance, into smaller herds and lent them to her male
relatives. The herds survived the first year of the drought with only minor losses. Rissa kept his animals together, and all of them perished.

Fadimatta considered this his most stunning stupidity. She argued
that she could not be expected to remain married to a man who could not
feed her. Rissa agreed to a divorce. Soon afterward she married a man
from her brother's camp.

Hassan hadn't seen his mother since 1968. When he emigrated to
Niamey, his father took the young children to Gao so they could beg
from relatives and look for menial jobs. Fadimatta moved to her new
husband's camp. She believed that Hassan was cursed by his education
and his father's blood, and she showed little interest in him.

In the spring of 1973 Fadimatta understood that her animals were
again threatened. She, her husband, an infant son, and her husband's
brother left their camp near Gao and made the kind of long, bold migration more common among the Peul. They discovered a valley north of
Menaka which was blessed by a series of short but concentrated showers in July and August. She and the two men divided the herd and led it
to different parts of the valley.

232

At the end of September, when they reassembled, practically all of the animals were alive. A week later they were nearly all dead. A final, freakish storm, an afterthought to the summer rains, triggered a flash flood. A huge wave rolled down the valley, drowning the cows, all but two of the camels, and nine tenths of the goats. Not enough animals survived to allow three adults and a child to remain in the bush.

Fadimatta took her infant son and climbed on one of the remaining camels to ride south to Niamey. She hoped that Hassan would loan her money to replace her losses. Before departing she gorged on the dead goats, trying to eat enough without vomiting to satisfy her appetite for days. She promised the men she would return in a month.

Hassan: "One night in November Sidi told me that some people were bringing my mother to the Belgian's. I had not seen her in four years and was surprised she had come. She was more intelligent than my father and I did not think that she would be a refugee.

"I remembered my mother as a large and beautiful woman. A Tuareg woman must be large in order to be beautiful. (The women who became prostitutes in Niamey were thin and we did not consider them beautiful.) I did not recognize my mother when I saw her. Her legs were as thin as wrists, her arms as thin as fingers. She was naked; she had sold all her jewelry and wore nothing except for a black rag wrapped around her waist and two amulets she clutched in her hand. She was sick; she had eaten the meat of dead animals she found along the roadside. The people who found her said she cried and fell off the donkey a number of times. This was why they tied her on.

"I cried when I saw that this was my mother. My patron and his wife came out of their house and they cried. My mother said nothing. We all took her into the house and washed her, wrapped her in a sheet, and gave her food that made her sick.

"The people who saved her lived in the Lazaret camp and were from her tribe. A woman who had walked to the camp from Menaka told them she was sitting by the road thirty miles from Niamey. These people then borrowed a donkey and walked toward Oullam. When they found her she was unconscious. They buried a dead infant that lay next to her, revived her with food and water, and put her on the donkey."

For a few weeks Fadimatta lived in the Belgian's garage. She followed Hassan around the garden, talking about her dead animals until she cried and collapsed on her blanket. Tuareg are suspicious about discussing dead relatives; a son is forbidden even to utter the name of a dead parent. Hassan asked what had occurred on the road, but she never told him coherently or explained the dead child. He begged her to stop crying over her dead animals and think about her future.

Hassan: "The two amulets that my mother clasped in her hand were gifts for me, one to protect me from insanity and the other to protect me from dying of sadness. She didn't know that when I came to Niamey I sold my amulets and bought European clothes. It is true that when we Tuareg become sad, we can die of it. I am certain that many of the refugees died of sadness because they could not stop talking and thinking about their dead animals. Before the drought I never saw men cry or become sad.

"When my mother handed me the amulets, she said that she had news she could tell me only when I was wearing them. She hung them both around my neck and asked me to sit next to her. Then she cried that all of my animals had been killed by a flood. She had saved my camel and was riding to Niamey to give it to me and ask me for money, but it was stolen while she slept. She bought the amulets because she had seen people become insane when they learned that their animals were dead. She wanted to protect me from this insanity.

"Every Tuareg has his own herd of animals. I owned the camel that was stolen, fifteen goats, and twelve sheep. It took fifteen years for my herd to become this large. When I was born I was given one goat by my mother's family and one by my father's. These two mated and produced more goats. A few years later some of these were traded for sheep and then a camel.

"My mother was ashamed that these animals died while in her care. She said it proved that she was no smarter than my father. But it was intelligent for her to buy these amulets. Since it requires so much time to build up a young man's herd, it is understandable that he should be sad when he learns that it is gone. But my mother could not have known that I never planned to return to the bush and become a herder with these animals."

Fadimatta's brother-in-law came to Niamey a month later. He reported that the rest of her animals had died and that her husband had also become ill and died. She left the Belgian's garage to begin a three-month period of mourning during which she would be hidden from every man but her son. Hassan was relieved. He had worried that the Europeans might become tired of her hysteria and dismiss him.

He rented a small banco house near the river and hired a woman to draw water, buy firewood, and pound and cook grain for his mother's meals. He paid for everything. Every day women from her tribe walked in from the refugee camp to visit her. They ate her millet, talked about their dead animals, and cried. When they left, Fadimatta was lonely, and after a month of living alone she decided to break her mourning and join them at the refugee camp.

Hassan: "When my mother moved to Lazaret I bought her a tent of old clothes sewn together by a blacksmith woman. I continued to pay a woman to prepare her meals. I visited her every day and brought chocolate, tea, rice, millet, and milk. Now my mother was one of the wealthiest women at Lazaret and she had to share her food with other women. These women knew that she was intelligent, and to them it seemed natural that she should be so rich.

"She liked to hear the stories about how my father had lost my money by trading cigarettes and goats. She composed songs about him and sang them to her friends. This made me more determined not to send my father the money he had requested in his letter since he would be embarrassed if he came here.

"It made me sad to visit my mother. The people at Lazaret lived too close to one another and it was dirty. When I left and walked back through the camp to Niamey, it was cold and dark and I often fell over people. Throughout the camp I could hear people—I think that some of them were asleep—crying, singing, and talking about their animals and families."

* * *

235

iv

*T*he United Nations Environmental Program and the Swedish Government Development Agency studied the Lazaret camp so carefully, asking each of 569 refugees an identical 91 questions, that they even compiled statistics on the refugees' dreams. Some of the refugees interviewed reported having happy dreams of returning to the bush with a herd of animals, of being reunited with relatives, and, most commonly, of trucks arriving with relief supplies.

Most of them reported nightmares. Thirty eight percent could not remember their content. Out of the 62 percent who could, 22 percent dreamed about animals dying, 13 percent about the time before compared with the time during the drought, 11 percent about what they would eat tomorrow, 9 percent about the future (presumably in bleak terms), and 7 percent simply said they had "somber dreams."

Unlike the gatherings of refugees in smaller cities or bush centers, the Lazaret camp was studied and scrutinized by foreign journalists, academicians, and relief experts. It was one of the largest camps, its inmates had suffered as much as any other sahelian people, and it was close to Niamey's hotels, restaurants, and four weekly flights to Paris.

Lazaret was also a magnet for Niamey's Europeans. They visited the camp with boxes of food and hired refugees to work at their houses. They recorded Tuareg music on cassettes and worked as unpaid volunteers, distributing food and working in the dispensary.

Lazaret was not only largely sustained by Niamey's Europeans; it was also founded by them. Before April 1973, the Malian Tuareg who came to Niamey were scattered, invisible, sick, and hungry. They camped along roadsides, in vacant lots, in the excavated open areas between shantytowns. Only two Catholic missionaries, Father Arnoux and the Bishop of Niamey, Monseigneur Berliet, brought them food and medicine. By April, over one thousand were gathered in Niamey. They were so wretched that the government could no longer ignore them. Since the government feared that they might start an epidemic and had proclaimed a national disaster and solicited foreign aid a month earlier,

236

President Diori finally permitted the missionaries to gather them into a single location where it would be easier to feed, vaccinate, and supervise them.

The priests brought the Tuareg together on a treeless, windy plateau a mile from Niamey on land rented from a Djerma farmer. Before the drought the area had been a millet field and it still contained a small banco house, which became the dispensary, and a thirty-meter well, which became the sole source of water. The well was operated almost continuously by bouzous employed by the farmer, and the refugees had to pay six cents for about four gallons. During the summer the camp grew, and even approaching the well to buy water became difficult. The space around it was congested with people, like the wells in the bush overpopulated with animals. Dirt and excrement fell into the unprotected opening, polluting the water and spreading dysentery.

Inspired by the hope that the Tuareg refugees, like Lazarus, could be restored to life, Fathers Arnoux and Berliet christened the camp Lazaret. If the Tuareg were to be restored, it was a miracle the priests would have to work themselves. During 1973, food, medicine, and shelter at Lazaret were donated by the Catholic mission, private relief organizations, and Niamey's European and wealthy African communities.

The Nigerien government felt that so many Nigerien citizens were so desperate that it was an act of generosity just to permit foreign food and energies to be channeled toward helping Lazaret's predominantly Malian population.

At Dakoro, in central Niger, 80 percent of the region's people were judged completely destitute by the government; they depended on food contributed by foreign donors and delivered sporadically to isolated relief centers. During the summer of 1973, 100,000 Nigeriens, mostly Tuareg, gathered at Agadez. The rains washed out all roads to the south, and the refugees at Agadez were saved only by a costly airlift of food in Belgian and Canadian planes. Twenty thousand refugees, mostly Tuareg women and children, lived in the open spaces of Maradi, Niger's second largest city. A survey showed they had lost 97 to 100 percent of their animals; their infant mortality rate had tripled; half of them had no shelter of any kind, not even a straw mat. Of these refugees

237

without shelter, almost half were orphaned or abandoned children under the age of fourteen.

In 1974 a survey of Niger's refugee camps was taken by John Buche, the deputy chief of Mission at the American Embassy. It showed that of 200,000 people in major urban refugee camps (a figure that does not include an equal number of destitute nomads clustered around remote food distribution centers in the bush), the majority were nomads who had lost their entire stock of animals. The survey also revealed that half of Niger's population, more than 2 million people, depended on relief food sent by foreign donors and distributed by the government.

Initially, conditions at the Lazaret camp were as bad as, if not worse than, those at other camps. (However, by 1974 the Lazaret refugees were benefiting from the attention of the foreign community, their proximity to food, and the opportunities Niamey offered for work, begging, and prostitution.) Almost half of the Tuareg arrived at Lazaret without cooking utensils, tents, or possessions of any kind. They slept under cardboard, pieces of cloth, or straw mats. Many lay in the open with no protection from sand, cold, or wind. One of the greatest problems they faced was that they had never lived so close to one another for so long. People who were accustomed to forty meters of distance were now separated by four or less. They were unable to cope with living so close to one another and the space between their shelters became filled with rubbish and excrement.[1]

Food and medical attention at Lazaret were dispensed by an eclectic group of volunteers that included a young Swedish doctor, a Norwegian customs inspector who flew to Niger at his own expense, members of the Volontiers du Progrès, the French equivalent of the American Peace Corps, various Nigerien and European residents of Niamey, and the Catholic missionaries.

Throughout 1973 and the first six months of 1974 the population of Lazaret increased steadily: from 1,000 in April 1973 to 2,500 in August, and finally to 20,000 by April 1974. The largest increase occurred

---

[1] Yet the refugees were not ignorant of the importance of hygiene. Thirty-six percent of those interviewed wanted toilets built around the camp; others suggested that people be encouraged to walk further into the bush.

between November 1973, when there were 5,000 inhabitants, and February 1974, when there were 12,000. Thousands of refugees also passed through Lazaret on their way to other cities or countries, or to Niamey itself.

Despite the harsh surroundings and crude living conditions, the refugees at Lazaret enjoyed the advantage of regular food distribution. By the beginning of 1974 the missionaries were giving each day to each person fifty cents worth of rice, sorghum, and a creamy, American-made corn/sorghum/milk/sugar powder (CSM) which the refugees called "delicious" or "sugared powder."

Table manners are not included in Tuareg etiquette. The Tuareg spit tobacco near their food, gorge themselves rapidly, regardless of how hungry they are or how much food is available, and in their haste to eat as much as possible as quickly as possible usually undercook millet and meat. This had been the case long before the drought. According to some early twentieth-century French desert travelers:

> These magnificent Tuareg, so noble and elegant, eat with a truly extraordinary savagery. Some of them will bite into a whole leg. When the meat offers any resistance, they will cut if off at the level of their mouth with a knife, and amiably pass on to us the remaining piece. Others will tear off a rib with their hands, and handle it and knead it well before presenting it to us. If the Tuareg get their hands greasy, they profit by the occasion by rubbing them over their faces, their legs and thighs, with the effect of making them shiny and beautiful.

The Lazaret diet contained 1,800 calories, less than the 2,344 average intake before the drought. When interviewed about these rations, 29 percent of the refugees said they were good, and 27 percent answered realistically that they were hungry, that the food was free, and that they were in no position to complain. Only 13 percent were unhappy with the lack of milk, and, believing that this lack made them ill, said that their rations were poor. Seventy-one percent of the refugees concluded that they were better off in Lazaret than in the bush.

While the food at Lazaret was more plentiful than in the bush, the Tuareg themselves did not raise, feed, milk, trade, and guard it. Instead, it was wrapped in plastic bags, delivered by trucks, and administered by Europeans. The link between the Tuareg and their animals was broken. As they lined up with their bowls to await the relief trucks, they were constantly reminded that their way of life appeared to have failed.

Before the drought, Tuareg children played "raid." They smoothed out miniature sand battlefields on which they reenacted famous battles adapted from the oral histories, sometimes inventing their own. Sticks, rocks, and pieces of skin represented animals, and camel puppets were made from sheep jaws.

Hassan's mother remembers playing "counting the herd." A large rock was the herder, and around it she arranged rows of small stones, each representing an animal. The family herd was reconstructed—so many goats, sheep, camels, and bouzous. She competed, cheated, stole, traded, and lent animals. She paid bouzous with goats, gave feasts and bridewealths. For variety, she played "watering the herd," and grouped the stones around a hole. At Lazaret, the children played games of "relief truck" and "Land Rover." They dragged pieces of wood, straw mats, and cardboard sugar boxes through tracks excavated in the dirt around their tents and shelters.

Fifty percent of the people at Lazaret said that they didn't want their children to become nomads, and 96 percent wanted to send their children to school. Sixty-six percent claimed that the most important lesson they learned from the drought was that "a sedentary life is better than a nomadic one." Before the drought, resistance to education had been a crucial part of Tuareg strategy to isolate and protect their society. Moussa, the marabout who accompanied Sidi on his journey from Gao, became an important figure at Lazaret. Since the chant he sang on the road between Gao and Niamey was performed often, he probably had a significant influence on these figures.

Moussa was chosen to be the leader of the Lazaret Tuareg from Bourem. At the camp there were only bits of families—six men and one woman grouped in one tent, eleven adults and five children in another. Everyone at the camp seemed to have lost a brother, sister, parent, or spouse. It was difficult to find children under five or adults over fifty-five; they comprised less than 3 percent of the entire camp. To replace the traditional social structure of the families as well as to facilitate food distribution and the taking of a census, tents and shelters were grouped according to the peoples' origin.

Moussa assumed the administrative task of ensuring that food was fairly distributed among the people from Bourem. He also made amulets and decreed religious punishments. He put his elbow on the upper thigh of a sinner and slapped his leg with the palm of his hand: a hundred slaps for failure to pray, three hundred for a woman who had a child out of wedlock. He wrote verses from the Koran on a slate and then dipped the chalk into a bowl of water. By drinking the water, people believed they could avoid further catastrophes. This was a popular treatment in Lazaret, and one that could continue for months as the suppliant drank a different verse each day.

For many of the Niamey refugees this was a rearguard action as they began to abandon marriage and class taboos as well as prejudices against education. Behavior in the bush was guided by a complicated code of etiquette. Its strict observance was necessary to gain respect. Gait, gesture, and posture were all meant to reflect elegance, refinement, and courage. Large expenditures for dress and ornament were integral to this compulsion to live gracefully. During the exodus, the Tuareg not only sold jewelry and clothes to survive but also abandoned the snobbishness and exclusivity that was basic to the maintenance of their self-esteem and national character.

Tuareg seldom married outside their class before the drought. There were occasional unions between vassals and nobles, particularly after the French occupation reduced the power of the nobles. But marriages between either of these classes (or the marabouts) and blacksmiths, bouzous, or another black people were almost unknown. Yet 50 percent of the refugees at Lazaret admitted that they would permit, if not encourage, their daughters to marry anyone. Said one noble from Mali, "Now, no matter who comes with food, even a blacksmith, I would give him my daughter." Another said, "Whoever has the means to marry my daughter, no matter who, may have her."

Even though the drought eliminated the remaining substance in the economic distinctions between the Tuareg classes, wealthier refugees from a lower class still deferred to the nobles, pretending that the nobles' status was unchanged by their poverty.

In 1961, when the Mali government abolished even the word "slave" and encouraged the bouzous, who were servants in name but slaves in fact, to leave their masters, one enterprising ex-slave from Kidal emigrated to Niamey and sold firewood to other bouzous. By 1973 he had monopolized the firewood business in one of Niamey's poorer quarters. He owned a motorbike, European furniture, and a large concession. When he learned that the son of his former master from Kidal was living in Lazaret, he brought him food and cooked it himself.

Other ex-slaves didn't care what happened to their former masters and were embarrassed by their one-time servitude. Beyna was seventeen when his family left a Tuareg camp and moved to a village of bouzous in the Adar in 1960. He left this village during the drought and traveled to Niamey. In Niamey he bought two ten-liter oil cans and tied them to the ends of a pole he could balance on his shoulders. For five cents he filled the cans with water at the nearest well and carried them to customers. As more farmers emigrated to Niamey and built villages of grass huts on the outskirts of the city, each further and further from existing water points, Beyna's trade flourished. He earned two dollars a day for the forty trips between wells and customers. During the winter, when demand slackened, he made less.

He used his earnings to pay the bridewealth of a young bouzou woman. After the marriage he bought a wooden table, pillows, a raised wooden bed, and a mosquito net, and he and his bride lived in a hut in one of the villages that surrounded Niamey. His bride was young and beautiful, and these gifts made her want more. She asked for blankets, clothes, and more cooking utensils. When a neighbor told him that the soap factory paid laborers to load cartons onto trucks, he went there and was hired.

Sidi: "Beyna never worked as a slave. It made him angry when the Tuareg from Mali called him one and gave him orders when he carried water. He told me that he refused to bring water to any clients who called him a slave. He preferred to work at the factory because no one there called him a slave and he received free soap."

242

*F*or some refugees Lazaret was a way station, helping to ease the transition between the bush and Niamey, a base from which they could visit, beg, and perhaps work in the city. They compared Lazaret to other camps. Sixty percent said its greatest advantage was the opportunity to beg in Niamey, 29 percent mentioned more food, and 20 percent talked of Niamey's "employment possibilities." The camp's greatest disadvantages, according to the refugees, were the possibility of traffic accidents (38 percent), the smell (31 percent), that they had to pay for everything (11 percent), and the ease with which their children got lost (4 percent).

Many of the "employment possibilities" required strenuous physical labor. Like the marriage of Tuareg women to blacks, this was a further attack on Tuareg prestige and exclusivity. However, one profession often open to Tuareg in Niamey and other West African cities was neither demeaning nor strenuous: guarding homes, shops, and factories from thieves.

Long after the last organized raids of the 1920s, Tuareg still distinguished between taking booty during a raid and thievery. The first was courageous, the second cowardly. It was shameful to creep into a village, around a wall, through a window, and snatch a piece of jewelry or drive away an animal. The thievery around In Waggeur was seen as a foreign virus, carried by strangers and spread by the drought. (But some of the educated Tuareg could excuse theft. Hassan said, "If a man cannot feed his family, then he must steal; it is his duty to feed them.")

Animals, jewelry, food, and slaves captured during a raid were not stolen; they were spoils fairly won. Rules were followed during a raid: Tuareg women were never harmed or carried off, and raiders who were tracked down and encircled before they could escape were allowed to continue unharmed if they returned whatever they had taken to its rightful owners.

A raid was a graceful, noble pageant. Men rode their finest camels with their most ornate saddles. They wore their finest clothes. Physical

243

prowess was important to success. To take their prizes, raiders had to fight, first on camel, poking nine-foot steel lances at the enemy, then hacking with swords, and finally on foot, stabbing at each other with stilettos as they tried to protect themselves with skin shields.

Although violent crimes are rare in Niamey, petty thievery is not. During the drought it increased. Europeans and educated Nigeriens lived a life of middle class comfort; the rest of the Nigeriens lived below what would be considered the poverty line in the United States. A small amount of cash, a modest possession, is capable of saving or transforming the life of a poor Nigerien. A watch can feed a family for months, a radio or cassette recorder finance the start of a small business, pay a bridewealth, keep a child in school. It is remarkable that there is not more theft in Niamey.

Niamey's thieves jimmy windows and doors, break locks, climb over walls, and enter a house or compound while its owners are sleeping or absent. Since the thieves are terrified of the disgrace and long prison sentences that accompany capture, a highly visible guard will often deter them.

During the drought, motivation and targets for theft increased as refugees and relief workers crowded into the city. Accordingly, more Tuareg were hired as guards. There had always been guards in Niamey, but since the Tuareg avoided cities, most guards were black Africans. In 1969 the Tuareg, who were willing to work for lower wages and who were believed by their employers to be more effective deterrents, started to replace the blacks. Would-be thieves, farmers, and nomads alike, had learned from their oral histories that the Tuareg were willing and skilled warriors; and while most of the guards hired during the drought were more adept at watering and riding animals than at battling with swords, their histories and myths convinced them, their employers, and potential thieves that the opposite was true.

A significant number of Tuareg became guards or were supported by the earnings of guards, not just in Niamey and Niger's other cities but also in those of Nigeria, Ghana, and other sahelian and coastal countries. Since being a guard required no physical exertion beyond keeping awake—no weeding, planting, or carrying that made a man appear to be

244

serving his "inferiors"—it was a coveted position. "It is as easy to make the sky fall as to change your character" and "To change your character is to disappear" are two favorite Tuareg sayings. By becoming guards, many Tuareg refugees were saved from disappearing, from changing their clothes (as they were encouraged to wear traditional clothing) from altering their work habits and etiquette, and from restructuring their myths, or so it seemed.

Some men guarded homes only to earn enough money to enable them to return to the bush. Others seemed perfectly content to remain in the cities as guards. They lost contact with their recent past—the drought and exodus—and, with the help of their myths and histories, returned to the precolonial past of heroics and warfare enjoyed by their ancestors.

Their new culture of urban heroics was confusing, an optical illusion. From one perspective it was a clever and creative adaptation to hardship and change; from another, a grotesque parody.

vi

*A*takor woke up two hours before sunset. Ever since he had arrived in Niamey he had been living in Goudel, a suburb of Niamey, with four other Illabakan men. All of the men were refugees and all were being fed and sheltered by the same Illabakan soldier who had assisted Atakor in Tahoua.

Atakor glanced about the small hut and gathered together his belongings. He slipped his callused feet under the leather straps of his sandals, pulled one blue robe and then another identical one over his head, and arranged the pouches with Koranic verses around his neck. He strapped two swords to his side, first his father's and then the copy that he had had Sidi make with his earnings from guarding the soap factory.

He pulled a swath of blue cloth through his right hand and rubbed his fingers over his forehead and sunken cheeks. He had bought the cloth in the Niamey market; it cost a few dollars and contained none of the indigo carbon that would color his skin. He wound it around his head and delicately drew the veil up to the bridge of his nose. He pulled down his baggy white trousers so that they covered his legs completely. "The veil and the trousers are brothers" said the Tuareg, believing that both were necessary to preserve modesty before parents-in-law or a foreign people.

He emerged from the hut in a crouch, straightened up, tightened his veil, smoothed his two robes so that the first hid the second, and knotted the two ropes that ran around his waist to hold the swords to his side. He walked away from the hut.

In a few minutes he had joined Niamey's stream of cars, bicycles, motorbikes, and pedestrians. Since many Tuareg in Niamey held jobs as guards, he was a common sight as he disappeared into clouds of red dust and walked toward his new job, night guard at Niger's soap factory. Like his shelter and food, the job was arranged by the Illabakan soldier.

Niger's industries employed only 9,000 workers in 1973. There were fledgling uranium mines at Arlit in the north, a cement factory at Malbaza in the middle of the country, peanut-processing plants in the south, and in Niamey a few rudimentary consumer industries: A plastics factory stamped out plastic sandals, molded black dress shoes, and rolled out sheets of plastic bags—large ones to protect exports and small ones for imported pears sold at the Pariscoa supermarket.

Braniger, the brewery, produced beer in irregularly filled green quart bottles and smoky twelve-ounce "export" bottles. It also concocted Yuki soda, whose motto was The Vanquisher of Thirst and whose trademark was a cowboy holding a bottle of Yuki and riding out of a landscape that could have been either Texas or northern Niger.

The soap factory that Atakor guarded made a harsh detergent and cakes of brown soap stamped with an Agadez cross on one side and the legend "Marseilles-type soap, made in Niger" on the other. (The soap was exported to English-speaking Nigeria.)

Atakor arrived at the soap factory as usual around 6:30, just as its workers left for the day. He exchanged greetings with the day guardian, a bouzou in oversized sunglasses, white veil, and purple robes dripping with ancient, self-awarded French medals. Atakor took up his customary post, standing near the wire-mesh gate leading to the factory.

246

What disturbed Atakor the most about Niamey was not, as with most other refugees, its food, noise, and unfamiliar smells, but that "things are not normal since bouzous wear swords and pretend they are courageous." He was also bothered that the camels belonging to the Djerma wood merchants were thin, covered with mange, and mistreated, never bedecked with beautiful ornaments or saddles.

The sun disappeared into Niamey's settling dust, and the daytime guard left with the workers. Atakor was alone. Next to the trucks that the workers loaded with cartons of soap was a line of empty oil drums. Atakor rolled one next to the gate, but away from its electric lamps. He slipped off his first blue robe and laid it over the drum. Then he unstrapped the sword that Sidi had made, placed it nearby, and took off his sandals, arranging them so that they peeked out from under the robe. He sat hidden by a nearby bush, watching the fence and dummy, waiting to catch anyone who tried to steal cartons of soap or detergent.

Atakor: "I wanted to guard a house instead of the soap factory. There was a greater opportunity to catch thieves at a house. But my cousin arranged this job and I did as he told me.

"To be known as a courageous guard it is necessary to have an exploit. The guards who had caught or chased away thieves were famous. The women sang poems about them and their patrons rewarded them with presents.

"One famous thief robbed eight houses before we caught him. The Europeans and the guards were both looking for this man. The guards swore vengeance against him because he had fooled them. The women made fun of the guards and called them cowards. In order to trap this famous thief, a guard who worked for an Italian pretended to be asleep by laying his sword, sandals, and veil on the ground and hiding behind a wall.

"When this thief jumped over the wall, he believed that the guard was asleep and he opened the door of the Italian's house with force. As soon as he entered the house the guard was behind him with a sword and his dog. He also had five knives strapped to his arms and legs. He hit the thief on the back of the head with his fist, and then the thief hit him in the eye. The dog bit the thief and the guard hit him with the flat of his sword. Then the Italian woke up and he and the guard tied up the thief.

The next morning they took him to the police and the guard went to the hospital with an injured eye.

"The police brought in the Europeans and the guards who had seen this thief and they identified him as the man who had stolen from them. One of these Europeans was the French ambassador, and he gave the guard 10,000 CFA (almost $50). He invited the Italian to eat with him and offered him money if he would give him his courageous guard.

"The Italian refused, and to keep this guard at his house gave him a mobylette [motorbike] as a present. All of the people in Niamey knew about this courageous guard and sang songs and told stories celebrating him. Soon other guards said that they too had fought with thieves and driven them away, but they were not believed because they could not prove their stories."

Atakor's decoy did not attract a thief. But within a month he caught a bouzou worker attempting to steal soap. The day laborers usually left the factory while the bouzou guard was still on duty. However, on one particular day Atakor arrived early and the bouzou guard left him in charge. Pilferage at the factory was not unknown and probably occurred with the connivance of the daytime guard.

When Beyna tried to walk out of the factory with soap hidden under his shirt, Atakor confiscated it and gave it to the foreman the next morning. The police were called and Beyna was arrested. When more cartons of soap were found in his hut, he lost his job and was sent to jail. He and the other workers blamed Atakor and promised vengeance.

Atakor: "The bouzou shouted that he would kill me with a knife. Then my patron at the factory gave me my wages and said that I should leave because I was in danger from his friends. I was not sorry for what had happened. The bouzou was a thief, and he had left his master. They [the bouzous] have a responsibility to their masters because of everything they have done for them. Some of the marabouts said that bouzous who deserted their masters during the drought should be punished. I agreed with them."

By early 1974 Sidi's forge had become a gathering place for the Tuareg guards. They spent hours exchanging their news and watching him make new knives and swords for them and jewelry for their women to replace that sold during the exodus. Sidi sat near the street all day, watching the movements of the guards and Europeans and joking with Nigerien functionaries who bought jewelry for their wives. He was the confidant for guards, bouzous, Europeans, and functionaries. He listened, observed, joked, and advised each on his purchases. He knew who were the best employers, and when they were hiring or firing guards or housekeepers.

When Hassan told him that the Belgian wanted a guard who could live in his courtyard and watch his house day and night, he told Atakor. It was a reward for his patronage. From the day he began work, Atakor never left the vicinity of the Belgian's compound. He paid other men to bring him food and he saved his wages.

There is a Tuareg saying that "A man and his woman friend are for the heart and the eyes, not just for the bed as among the Arabs." Like Sidi, Atakor's "heart and eyes" were lonely for his wife. But unlike Sidi, Atakor knew where to find his. By April 1974 he had worked at the Belgian's for three months. He could afford to give transportation money for Miriam to an Illabakan who was traveling north to Tchin-Tabaraden.

As soon as Miriam received Atakor's money she paid the driver of a relief truck to take her and her infant daughter to Tahoua. From there she bought a place on a truck bound for Niamey.

9

Niamey
April 1974–October 1974

. . . myth and music share of both being languages which, in their
different ways, transcend articulate expression, while at the same time—like
articulate speech but unlike painting—requiring a temporal dimension in
which to unfold. But this relation to time is of a rather special nature: it is as
if music and mythology needed time only in order to deny it. Both, indeed,
are instruments for the obliteration of time.

—Claude Lévi-Strauss,
The Raw and the Cooked

i

*E*arly in the morning of April 15, 1974, troops of Niger's 2,000-man army, commanded by Chief of Staff Lieutenant-Colonel Seyni Kountché, occupied Niamey's radio station, electric works, and telephone exchange. They attacked the presidential palace and overthrew the Hamani Diori government. By 5 A.M., three hours after the coup had begun, Niger was ruled by a Supreme Military Council commanded by Lieutenant-Colonel Kountché.

When the army attacked the palace Madame Diori urged the Tuareg guards to resist. They were outnumbered and, after a brief clash on the grounds of the palace, were quickly overwhelmed by the regular army. Thirty men were killed, and President Diori was taken prisoner (he is still incarcerated on an army base in Zinder). Madame Diori was killed when she fired at the soldiers storming into the family's private quarters.

Diori was Niger's tolerant father figure, a political moderate who, until his efforts to become more independent from France in 1972, was trusted by the French and respected by other moderate African leaders. He was considered an example of the success of the French colonial policy of assimilation and creation of a French-African elite. Every summer he vacationed at a villa in Contrexéville, France.

Although Diori's honesty was unquestioned, he was too tolerant of

253

the incompetency and corruption of his subordinates. The director of his cabinet, Mai Tourare; a close relative, Boubaka Moussa; and Madame Diori were known to critics as the "clan of guzzlers" because of the profits they allegedly made from the drought. Madame Diori was an extremely rich woman; she owned a number of large houses in Niamey, which she rented to foreigners, as well as large areas of fertile land. Four months before the coup, some members of Diori's cabinet presented him with proof that other ministers were profiting from the drought relief programs. Diori prepared decrees to expose the guilty ministers, but his wife persuaded him to wait.

Seyni Kountché is thin and taut. He wears an immaculate khaki uniform and a few modest medals. He always seems to be sitting on the edge of hard chairs and he never smiles for a photograph. He appears tense—clenching his fists, his veins standing out, ready to spring.

Since taking power, Lieutenant-Colonel Kountché has terrorized Niger's bureaucrats. In a radio address one week after the coup, he referred to a "bourgeois elite minority who have inflicted on our people a policy of inactivity and submissiveness." He scolds prefects in front of subprefects and teachers in front of their students. Unlike many military leaders, he detests expensive ceremonies, and Niger's Independence Days are less impressive than a small-town Memorial Day parade in the United States. When flag-waving schoolchildren and officials greeted him at the Agadez airport, he turned to the prefect and told him curtly that Niger was too poor to support even minor spectacles and that the children should return to their schools and the functionaries to their offices.*

When Kountché assumed the presidency, his efficiency and honesty

*Also in the spring of 1975 Kountché visited Farley Winson's Tara plantation. He asked if there was a Nigerien who could explain the project to him. There was none. The Nigeriens drew water, cut wood, dug ditches, and labored in the irrigated fields. Only Winson knew how Tara was managed.

Kountché announced that a Nigerien manager had to be placed in charge immediately and Nigeriens trained to perform managerial and administrative tasks. Rather than remain under a Nigerien supervisor and fearing further action by the government, first Winson's family and then Winson himself flew out of Niger. Their destination was Belize—formerly British Hondouras, one of the world's last colonies.

matched Niger's needs. The principal cause of the army rebellion was the Diori government's mishandling of the drought, and particularly of the food distribution within Niger. Cited too was Diori's inexplicable failure to use the army's trucks, personnel, and logistical expertise to deliver food to distribution centers in the bush. The drought was the greatest crisis Niger had faced since independence, yet the one institution that was trained to deal with catastrophes and threats to the national existence—the army—was ignored.

In the six months following the coup, Kountché's military government succeeded where Diori's civilian one had failed: in emptying warehouses of long-stored grain and delivering it to the people who needed it. Immediately after seizing power, Kountché ordered the army to search the property of former government ministers, prefects, and other functionaries suspected of hoarding. The army found private storerooms bursting with grain; it was confiscated and its owners arrested. Fraudulently obtained relief Funds were also seized from eighteen members of Diori's regime.

Next, official representatives from all of Niger's regions were summoned to Niamey and instructed in the army's new system of food distribution. Before the coup (sometimes delicately referred to as "the events of April 15"), OPVN had been so concentrated in Niamey that officials in the bush rarely knew how much food was going to be delivered to them and when. Sometimes they distributed their entire supplies, and were without any for weeks. More often they were cautious and distributed too little. Kountché restructured OPVN and forced many of its employees to live in bush centers, and to send back firsthand reports to their counterparts in Niamey.

Before the coup, Captain Ali Saibou had been the head of the army

A year later in 1976, the Tara plantation was virtually deserted. The quarter of a million dollars invested by the Lilly Endowment had purchased two gigantic landing strips (for Farley's two private planes) which were cracked, overgrown with weeds, and never used; an unfinished guesthouse that Winson was building for visiting government and foreign dignitaries; a forty-yard-long Tudor-style house that was slowly sliding into the Niger River; and various tractors and other agricultural machinery that was broken and mired in the flooded fields. None of the handful of Nigeriens who remained on the plantation had been trained to repair the equipment. Instead, they had learned a few phrases of English. Some of them wore Rhodesian bush hats, gifts from Farley.

255

post at Agadez, where he witnessed the confusion and corruption of civilian authorities. When he suggested to the Agadez prefect that the army be allowed to transport food to remote villages in the Air Mountains, he was told, "You are a soldier, not an administrator. You should stay in your fort."

After the coup, Ali Saibou was appointed minister of rural economy. His responsibility was to ferret out food from warehouses and deliver it quickly to refugees. He had the skills and temperament suited to this task. He was an energetic and innovative administrator, and he knew, or claimed to know, the location of every one of Niger's vehicles.

He requisitioned trucks from the army, the peanut cooperative (SONARA), the electric company, the government water and forestry commission, and other agencies previously excluded from the relief effort. He then traveled throughout Niger so that he could personally supervise the distribution of food in these trucks. Some refugees saw him so often they called him "the pilgrim."

One example of the innovation and common sense that Saibou and the army brought to the logistical problems caused by the drought occurred in August 1974. The summer's strong rains created a flash flood which washed out the bridge connecting Tahoua and Agadez with Birni-n'Konni and Niamey. When Ali Saibou arrived on the scene, 50 trucks carrying 150 tons of food were lined up on the river's southern bank waiting for the waters to recede. Saibou ordered prisoners and wooden planks to be sent north from Birni-n'Konni and 50 empty trucks south from Tahoua. The prisoners laid the planks over the river and then walked across, transferring sacks of grain from one set of trucks to the other. In twenty-four hours the food was moving north to Tahoua and Agadez.

Ali Saibou's willingness to suspend ordinary bureaucratic procedures was contagious. By the spring of 1974 the donors were sending between 1,000 and 1,350 tons of food a day to the Nigerian ports of Lagos and Port Harcourt, and from these ports the food traveled by rail and road to eastern and northern Niger. In May shipments to Niger were suddenly halted by a strike of Nigeria's railway workers. This was a crisis. It

256

would prevent the government from stockpiling food in the northern cities before the monsoon made roads impassable.

The donors' representatives at the ports were responsible for handling customs and shipping formalities and making certain that food was sent to Niger as quickly as possible. When the strike began they sent cables alerting their superiors, but their own attempts to transport the food to Niger were ineffectual.

Trevor Page, a famine troubleshooter employed by the United Nations and a veteran of Bangladesh, was immediately sent to Lagos. Twenty-four hours after his arrival he had hired 600 Nigerian trucks to transport grain to Niger. After signing contracts with the trucks' owners, he called together the donors' representatives and told them they had twenty-four hours in which to pay the truckers. If they failed, he would hold them responsible for the starvation that would occur in Niger. Two days after Page had come to Lagos, the food was loaded into trucks and sent north.

Al Baron, the AID representative in Niger, was an equally compassionate and innovative bureaucrat. He was the only member of the AID mission who had already served a tour of duty in Niger during the 1960s; he had liked the country so much that he requested that he be sent there during the drought. (Some AID personnel considered Niger such an unattractive posting that they began plotting their escape from the moment they arrived at the airport in Niamey.) Baron persuaded the Kountché government to return to Niger's traditional transportation and hire camels to deliver food to regions in the far east and north that were often made inaccessible by the rains. Camels were more dependable than trucks, less expensive, and eliminated fuel and repair problems. The fees paid for their rental helped the rural economy. Wages paid to truck drivers and money for gasoline and repairs were more likely to benefit Niger's cities.

During a visit to Gao, Baron also conceived the idea of supplying it and other northern sahel cities from Algeria during the rainy season. Despite initial resistance from Washington, he lobbied forcefully until his plan was approved. During August and September two caravans to-

257

taling 165 trucks carried sorghum from Oran and Algiers more than 1500 miles across the Sahara to Agadez and Gao.

The 1974 rains that prompted these innovations were 50 percent greater in quantity than those of the previous year, and only 10 percent below Niger's twenty-year average. In most regions they were also well spaced. However, pasture and crop lands were now so eroded that they were unable to hold the water. In August, floods washed away bridges, cut roads, destroyed crops, and drowned people and animals who had survived the drought.

Optimistically, the Kountché government had already prepared Niger's farmers for a better harvest. As part of a "back to the village" program, they were given seeds and a two-month supply of food and urged to leave the refugee camps and return to their own villages. Many did, and despite the floods and the plagues of rats and insects, Niger's grain harvests were 25 percent better than they had been during the drought.

Most Tuareg refugees had no herds or villages. Nevertheless, the government gave them food, seed for wild grasses, and encouraged them to leave the camps and cities. Many refused; they were afraid to return to the bush, and when the camps closed they moved to the cities and lived with friends and relatives who had already found employment. Others went to the camps that remained open. The refugee population of Maradi, Niger's third largest city, increased from 25,000 in April to 40,000 in August. Still others continued in the southward direction of their original exodus, going to Nigeria and other coastal countries. Those who returned to their former homelands found them less hospitable despite the return of the monsoon.

The green carpet that now covered previously barren pasturelands was deceptive. Much of it consisted of spiny, poisonous plants, unpalatable even to goats. Around In Waggeur the tastiest and most easily harvested strains of fornio had disappeared.

The landscape had a new appearance. It would take years for new trees to grow to replace those cut by desperate herders. Until then, there would be less vegetation capable of breaking the speed of the Saharan winds and reducing their capacity to carry away topsoil and push sand dunes across pastures.

258

Many of the Nigerien Tuareg who returned to the bush during the rainy season trekked south again in the late fall, as soon as the seeds and food given them by the government were gone.

Even fewer of the Malians returned to the sixth region. As at Maradi, the population of Lazaret increased by thousands every month in spite of the improved rains. The Kountché government was in a dilemma. It wanted to avoid the spectacle of loading the Malians into trucks at gunpoint and dumping them across the border. Yet it was embarrassed by the impression the camp gave visiting journalists, and worried by the friction between Malian and Nigerien refugees who were now competing for Niamey's scarce jobs.

The government was proud that it had ended the most flagrant corruption, evolved an efficient system of food distribution, and returned so many farmers to their villages. But the problem of the Malian Tuareg dominated foreign perceptions of Niger. Foreign photographers found stick-legged, swollen-bellied, skeletal children with more difficulty than before, but they found them.

In July the government closed Lazaret and, with the assistance of $100,000 donated by the United Nations, opened a new camp, Lazaret II, thirty miles north of Niamey. Lazaret II had more space for the refugees and more pasture for their few surviving animals. Nearby trees could be cut for firewood and neighboring land cultivated, if the refugees chose. The International Red Cross supplied a doctor and a fulltime medical assistant. Outdoor classes in French were held for Tuareg children. Lazaret II's greatest drawbacks were the paucity of water, which had to be brought by tank truck until a well could be sunk, and its distance from Niamey, which was too great to allow the camp's residents to work, beg, or visit friends in the city.

Fadimatta and her entourage moved to Lazaret II. Hassan could only afford the time and money to visit her on Saturdays. She told him that she would follow her new friends: If they returned to Mali, so would she, but she would prefer to remain close to Niamey.

By October 1974 the government had closed many refugee camps. The donors considered the emergency relief stage of the disaster to be over. They began to plan long-range programs aimed at reconstructing

259

and rehabilitating the sahel. However, the rains had done little for the Tuareg. Their animals were dead. They had nowhere to go and nothing to return to. Thousands of Tuareg refugees were marooned in Niamey, in Lazaret II, and in other West African cities. They huddled on little islands of blankets and mats around the men who had found work as guards. They talked, dozed, daydreamed, and drank tea; the men in dirty, drooping veils, the women in dusty black cloaks, like seals stranded on rocks after the tide has ebbed.

ii

*D*uring the summer of 1974 Miriam became accustomed to Niamey. Both she and Atakor said that they were "happy" to be reunited but refused to elaborate any further. When she wasn't buying food or wood, she and her daughter lay outside the grass hut that the Belgian had encouraged Atakor to build within the compound. When Miriam wanted company she placed her blanket outside the Belgian's gate and invited other women and children to join her.

She was often surrounded by half a dozen dusty children and their mothers. The children were naked except for the red amulet pouches hanging around their necks. Their heads were shaved except for a small tuft of hair at the very front. Miriam always tried to have an orange with her when she sat in the driveway. She peeled it with her teeth, broke it into sections with her red fingernails ("Red is a beautiful color and the dye from the red berries keeps my fingernails hard"), and put a section in each small hand.

During the rest of the day she kept her hands on her daughter. She cleaned her ears, examined her head for ticks, tickled her belly and the soles of her feet, threw her into the air, caught her, and then stroked her, like a sculptor smoothing clay into a pleasing shape.

As she and the other women played with their own and each others' children, they told stories and recited poems, some old and some new compositions about the drought and Niamey.

Miriam: "Of course I was happy in Niamey. My daughter was alive. Many people in Tchin-Tabaraden lost their children. In Niamey I was told by women from Mali that their friends had sold children in Nigeria.

"In Niamey I worried that my daughter would become as bad as Ibrahim [Sidi's son]. Everyone who visited that blacksmith spoiled Ibrahim. They gave him sweets and beignets [a solid doughnut cooked in a tub of fat]. He asked the clients for five CFA coins and they gave him those, too. He pulled men's veils and threw dirt at the other children, but his father never scolded him.

"I liked Niamey because there was food and I had joined Atakor. But the food was not good, there was not enough milk, and it was cold [It was actually warmer in Niamey than in the Azawak, but many of the refugees believed otherwise, probably because many had sold their blankets and clothes]. This was why Atakor became ill, because of the cold and the food in Niamey.

"I know nothing about Niamey because Atakor never left the Belgian's concession and I bought what we needed in Yantala [a small market close by]. I did not visit the city."

Atakor was skilled at surviving in one of the harshest environments on earth, but it had been over a year since he had ridden a camel or led animals to pasture and water. He had been accustomed to walking or riding ten to twenty miles a day in the plains of northern Niger, but now the greatest distance he walked was the ten yards separating his hut from the driveway gate.

Other men were equally inactive and parochial. They reclined, kneeled, and squatted on mats, guarding houses or providing companionship for those who did. Every evening Atakor, Sidi, Hassan, and other off-duty guards, members of Niamey's large floating community of Tuareg men, gathered around a pot of tea balanced on embers carried from Sidi's forge. To stay awake they drank and talked. After tea, they pulled the patio furniture into a small circle. They whispered at first, and later, when the Belgian's air conditioner began to rumble, they punctuated a well-told or amusing story with a "Yeee . . .," then a chorus of agreement and praise.

When men first came to Niamey, they discussed beautiful women, ancient histories, and friends who had returned to the bush. By the fall of 1974 Atakor and his friends were replacing these with new subjects: brave Tuareg guards and their European patrons.

Atakor, Hassan, and the Tuareg employed in the Plateau compared, criticized, and savored the foibles of their patrons with an interest and fervor usually reserved for camels and women. The guards identified closely with their patrons. If they were important and generous, or if their houses were impressive, then the men who guarded them gained prestige among women and other guards. The activities of the patrons, especially European patrons, became daily soap operas that provided the Tuareg with grand entertainment and subjects for endless gossip.

Atakor and Hassan: "In the bush we discussed who had the most beautiful, most intelligent animals. In Niamey we discussed who had the most intelligent patron.

"An intelligent patron pays his guard generously, at least 15,000 CFA [about $70] a month. [Most guards earn considerably less, around $50 a month, even if they are on duty day and night.] He gives him a long paid vacation so he can visit his relatives and does not become angry when he is late or falls asleep. An intelligent patron also gives his guard European clothes, shoes, and medicine, especially Nivaquine.

"A patron with 'great intelligence' is like an intelligent patron except that he also includes his guards in his family. He eats, jokes, and drinks tea with them."

"The Belgian and I are friends," said Hassan, "because we are both white and the blacks hate us both. Often the black people make rude jokes about the Europeans and talk about how much they hate them. We always tell the Europeans what the blacks say about them. The Europeans are helping us because we are both white and want to help other whites." [The Tuareg exaggerated their contempt for the blacks, especially when talking to Europeans, and magnified the injustices committed against them by the blacks during the drought.]

The guards wanted their European patrons to treat them as equals because they believed that they were. They noticed that Europeans ordered around black servants as they themselves once had, and always avoided any unpleasant physical labor. It seemed natural to the Tuareg that the blacks' new masters should treat their traditional ones with respect and when a patron accused his guards of being lazy, they were bewildered.

A Kel Dennik vassal, who had left the Azawak in 1968 after all his animals died and walked for two months to reach Niamey, said that he disliked being a guard and disliked the Europeans. He lived in a grass hut built in the courtyard and driveway of a two-story building of apartments rented by young, single Europeans and Nigeriens.

The apartments were on the outer edge of the Plateau. Their location enabled this guard to begin reconstructing his herd in a neighboring field. He pulled his goats through a hole cut in a wire-mesh fence whenever he wanted to milk, feed, or simply touch them. By the end of 1974 he owned eight goats.

"I proved my courage," he said, "because I walked to Niamey. If there had been no work in Niamey, I would have walked until I came to America. It took me three months to find work in Niamey. I went to every villa and asked the patron to hire me. When he refused, I asked him to give me food so I could eat until I could find work. This was courageous.

"Even though they gave me food, the European patrons are cruel. They hit me on the head when I sleep and when something is stolen they blame me for allowing it to be taken. They don't understand that I must sleep too, especially since I am here alone and I must pay people to bring me whatever I need. I have not left this house for six months. I sleep in the daytime when they go to work and cannot see me.

"The problem with the Europeans is that they never allow faults. They don't understand that Tuareg, like all men, have faults. It is God that gives us these faults, so what can we do?

"I have lived in Niamey for seven years, but I would still prefer to be a herder in the bush. The Europeans only stay in Niamey for a while and then they return to their homes. Why shouldn't I?"

* * *

The drought and the passage of time had erased the myths of Tuareg treachery and cruelty. The Flatters expedition was forgotten and Duveyrier's romanticism resurgent. Some patrons, Nigeriens as well as Europeans, found it difficult to picture these broken people as their feared and cruel former enemy, and they "adopted" entire Tuareg families.

When the Lazaret camp was moved thirty miles to Hamdallaye, the guards who worked in Niamey and their families stayed behind. Thirty miles was too long and too costly a commute. Some, like Atakor, built a straw hut or pitched a tent on their patron's property.

The patrons benefited. They no longer had to hire separate day and night guards. The same man and his family were on duty continuously, living, eating, and sleeping on the grounds, a much greater deterrent to thieves than a single guard. For the Europeans, it was also a more personal charity than their studies, programs, and administrative routines.

As refugees left the camps, the communities that grew up around the guards' huts became larger. Children, parents, friends, and fellow tribesmen of the guard congregated in open yards, driveways, next to gates, in the center of grassy turnarounds, and between the villas. The guards bought chickens and goats and supported everyone on their salaries. Their wives pounded millet, made handicrafts, and nursed children. These communities were livelier, but remarkably similar to the exhibits at the nearby National Museum.

The last time the Tuareg had settled among Europeans in a similar fashion was in Paris during the summer of 1909. A French anthropological society re-created an entire Tuareg camp complete with weapons, pots, jewelry, camels, donkeys, slaves, and a dozen open skin tents pitched in an open park at the corner of the Rue Blanche and the Boulevard Clichy. The principal "exhibit" was the people themselves, a mixture of a hundred Saharan people: Tuareg, their slaves, Arabs, and their dancing women. "Events" were scheduled throughout each day. The Arab women twirled, undulated, and gave high-pitched cries of "Yoo . . . yoo . . . yoo." Two veiled men faced off in the field and fought a mock gladiators' battle. They hurled their lances at each other's feet and then charged to slap at skin shields with the flats of their swords.

Large crowds of Parisians gathered twice a day to watch a "caravan." Slaves and blacksmiths beat drums while a veiled Tuareg warrior on a camel led the rest of the exhibits in circles around the park. Tuareg women rode sidesaddle on donkeys; they were followed by the Arab women, dancing and trilling, making music with the tiny cymbals on their fingers.

Bringing up the rear was Bala Mohammed. A French-speaking Tuareg, described as the "most intelligent" of the Tuareg, Bala Mohammed was also, perhaps not coincidentally, the one with the lightest skin and the most European features. "In spite of the brownish, tan tint to his skin," the guidebook to the exhibit stated, "he has absolutely the facial features as well as the profile of a French Basque."

The article also listed the measurements of Bala's face, lips, and body, and pointed out that although "many Tuareg have intermarried and mixed with black peoples, their white characteristics still predominate." Except for Mohammed, the light-skinned Tuareg nobles had refused to leave their desert camps to entertain the Parisians. Most of the people in the exhibit were dark-skinned vassals and their slaves.

Beyna, the ex-slave, was sentenced to six months in prison for stealing soap. He and the other prisoners were often packed into dump trucks and hauled to different parts of Niamey where they were made to wade into clogged sewers and dig out garbage and excrement. It was a punishment that would encourage visions of vengeance.

When he was released, Beyna returned to his first profession, water carrier. When he had saved enough money he went to a good blacksmith, Sidi, and ordered bracelets and rings to reward his wife for her fidelity. To reward himself he paid Sidi to make a knife, and plotted the revenge he had promised Atakor at the soap factory six months ago.

Sidi: "A blacksmith is not a Tuareg vassal or noble, nor is he a bouzou. He should not choose between these clients when they quarrel. He must be friendly with everyone.

"I had bouzou clients who pretended to be courageous so they could be guards. They didn't own knives or swords so they commissioned me to make them. I could not know that one of these bouzous wanted to kill another client with a knife he had bought from me.

"Beyna had been a good client. He had bought rings and bracelets, and the knife he ordered was expensive. While I was making it he visited me twice. He sat in my chair, brought gifts to Ibrahim, and told me about his wife and his life before the drought.''

In a city as small as Niamey, it was not an astounding coincidence that Beyna should have chosen a blacksmith who worked near Atakor. He could have located Atakor without difficulty in any case, whenever he chose. But when he saw that Atakor worked nearby, he returned on purpose to have Sidi make his knife.

Sidi: "Atakor only saw Beyna when he paid for the knife and took it. Atakor said nothing. After the bouzou left Atakor told me he was certain Beyna would revenge himself with my knife.

"I asked my other clients about this man and learned that he had boasted that he would kill Atakor. When I told Atakor this he said that I must find a rifle so he could defend himself.

"This was difficult, because after the events of April 15 the police confiscated rifles, even the ancient ones. However, I was able to rent one from a blacksmith in Yantala. I explained how it worked to Atakor because he had never fired a similar rifle before.''

iii

*F*rom his perch in the Belgian's tree, Atakor stared into the pools and shafts of yellow light that illuminated Niamey's Plateau neighborhood. He squinted down the sights of the antique rifle and pointed it at each shadow, sound, and silhouette, hoping, imagining that finally Beyna had come.

Lines of yellow street lamps hummed over an empty boulevard a block away. The porch and gate lamps of the villas of expatriate Europeans and government functionaries were ringed by halos of mosquitoes, gnats, and crickets spawned by the summer rains. Out in the countryside they were devouring the first plentiful harvest in six years.

Other lights on the Plateau were mobile. A houseboy pedaled home to one of the surrounding African neighborhoods, his bicycle light glowing, fading, and glowing again in cadence with the clicking pedals. The headlights of a taxi swept across a dark road as it turned a corner. Atakor strained his eyes but saw only children flitting in front of the long yellow shafts, like insects crossing the beam of an outdoor cinema.

There was no moon. Ramadan, the Moslem feast that lasted for a lunar month, would end when a marabout sighted a sliver of new moon at sunset. Already the moon had been seen to the west, in Senegal and Mauritania. Tomorrow it would appear over Niamey, the fast would be lifted, and the evenings would become brighter. But this last evening of Ramadan was black. Sidi had warned Atakor that Beyna would come on just such a night.

Atakor had taken precautions. Every evening at dusk he climbed into one of the two large trees flanking the gate to the Belgian's villa. He dragged up a can of water and the rifle. Hidden by the branches and leaves of the tree, he could guard the villa as well as watch for the bouzou.

Tonight, as on every other night, as soon as the Belgian's Renault pulled into the short driveway, Atakor jumped from the tree, looking with his veil and billowing blue robes like a prehistoric bird, and opened the gate. The Belgian never asked why he preferred to guard the house from a tree. Their greetings remained the same.

"Bon soir, patron," said Atakor.

"Bon soir, Atakor."

"Ça va?"

"Ça va bien."

When the porch lights had been dimmed from a switch inside the house and the air conditioner had begun to rumble, Atakor hitched up his veil so that only his eyes were visible and climbed back into the tree. He had never been inside the house.

Atakor's house was also located within the compound, directly beneath the tree and near the gate. It was a conical hut made of woven grass mats strapped to a wooden frame. Tonight Miriam lay inside surrounded by the round grass walls of the hut and the square cement walls of the courtyard.

Ever since the blacksmith's warning Miriam had spent the nights lying outside the hut, awake. Atakor told her that when he dropped a pebble from the tree she was to get up, open the gate, tell the bouzou that Atakor had left, and then lure him into the light of the gate lamps. But tonight she was ill. She lay on a mat inside the hut, shaking with fever.

Atakor invented another strategy. During Ramadan young boys dabbed designs on their bodies with white paint, stuck tufts of cotton on their faces, and tied white streamers to their shorts. The streamers were white cloth or the squiggles of styrofoam that came packed in cartons of Japanese radios. The boys were supposed to be rabbits, a traditional Ramadan disguise.

They roamed the streets in threes and fours, floating white dots and lines that raced out of the dark and surrounded pedestrians. When they cornered someone they jumped up and down and chanted "Tobaye, tobaye, tobaye-aye" ("Rabbit, rabbit, rabbit"). One of them pounded a long staff on the ground in time with the chant, moving it closer to the victim's feet until he gave the rabbits a small coin or a gift. Then they vanished to continue the hunt.

Tonight a group of rabbits stood at the juncture of the Avenue Charles DeGaulle—the Plateau's principal boulevard, and the side street leading to the villa. Atakor had bribed them with sugar and money to accost anyone who passed the corner and maneuver them under a gate lamp. With Miriam sick, the rabbits would be Atakor's trip wire.

Beyna left the mud-brick house he shared with two other bouzou families in one of Niamey's African quarters and walked toward the Plateau. In these neighborhoods the lights were weaker but more numerous than in the Plateau. The beam of a flashlight or a taxi's headlights sweeping across a silent street illuminated for an instant rows of people sleeping on mats, men squatting to urinate, a camel or a donkey swaying under a load of firewood—random bursts of light that shattered the deceptive quiet of Niamey's evenings, showing them to be pulsating with the hidden activities of a people accustomed to darkness.

As he approached the Plateau, Beyna passed small kerosene-burning hurricane lamps that flickered across wooden tables piled with toffees, hard candies, soap, cigarettes, and purplish kola nuts from the coast. He passed yellow fires that warmed pots of food stirred by enormous women. The customers sat opposite on wooden benches as if waiting to be taught a lesson while the women filled tin bowls with rice and hot sauce or millet and milk.

In ten minutes Beyna was in Niamey's commercial sector where Africans and residents of the Plateau mingled. During the day, the Africans sold their wares to the Europeans and government functionaries, either in the small triangular marketplace or at the Pariscoa, Niamey's supermarket.

Slivers of a faded Technicolor movie shown in an outdoor theater, the Rex, were visible from the surrounding streets. When the Harmattan wind was silent, the neighborhood throbbed with roaring engines, squealing tires, rapid metropolitan French, and the staccato gun duels of Westerns and spy dramas.

With the sounds of cinema violence echoing behind him, Beyna stepped in and out of the pools of light thrown by the street lights along the Avenue DeGaulle as he climbed the hill leading to the Plateau. At the top of the hill he walked halfway around a traffic circle and turned left with the avenue. The street lights followed the Avenue of Independence to the President's palace, the government ministries, and the army camps. Here the Avenue DeGaulle was dark. Even when the moon was full, the tall, leafy trees made it seem like a French country road.

Beyna reached under his white robe and slipped the knife out of the scabbard he had strapped to his chest. Pulling it free from the folds of his robe, he held it close to his side. The curved blade was a foot long and miniature crescent designs ran along its middle from hilt to tip. Another shorter knife was strapped to the calf of his left leg. It was the kind of knife that Tuareg warriors had once worn openly, tied to their left wrist so that during a battle they could draw it quickly with the right hand.

The Plateau was silent except for the coughs of the Tuareg guards whose lungs had not recovered from last winter's cold evenings.

Beyna knew that within most of the wood fences and concrete walls that surrounded the villas was a courtyard with carefully tended shrubs and plants, a large one-story house with bars on the windows and locks on the doors, and a Tuareg guard sitting, often sleeping, in the shadows. He counted the houses on the avenue until he arrived at the road that led to the Belgian's villa. He crossed the road diagonally, avoiding the rabbits who stood under a gate lamp. They were arguing over the division of alms they had just received from a pedestrian and they failed to notice Beyna or alert Atakor.

Sidi had made Beyna's knife. He had also warned Atakor of Beyna's intentions and rented the rifle, repaired its trigger, and cleaned its barrel. As Beyna approached, Sidi sat with Hassan ten yards from the Belgian's villa, awaiting the outcome.

Fifty years ago, when Atakor's Tuareg ancestors were warriors and the bouzous slaves, Sidi's were the Mata Haris and Metternichs of the sahel—spies, advisors to chiefs, intermediaries and negotiators between warring tribes and lovers. Now the drought had forced Sidi into a role more familiar to this earlier generation of blacksmiths.

He and Hassan drank green tea to keep awake. The teapot stayed warm in a wicker basket holding hot embers from the forge. When the tea boiled Sidi poured it into two shot glasses that rested in a brass tray. He poured from two feet above the glasses and filled each exactly to the rim. Hassan lifted his veil, which he wore tonight for the first time in almost two years, and drank the tea in three slurps.

The headlights of a taxi turning into the side road picked out Beyna's silhouette. He was crouched next to a wall fifty yards from Atakor's tree, opposite the rabbits. Atakor sighted him, pulled back the hammer on his rifle, and waited for him to approach the compound. His legs shook with fear and the branches of the tree rustled.

Even though the Tuareg people were famous for courage and skill in battle, Atakor was a herder, not a fighter. He had never fired a gun, never fought at close quarters with a knife or a sword, never killed or wounded an enemy.

Fifteen months earlier when he had attempted another act of courage, by trying to save himself in the bush, he had failed. Now, by repeating the strategy Najim had used to protect In Waggeur from Arab raiders in 1920, he hoped to succeed.

The ancient rifle wavered as Atakor lined up Beyna in the sights. The

270

bouzou was trapped, frozen in the taxi's yellow headlights. He had drawn his knife. He was at the foot of the wall surrounding the Belgian's compound.

The taxi passed, and as if a light had been switched off, the street was instantly dark. With his rifle still pointed at the foot of the wall, Atakor jerked the trigger.

Beyna screamed and fell. The painted rabbits, whispering and shuffling under the street lamp, fled. Hassan and Sidi ran to the Belgian's gate. Miriam woke from her fever and stumbled from the hut. She joined the men gathered in the driveway.

Atakor cried "Yeee . . . eee" and jumped from the tree, the gun in his hand. He drew a knife from a scabbard tied to his calf and, finding Beyna, dragged him into the center of a pool of light. The bullet had ripped through his forearm, making him drop the knife. He was stunned but conscious.

Atakor bent over him, pulled Beyna's wounded arm free from his cloak, and drew his own knife across Beyna's wrist. Blood filled the shallow line of the cut. Hassan grabbed Atakor's arm and shook it. He dropped the knife.

Beyna had recovered from the slight shock of his wound, and now he ran. Atakor hardly noticed. He was on his knees by the wall, sweeping the ground with his hands, searching for Beyna's knife. Instead of cutting off the bouzou's hand, he would save his knife, as a trophy which would prove his heroism to his patron and perhaps bring a reward.

A few days later Miriam, another woman recently arrived in Niamey from In Waggeur, and half a dozen other women sat on a carpet of blankets in front of the Belgian's driveway. Some propped their heads on their elbows and others sat cross-legged, cradling children in their laps and leaving their hands free to clap.

Their black robes flowed together. Their hands and feet touched, hands resting on knees or other hands. Like cats cleaning each other, they absentmindedly brushed dirt from one another's garments.

They drew their cloaks around their bodies so that they appeared to be inhabiting small black tents, dusted with dirt stirred from Niamey's

271

streets by the private cars and taxis bringing their patrons back to the Plateau at dusk. Hands emerged from the tents to clap and create a counterpoint to the poems they were setting to music.

Ibrahim ran around them in circles. Sidi listened from his forge and Hassan from his garden. Atakor stood a few yards away, on the other side of the driveway gate, on duty. The women could see him but he ignored them, or pretended to. He paced in a triangle from the gate to his hut to the edge of the garden, his expression hidden under his veil.

The woman from In Waggeur repeated a song composed by the people who had stayed in the Azawak during the drought. It was one of many "sorghum songs" popular with the small group of Tuareg who still assembled at In Gall in August for the Cure Salée, where they came not to water their animals but to receive free sorghum.

First the woman recited the verses herself. Then the others joined in, repeating them again and again.

> Welcome to the food sent us by Kountché
> Food that is distributed by Boucli.
> Welcome to the food, especially the American milk
> And sorghum in plastic bags,
> Food that is transported in Belgian trucks.
> Long live Ahmadou in the region of Agadez!
> We thank the government of Kountché.
> Long live the United States of America
> Who sends us aid without ceasing.

Now Miriam sang her newest composition in a monotone that, like a priest's chant, dropped to a lower register at the end of each line:

The guards come from Mali; from Kidal, Menaka, and Gao.
They come from Niger; from In Gall, In Waggeur, and Tchin-Tabaraden.
The thieves are numerous, like grasshoppers after the rain,
Like desert rats when the pools are full.
They are not courageous, and when they see our guards,
They are like sheep.
Atakor, our chief, has saved the Europeans.
His courage merits a beautiful camel,
Decorated with beautiful ornaments
That will sing praises to his courage as he rides.

272

Epilogue

Precise statistics, even estimates, of how many Tuareg and other sahelian peoples died as a result of the drought are unreliable. The United Nations Food and Agriculture Organization claims 150,000 deaths. Other estimates range from zero to half a million. The most sensible statement about mortality rates during the drought has been made by John Caldwell, an Australian demographer: "What conclusions can one draw about the extra mortality arising from the drought of the early 1970s? Primarily that no one knows."

Perhaps the most startling aspect of the drought is not how many people may have perished but how so many survived even as their societies, economies, and environments were being devastated; and how, before large amounts of relief food arrived in the sahel, so many individuals saved themselves by using every physical and cultural resource at their command, including their myths and histories.

Since 1974, AID, other donor agencies, and the Nigerien government have been experimenting with various programs meant to reconstitute the nomadic herds and thereby enable the nomadic survivors of the drought to return to their homelands. However, in the three years since the drought ended very little has actually been done. Academic experts hired by the donors continue to study the proposed programs.

275

The interviews with Tuareg living in the vicinity of In Waggeur before the drought show that they had a sophisticated appreciation of the fragility of their environment. Now that the drought is over, instead of imposing more borders and rules and continuing with the repetitive expert studies which delay the implementation of programs, the real experts in sahelian livestock—the Tuareg and the Peul—should be given the animals which will allow them to reconstitute their herds. Before the modern wells were sunk, control of pastures and water points was in the hands of the Tuareg chiefs. Now that the modern state has given these chiefs the responsibility for administrative tasks such as census taking and tax collection, it should not be difficult to allow them to regulate the use of water points and pastures.

However, while the experts and governments argue over how the nomadic herds should be reconstituted, many of Atakor's generation are being sacrificed. They are losing their skills, many of the younger generation are not being trained as nomads, and the genius and stamina that enabled the Tuareg people to survive is being lost. If any of these programs are ever fully implemented, it may be discovered that reconstituting a herd of cows is easier than resurrecting a family, a tribe, and an entire people.

Although no one knows how many people died because of the drought, it is certain that without the emergency relief programs the suffering and starvation would have been much greater. However, the shortcomings of these relief programs, their tardiness and inefficiency, underline the fact that famine relief is essentially a military operation. It calls for the logistical skills, the transportational resources, and the organization and discipline found in the military forces of the donor nations, not in their bureaucracies. If the American armed forces could supply marines under siege at Khe Sahn and the entire city of Berlin during the 1948 blockade, they certainly could have overcome the logistical problems of landing large quantities of food in the sahel.

The French army has a *force de frappe* of paratroops who are prepared to intervene almost anywhere in the world on short notice. The international community needs a disaster *force de frappe*, comprised of

276

the finest logistical and transport specialists from a number of national armies, under the supervision of the United Nations, and able to respond instantly and effectively to disasters, particularly to famines. Some of the troops in such a force would be from Asian, African, and South American countries, and all would be unarmed.

This multinational force would tend to eliminate the profiteers, organizational and political rivalries, and bureaucratic inefficiency which have hampered famine relief in the past. It would also eliminate some of the problems of pride and sovereignty which have prevented or delayed poor nations from asking for famine aid from the rich nations. There are political obstacles to any multinational undertaking, but if an armed international peace-keeping force is feasible, so is an unarmed one to prevent starvation.

If such a force had been at work in the sahel during the early years of the drought, the disaster that befell the Tuareg people might have been mitigated or prevented. Instead, the unraveling of the Tuareg families and the deaths of so many animals has had a serious and perhaps lasting effect on the ability of the surviving Tuareg to live as they did before the drought, as a distinct and self-sufficient people. The fate of the individuals in this book is representative of the uncertain future of the remnants of the Tuareg people.

Hassan was fired from his job as gardener during the summer of 1975 for refusing to perform tasks he considered demeaning. A year later he was still living in Niamey, unemployed and supported by Sidi and his European and Nigerien friends. He has sold most of his European clothes and stopped sending money to Rissa, and since the end of 1975 he has not heard from him.

During the winter of 1976 Rissa and his family were still in Gao living under their Scandinavian sail. The Mali government is following a strict program of encouraging all Tuareg refugees to become either farmers or laborers. Those who refuse find it difficult to receive free or subsidized food.

The refusal of thousands of Malian Tuareg to return voluntarily to their country after the drought embarrassed the Mali government. It was unofficially charged that the Nigeriens were holding the Malian Tuareg

277

against their wishes in order to inflate their relief rolls and receive more free food from the donors. Finally, in the spring of 1975, the Kountché government acceded to Malian demands and closed the second Lazaret refugee camp. The refugees were shuttled back to the sixth region under guard in Malien army trucks.

At first Fadimatta, like many of her friends, fled to Niamey and hid. But since Hassan could no longer support her, he advised her to take advantage of the free ride and see if conditions in Mali had changed. She took his advice and returned to Gao. Many other refugees who went back have since returned to Niamey where, again, they live scattered throughout the city, much as they did before the Catholic missionaries opened the first Lazaret camp. Fadimatta did not return, and Hassan has heard nothing from or about her since her departure.

Sidi remained in Niamey. He has moved his forge a couple of times between the Plateau and Terminus neighborhoods. During the summer of 1976 he traveled to Kano to search for his wife. He failed to locate her. He has decided to "follow Moussa's advice" and send Ibrahim to school instead of training him to become a blacksmith.

Beyna disappeared from Niamey after the Plateau incident.

Late in 1975, before completing the interviews for this book, Atakor died of a respiratory ailment, probably tuberculosis. This was an occupational hazard for guards, who had to stay outdoors during Niamey's winter evenings. The practice of hiring Tuareg guards has become widespread in many West African cities. It is still the preferred labor for Tuareg men and since each guard supports a number of people, the importance and symbolism of the profession extends well beyond the number of men actually employed.

Miriam returned to Tchin-Tabaraden after Atakor's death. In the winter of 1976 the Tuareg living around In Waggeur and Tchin-Tabaraden were again shaking hard red berries from trees and gathering cram-cram and wild melons. They were on the brink of another exodus and free grain had to be distributed at In Gall. (Although the rains since 1974 have been satisfactory, Niger's farmlands have not yet recovered from the drought and in 1976 the government again had to ask the donor nations to supply famine relief.)

* * *

For many Tuareg their first exodus from their homelands was indeed a "last caravan," and they died or remain scattered throughout the cities and sedentary regions of West Africa. They continue to live on charity or on their earnings as guards or laborers.

Others tried to return to their homelands after the rains of 1974, 1975, and 1976. Most have been unable to rebuild their herds to a level that would support them in the bush and they have reappeared in the cities during the soudure—shuttling between two worlds, their fate depending on the quality of the rains and the opportunities for salaried employment. As in the case of the drought-related mortality rates, there are no reliable figures for how many Tuareg managed to remain in their homelands and how many have been forced to settle in other regions. My own estimate is that between 50 and 75 percent of the Tuareg people were uprooted by the drought. The most seriously affected nomadic regions were almost entirely depopulated.

The Tuareg who have managed to remain in the bush will continue as herders. Eventually, some may be included in the livestock programs being planned by the donors. But these herders will represent only a fraction of those who lived in the bush before the drought and in a few decades they, like the guards, will become a weak and distorted echo of an earlier generation.

Index

281